THE RESURRECTION OF HUNGARY

CLASSICS OF IRISH HISTORY
General Editor: Tom Garvin

THE RESURRECTION OF HUNGARY

A PARALLEL FOR IRELAND

Arthur Griffith

with an introduction by
Patrick Murray

UNIVERSITY COLLEGE DUBLIN PRESS
PREAS CHOLÁISTE OLLSCOILE BHAILE ÁTHA CLIATH

First published 1904
This third edition first published 1918
Reprinted with a new introduction by
University College Dublin Press, 2003

Introduction © Patrick Murray 2003

ISBN 1 900621 96 7
ISSN 1383–6883

University College Dublin Press
Newman House, 86 St Stephen's Green
Dublin 2, Ireland
www.ucdpress.ie

Cataloguing in Publication data
available from the British Library

Typeset in Ireland in Baskerville by
Elaine Shiels, Bantry, Co. Cork
Printed on acid-free paper in Ireland
by ColourBooks, Dublin

CONTENTS

INTRODUCTION
Patrick Murray

On 3 March 1848, the year of revolutions, the Hungarian nationalist leader, Louis Kossuth, demanded self-government for Hungary. Within weeks, an elected parliament replaced the Hungarian Diet. The Austrian government, confronting revolution in Vienna and among its Czech subjects, was obliged to acquiesce in virtual independence for Hungary. In the autumn of 1848 following the defeat of the Czechs, an Austrian invasion of Hungary was repelled by an army led by Kossuth, who was elected first president of an independent republic of Hungary. Within a year, however, this arrangement was overthrown, and Austrian control resumed, when the combined forces of Austria and Russia defeated Kossuth's army on 9 August 1849, at the battle of Temesvar. This was not the end of the Hungarian resistance to Austrian hegemony. By 1867, the Austrians were obliged to concede a large measure of independence to the Hungarians, not in response to violent revolution, but as a result of a campaign of passive resistance and non-co-operation led by Franz Deak. The essential, and most successful, aspect of Deak's policy was the steadfast refusal of the Hungarians to send representatives to the Imperial parliament in Vienna, as a means of securing the re-establishment of a separate Hungarian parliament in Budapest. The outcome of this strategy was an agreement between Deak and the Austrian Chancellor in 1867, known as the *Ausgleich*, or compromise. This recognised Austria and Hungary as separate political entities, each recognising the Austrian Emperor as their monarch. Franz Josef retained his imperial status in Austria, but was King of Hungary. Full Hungarian autonomy was, however, significantly circumscribed by the provision for common ministries of war and foreign affairs and the retention of close economic ties between Austria and Hungary, although fiscal autonomy and economic protectionism were conceded to Hungary.

Many observers, politicians as well as political theorists, British as well as Irish, saw, or professed to see, important parallels between the relation of Hungary to Austria from 1848 to 1867 and that of Ireland as a whole to Britain from the Act of Union of 1801. Sydney Smith found it impossible to think of the affairs of Ireland "without being forcibly struck by the parallel of Hungary". In 1885, Lord Salisbury, the Tory leader, then contemplating outmanoeuvring the Liberals by offering Parnell a measure of local government for Ireland, considered the Austro-Hungarian constitutional arrangements of 1867 as a possible framework. In 1886, in the course of the debate on his first Home Rule Bill, Gladstone made reference to the possible relevance to Ireland of "the altogether new experience of Austro-Hungary". It is not surprising that in the immediate aftermath of the events of 1848, Young Irelanders, among them William Smith O'Brien, John Mitchel and Michael Doheny, should have seen parallels between Hungarian and Irish attempts to win political independence, and that contemporary Irish journals took an active interest in the Hungarian question.

It was Arthur Griffith who undertook the first serious investigation of the historical evolution of the Austro-Hungarian constitutional settlement, and who provided the first thoroughgoing analysis, in *The Resurrection of Hungary*, of how this settlement might be applied in the Irish case. The work attracted unprecedented interest: over 20,000 copies had been sold within three months of publication. Griffith's analysis, and his detailed outline in 1905 of how his Hungarian policy of dual monarchy could apply in Irish circumstances, provided the basis for the concept of independence advocated by his new

Sinn Féin movement. His main proposal was to revive what he called "the one statesmanlike idea" that had occurred to Daniel O'Connell in the later phase of his career but which was not implemented by him. This involved summoning an Irish parliament to be called the Council of Three Hundred, to meet in Dublin; this body would proceed to legislate for Ireland and ignore the Act of Union. Griffith suggested that following the withdrawal of the Irish Parliamentary party from Westminster, as an act of defiance on the Hungarian model, Irish national leaders should summon a Council of Three Hundred to meet in Dublin "and initiate, discuss, and pass measures calculated to benefit the country", such measures to be implemented by local representative bodies such as County Councils, Urban Councils and Poor Law Boards.[1]

Later, Griffith was to be criticised for building a serious and influential argument upon insecure foundations. It has, for example, been alleged, most notably be F. S. L. Lyons, that his understanding of nineteenth-century Hungarian history was sketchy, and by Edward Norman that his work was the fruit of "slight but excited readings". This is almost certainly unfair, as the opinions of some authoritative commentators will suggest. In an early notice of the articles in the *United Irishman* on which Griffith based *The Resurrection of Hungary*, published in *An Claidheamh Soluis* in December 1904, Kuno Meyer, the German Celtic philologist, who was familiar with the historical background, found Griffith's comments on Hungarian history both brilliantly expressed and instructive.[2] A modern Hungarian scholar, Thomas Kabdebo, who analysed Griffith's book in the light of the Hungarian sources cited in it, describes it as "a clear and authoritative document drawn upon facts and views of Hungarian history as chronicled by Hungarian historians and foreign observers of Hungary", and as containing few errors.[3] Whatever the status of the work as history, to focus attention exclusively on its scholarship is to misunderstand Griffith's aim in writing it. He was using a particular set of historical circumstances, Irish and Hungarian, in a selective way as material on which he could base a political parable for his own time, omitting details that did not suit his argument and throwing into strong relief those that did. His method is thus inseparable from myth-making; he could represent the period from 1782 to 1800, during which, as he put it in *The Resurrection of Hungary*, "the English Parliament removed all claim or title to govern this country" as a golden age in Irish constitutional history and an ideal to strive for in the present and to adapt to contemporary conditions.

Griffith, however, was reluctant to associate the "independent" Dublin Parliament with Grattan, whom he regarded as little better than the Irish Party members sitting at Westminster in 1904. To Griffith's mind, Grattan's political incompetence and faith in English benevolence anticipated Redmond's. In *The Resurrection of Hungary*, he acknowledged that Grattan was "an excellent orator, sincerely patriotic", but regarded him as "neither a statesman nor a leader of men". If Griffith had an eighteenth-century hero, it was Henry Flood, the author of the Renunciation Act of 1783.[4] Two years before *The Resurrection of Hungary* was published, Griffith enunciated the political doctrine which it advocated to a convention of Cummann na nGaedheal on 26 October 1902. Cummann na nGaedheal, then two years in existence, was a movement founded by Griffith: all that was expected of its members was that they should declare themselves in favour of an Irish Republic and be persons "of decent character". Griffith, having denounced the members of the Irish Parliamentary Party at Westminster as promoters of "a useless, degrading and demoralising policy", called on Irish people abroad to withdraw all support from them until they adopted "the policy of the Hungarian deputies in 1861, and refusing to attend the British parliament or to recognise its right to legislate for Ireland, remain at home to help in promoting Ireland's interests". The idea that Ireland's parliamentary representatives should withdraw permanently from Westminster was not new, but Griffith's determination to persist with this as part of his grand Austro-Hungarian strategy of dual monarchy was.

During the Treaty negotiations in 1921, Griffith believed that the dual monarchy, which would have meant that Ireland and Britain would have had separate legislatures but a common monarch, might provide the solution to what he regarded as an otherwise intractable problem. In canvassing the idea he was, above all, anxious to avoid partition, which he believed would create massive political difficulties. He was certain that a Northern State could never function with a huge dissenting nationalist minority, and at the same time that a million unionists would not accept a united Ireland independent of Britain. Griffith's friend P. S. O'Hegarty remembered telling Griffith during the Treaty negotiations that the only way to avoid partition "which was to be avoided at any cost", was the old Sinn Féin alternative of King, Lords and Commons, a free Ireland with full powers and the same King as England. This, both he and Griffith believed, was "the one thing which Ulster Unionists, with their emphasis on loyalty to the King, could not hold out against". Cobban, like O'Hegarty, argues that partition was not the only possible outcome of the Ulster problem, suggesting that "on the basis of territorial nationalism, the union of all Ireland was undoubtedly a possibility". This might have been achieved had the leaders of southern nationalism advocated less militant policies and stopped short of demanding a totally independent Irish state, and had the British governments been more even-handed. Cobban found nothing inevitable in "the victory of the tradition of Wolfe Tone over that of Grattan and Flood", while British policy, "diverging from the sounder lines it had followed in Canada, by supporting the Protestant loyalists at all costs, laid the foundation of partition".[5] Before 1916, there might have been a remote possibility that a dual monarchy, as visualised by Griffith, might have served the unifying purpose O'Hegarty attributed to it. In 1921, it was not a solution likely to recommend itself to any of the parties.

Griffith's proposals for a "Hungarian" solution to the Irish question are most vulnerable when he proposes an idealised version of the parliament of 1782 as model for a constitutional settlement. It was, in the light of a respectable Irish precedent, perfectly plausible to advocate the withdrawal of Irish parliamentarians from Westminster, a course considered by O'Connell and Parnell, and advocated by Thomas Davis in 1844. What Griffith thought of as his next step, the establishment of an Irish parliament on Irish soil, after the pattern of Grattan's Parliament of 1782, was much less convincing. This would have involved an Anglo-Irish version of the Austro-Hungarian *Ausgleich*, the only institutional link between the two countries being a shared monarch with separate crowns. The self-governing Ireland which would, Griffith believed, result from this arrangement would begin to enjoy the kind of prosperity Griffith associated with Grattan's Parliament. He based this sanguine view on what the Volunteers who had made the 1782 Parliament possible had been able to achieve by way of economic pressure when a measure of legislative independence afforded some economic independence. They bound themselves not to import any goods of English manufacture, or to consume such goods, when Irish manufacturers were competent to supply them. The result was, as Griffith put it, that "Irish manufactures revived to an unprecedented degree".[6]

It is curious that Griffith appears to have had a better understanding of nineteenth-century Hungarian politics than of British constitutional theory. He argued, for example, that Grattan's Parliament had acted unconstitutionally, and beyond its legitimate authority in 1800, in voting for its own dissolution, since, as he believed, the Renunciation Act passed by the British Parliament in 1783, abrogating all future claims to legislate for Ireland, was still valid, despite the passage of the Act of Union eighteen years later. In Griffith's view, this meant that the re-establishment of the Irish Parliament in the twentieth century would restore the proper constitutional position. This argument faced one disabling difficulty, failing as it did to take account of a fundamental feature of the British Constitution: what Nicholas Mansergh terms the "transcendent competence of parliament".[7] This principle deprived Griffith's view of the Act of Union of its validity, since any British Parliament had the authority to repeal any previous enactment, even the Renunciation Act of 1783, which, until it was repealed in 1801 by the passage of the Act of Union, had circumscribed its own powers to legislate for Ireland. All Griffith could then rely on as the foundation for his revived Irish parliament was the continental precedent provided by Hungarian nationalists in defence of their constitutional rights.

Griffith's tendency to idealise the Parliament of 1782, and his advocacy of an Irish settlement based on what he thought the revival of such an assembly might achieve for Irish separatism, made his work vulnerable to serious criticism. That parliament, because it was based on a limited franchise, was representative of only a small minority of propertied Irish people. Membership could be purchased: Grattan, for example, followed this procedure when, having retired, he wanted to re-enter the Parliament to protest against its dissolution. Its most striking defect, from a nationalist point of view, was its exclusion of Catholics from membership. It was a legislature without power to control the executive, while its enactments were subject to a royal veto, which in practice meant a British government veto. Against this, it might be urged that Griffith was all too conscious of the deficiencies of the Hungarian scheme, and of the Irish Constitutional settlement of 1782, from the point of view of advanced nationalists, many of whom believed that only armed force could achieve the separation of Ireland from Britain. Griffith did not regard the policies he advocated in *The Resurrection of Hungary* as representing the ultimate Irish demand but as a distinct advance on what he saw as the acquiescence of the Irish Party at Westminster in the "usurpation, tyranny and fraud" perpetrated by "a foreign government". While emphatically rejecting the sterile parliamentarianism which had failed to advance the cause of Irish self-rule, Griffith also rejected violent revolution. His *Resurrection of Hungary* was an honourable attempt to find a middle way which he hoped might earn further increments of freedom. Its emphasis on dual monarchy, on "king, lords and commons" was calculated to appeal to the large body of conservative nationalists whose views on Home Rule did not involve the exclusion of Ireland from the Empire. Some of Griffith's proposals, particularly the one advocating the withdrawal of Irish members from Westminster, represented a significant departure from the policy of the Irish Party whose leader John Redmond was, as Mansergh remarks, "more loyal to Westminster than Westminster was to prove to him". [8] In 1904, however, as *The Resurrection of Hungary* makes clear, Griffith was content to work within the monarchical framework which characterised his ideal settlement, the Austro-Hungarian *Ausgleich*, while the two main strategies he derived from the Hungarian example, abstentionism and passive resistance, marked him out as a Deak rather than a Kossuth. This was recognised by D. P. Moran, editor of *The Leader*, who condemned Griffith and his followers, whom he characterised as the "Green Hungarian Band", for preferring a monarchical constitution and the sacrifice of the Irish national character to the separatist Gaelic republic which was Moran's ideal. In December 1921, Griffith found it possible to subscribe to an Anglo-Irish settlement based on loyalty to the Crown. It is worth noting that Document Number Two, de Valera's alternative to that settlement, envisaged an Irish association with the states of the British Commonwealth, and the recognition of "His Britannic Majesty as head of the Association". This scheme had close affinities with an essential detail of the Hungarian policy advocated by Griffith in *The Resurrection of Hungary*.

It is instructive to consider the proposals formulated by other pre-1916 Irish nationalists, and by Irish unionists, for an Anglo-Irish settlement in the light of *The Resurrection of Hungary*. Most of these make Griffith's proposals appear relatively advanced, although the preservation of a monarchy shared by both countries is a feature common to all. During the first decade of the twentieth century, Redmond, leader of the Irish Party, was making it clear that his vision of Home Rule was in accord with what Paul Bew has called "his always latent liberal imperialism".[9] In 1908, he told the journalist A. G. Gardner that "our stake in the Empire is too large for us to be detached from it. Our roots are in the Imperial as well as in the national."[10] In 1910, Redmond and his ally T. P. O'Connor were explaining to North Americans that Home Rule for a thirty-two county Ireland did not mean a break with the British Empire. On the contrary, as Redmond put it, the Irish people desired "to strengthen the imperial bonds through a federal system of government". He was content to accept a measure of Home Rule which would give Westminster "the final authority over local legislation enacted in Ireland as it has over [British] legislation". The Irish Party would not look for such complete local autonomy as the self-governing British colonies enjoyed, would abide by any fiscal system enacted by the British parliament and would favour continuing Irish representation at the House of Commons. "Once we receive Home Rule" Redmond promised, "we shall demonstrate an Imperial loyalty beyond question".[11] Redmond disowned these sentiments when they were comprehensively criticised by Irish politicians and in the Press. In the immediate post-Treaty period, the Redmondite vision of an Ireland united in its loyalty to the Empire was shared by Churchill, who, in the Commons debate on the Treaty, hoped that "Ulster" would join the south and that as a consequence "the national unity of Ireland within the British Empire would be attained". He liked to believe that it was this dream of a united Ireland, and not the British threat of war, that had induced the Irish Treaty delegates to accept allegiance to the Crown.

In 1917, an Irish Convention was summoned by the British Government in the hope that 101 "representative Irishmen", Unionist and Nationalist, could formulate proposals for presentation to the Imperial Parliament for the future self-government of Ireland within the Empire. These proposals were less radical than those advocated more than a decade earlier by Griffith in *The Resurrection of Hungary*. The scheme, accepted by a majority vote of the Convention, if implemented, would not have involved the partition of the country. It provided for the establishment of a parliament for the whole of Ireland, with an executive responsible to it. The parliament was to consist of a King, a

Senate and a House of Commons with a general power to make laws for Ireland. However, the Imperial Parliament was to retain supreme power and authority over all persons in Ireland, and over the matters of peace and war, treaties and foreign relations, as well as the protection of the Protestant minority. Irish members would still sit in the Westminster Parliament. The Sinn Féin boycott of the Convention made it a largely futile exercise, this futility further compounded by unionist unwillingness to accept even so qualified a measure of self-government as that embodied in the majority report.

Political developments in Southern and Northern Ireland, particularly from 1912 on, made Griffith's *Resurrection of Hungary* look increasingly like a historical curiosity, especially to advanced nationalists. These developments included the growing dominance of physical force nationalism following the 1916 Rising, the failure of the British government to grant even a limited form of Home Rule to Ireland, British acquiescence in the unconstitutional methods employed by Ulster Unionists, the evolution of Griffith's moderate Sinn Féin into a much more militant movement led by de Valera, and the growing demands for an independent Irish republic. The fact that it was overtaken by events cannot detract from the importance of *The Resurrection of Hungary* as one of the indispensable documents of twentieth-century Irish history, and as an influence on the debate within Irish nationalism between 1904 and 1921. Its central proposal, the withdrawal of Irish elected representatives from Westminster, was to become a cornerstone of Sinn Féin policy, while the protectionist economic policies Griffith advocated had an enduring influence. The possibility of a dual monarchy was still being canvassed by a few Irish politicians, most notably Kevin O'Higgins, in the mid-1920s. O'Higgins believed that the coronation of the King of England in Ireland as King of a separate Irish Kingdom in which the north-eastern counties could have a local administration offered a possible alternative to partition, since it would provide the means of reconciling unionist loyalty to the Crown with the separatist urge of southern nationalism.[12] W. B. Yeats, however, although he regarded O'Higgins as the greatest of the post-Treaty politicians, nevertheless suggested that a royal opening of the Dáil might be too great a price to pay for the unity of Ireland.[13]

NOTES

1   *The Resurrection of Hungary*, pp. 91–2.
2   See Brian Maye, *Arthur Griffith* (Dublin, 1997), p. 98.
3   Thomas Kabdebo, *The Hungarian–Irish Parallel and Arthur Griffith's Use of His Sources* (Maynooth, St Patrick's College, 1988).
4   See Patrick Maume, "Young Ireland, Arthur Griffith and Republican Ideology", *Éire-Ireland* (Summer 1999), p. 165
5   Alfred Cobban, *Self-Determination* (New York, 1970), p. 164
6   *Resurrection*, pp. 84–5.
7   See Nicholas Mansergh, *The Unresolved Question: The Anglo–Irish Settlement and its Undoing* (London, 1991), p. 24
8   Ibid., p. 26
9   Paul Bew, *John Redmond* (Dundalk, 1996), p. 30
10 Ibid.
11 See Michael Wheatley, "John Redmond and federalism in 1910", *Irish Historical Studies* (May, 2001), pp. 354–5.
12 See Terence de Vere White, *Kevin O'Higgins* (Tralee, 1966), pp. 216–17.
13 W. B. Yeats, *On the Boiler* (Dublin, 1939), p. 30.

NOTE ON THE TEXT

This edition has been reprinted as a facsimile of the Third Edition, 1918. The original illustrations on unnumbered pages have been printed on pp. iv and vi–viii of this edition.

THE RESURRECTION OF HUNGARY

FRANCIS DEAK.
(Circa 1867.)

THE
RESURRECTION OF HUNGARY:

A PARALLEL FOR IRELAND

WITH APPENDICES ON

PITT'S POLICY AND SINN FEIN

By ARTHUR GRIFFITH.

" The case of Ireland is as nearly as possible parallel to the case of Hungary."—WILLIAM SMITH O'BRIEN.

" It is impossible to think of the affairs of Ireland without being forcibly struck with the parallel of Hungary."—SYDNEY SMITH.

" Whenever the people of England think one way in the proportion of two to one, they can outvote in Parliament the united force of Scotland, Wales, and Ireland, although they should think in the other way in the proportion of five to one. And if England thinks one way in the proportion of three to one, she can outvote Scotland, Ireland, and Wales together, although they were each and all to return the whole of their members to vote against her."—GLADSTONE.

" A country is prosperous, not in proportion to its fertility, but in proportion to its freedom."—MONTESQUIEU.

THIRD EDITION.

Dublin :
WHELAN AND SON.
1918.

LOUIS KOSSUTH.
(Circa 1848.)

FRANCIS JOSEF.
(Circa 1867.)

THE QUEEN OF HUNGARY.
(Circa 1867.)

Preface to the Third Edition.

In the fourteen years that have passed since "The Resurrection of Hungary" was written, Ireland continuing to pursue the policy rejected by Hungary in its conflict with Austria, has had its population further reduced by eighty thousand souls and its taxation trebled.

In the British Parliament, whither it sent its representatives, those representatives during that period supported in office four successive English Governments; associated Ireland with England's declaration of war upon Germany; aided England's Government to impose English war taxes upon this country; declared that Irish manhood must subserve the war aims of England; announced willingness to aid England to conscript Irish youth should it be necessary to English victory; and agreed with England to partition Ireland in the twentieth century as Russia, Prussia and Austria partitioned Poland in the eighteenth.

In the same space of time sixteen Irishmen were executed and two thousand five hundred Irishmen deported and imprisoned on proof or suspicion of seeking that measure of independence for Ireland which England claims for nations that lie within the dominion of the Powers upon whom she declared war.

In the past year the British Premier stated in the British House of Commons (a) that Ireland is still as unreconciled to England as it was in the days of Oliver Cromwell; (b) that the Irish representatives in England's Parliament had never claimed for Ireland that sovereign independence England claims for Belgium, Serbia, Rumania and Poland; and (c) that England would never yield Ireland back her sovereign independence.

These are the evil fruits of Parliamentarianism masquerading as Constitutionalism—physical and economic decay, moral debasement, and national denial.

The constitutional leader of Hungary—Francis Deak—refused to associate his country with Austria's war against Prussia even when Austria bid the restoration of Hungary's independence as the price. None but the Government of a free Hungary might pledge the lives and property of the people of Hungary. The pseudo-constitutional leaders of Ireland pledged Ireland's blood and treasure to England's war upon Germany and Austria-Hungary without even offer of the bribe of Irish independence, and without reference to the Irish people. The Irish people have disowned their false leaders, but the sin was less in the men than in the system. Irish Parliamentarianism, born of the Act of Union and based upon admission of English right over Ireland, was inherently vicious. It constituted not a national expression, but a national surrender. It was the acceptance of moral and constitutional right in another country to shape our destinies; and whither it led the Irish people—to the attempted renunciation of their national past and their national future—to provincialism, partition, and foreign conscription—was whither it tended by the law of its being.

When Mr. Pitt, having struck down an organised and centred Ireland, induced the Irish to send their representatives to a foreign Senate to discuss with a foreign majority the affairs of this country, and to accept the vote of the foreign majority as the deciding factor—Mr. Pitt came nearer to conquering Ireland than came Mountjoy, who handed over Ireland to Elizabeth "carcases and ashes," or than came Cromwell when, with fire, sword, and slaveship, he "settled Ireland for all time." For Mr. Pitt achieved by fraud what the warriors failed to gain by force. He confused the moral standards of the nation. He caused Ireland to revolve on an axis not its own. He made Irish nationality a doubter of its own existence, and in Irish politics he made a chaos.

Thus most Irishmen lost the instinct of thinking nationally, and came to think of Ireland in terms of English Toryism or English Whiggery, English Radicalism or English Socialism. They grew to look upon this English party or class as a friend, and that English party or class as an enemy. Hence they ceased to recognise in all English parties and classes the same England in different garments. Mesmerised by London—whither its eyes were turned away—Ireland permitted, one by one, the attributes of nationhood to be filched, and in the end the Irish Nation, dwindling from the earth, listened to the spellbinders who half-persuaded it that duty and allegiance lay outside itself, and were in fact due to that country which had erased its name from the list of independent nations.

Ireland was sick—mind-drugged by Parliamentarianism—but Ireland is convalescing. The memory of what she was and the realisation of what she is are restoring her to national health. She sees herself as Hungary came to see herself—through eyes no longer fitted to foreign spectacles. She sees Finland stand up a free Republic, Poland arise a sovereign Kingdom. She asks shall she, their elder sister, be less in the world's account, and she demands to-day an equal independence. It is the story of the Sibylline Books.

Fifty-seven years ago the London " Times," writing of the struggle then waging, said of the Hungarians—

> They wish to be Hungarians, and not Germans, and they have no desire to be dragged by Austria into German politics and be compelled to spend their money and lives in pursuit of objects in which they have no interest.

That is to-day the position of the people of Ireland. They wish to be Irish, and not English, and they have no desire to be dragged by England into British politics and be compelled to spend their money and their lives in pursuit of objects in which they have no interest.

ARTHUR GRIFFITH.

January 20, 1918.

Preface to the First Edition.

(1904).

The series of articles on the " Resurrection of Hungary " originally appeared in "The United Irishman " during the first six months of the present year [1904]. The object of the writer was to point out to his compatriots that the alternative of armed resistance to the foreign government of this country is not acquiescence in usurpation, tyranny, and fraud.

A century ago in Hungary a poet startled his countrymen by shouting in their ears: "Turn your eyes from Vienna or you perish." The voice of Josef Karman disturbed the nation, but the nation did not apprehend. Vienna remained its political centre until, years later, the convincing tongue of Louis Kossuth cried up and down the land: "Only on the soil of a nation can a nation's salvation be worked out."

Through a generation of strife and sorrow the people of Hungary held by Kossuth's dictum and triumphed gloriously. The despised, oppressed, and forgotten province of Austria is to-day the free, prosperous, and renowned Kingdom of Hungary.

Sixty years ago, and more, Ireland was Hungary's exemplar. Ireland's heroic and long-enduring resistances to the destruction of her independent nationality were themes the writers of Young Hungary dwelt upon to enkindle and make resolute the

Magyar people. The poet precursors of Free Hungary—Bacsanyi and Vorosmarty—drank in Celtic inspiration, and the journalists of Young Hungary taught their people that Ireland had baffled a tyranny as great as that which threatened death to Hungary. Times have changed, and Hungary is now Ireland's exemplar.

It is in the memory of men still living when Hungary had not five journals in which a word of the Hungarian language was permitted to appear, when she had no modern literature save a few patriotic songs; when she had no manufactures of moment, and no commerce, save with her enemy, Austria; when she was cursed with an atrocious land-system and ruled by foreign bureaucrats; when her whole revenue did not reach £6,000,000 yearly, and her finances were robbed to perpetuate her oppression.

To-day the revenue of Hungary is £42,000,000 —800 newspapers and journals are printed in the Hungarian language. She possesses a great modern literature, an equitable land-system, a world-embracing commerce, a thriving and multiplying people, and a National Government. Hungary is a Nation.

She has become so because she turned her back on Vienna. Sixty years ago Hungary realised that the political centre of the nation must be within the nation. When Ireland realises this obvious truth and turns her back on London the parallel may be completed. It failed only when, two generations back, Hungary took the road of principle and Ireland the path of compromise and expediency.

Contents

Introduction.

Look on the Map of the World at Hungary. It is a fair and fertile country, inhabited by a brave and intelligent people. Sixty years ago it was enslaved, as is Ireland. To-day it stands, a free and prosperous nation, in the front rank of European States. Within the lifetime of men not yet too aged, the Eagles of Austria, bathed in Hungarian blood, flew in triumph over a vanquished land. Ireland, at the end of the great Artificial Famine, looked not so hopelessly crushed as Hungary at the close of the same year —1849. Ireland after Aughrim seemed a nearer parallel. Therefore, when gazing out from Ireland to-day you behold Hungary as free, as prosperous, as strong, and as renowned as the Austria which, less than seventy years ago, erased the name of Hungary from the map, you may well rub your eyes, remembering that Hungary never once sent a Party "to fight for Home Rule on the floor of the House" in Vienna—never once admitted the right of Austria to rule over her—never once pretended to be loyal to the Power that manacled her—and, notwithstanding, forced Austria to her knees and wrung from her unwilling hands the Free Constitution that has made the potent Hungary we see to-day.

Before we tell the story of how it was done, we must briefly sketch the history of Hungary to the day of Vilagos in 1849, when Europe wagged its head and said: "Hungary is no more!"

In the eighth century of our era the warlike Magyars burst in upon the rich plains ringed by the Carpathians, and raised their standard above the fertile land. Christendom, alarmed, went forth to drive the infidels back through the Eastern Gates of Europe, but got the worse of the attempt, and Hungary remained a nightmare to Christendom until a miracle happened and a King arose—the good King Stephen, whose Iron Crown each King of Hungary must don in Budapest before the Hungarian owes him allegiance—who converted the invincible Magyar warriors to the Christian faith. Thenceforward Hungary from being the menace became a sentinel of Christendom, standing by the Asiatic Gate, and holding it against the unbelievers who sought to force an entrance with the sword. John Hunyadi, by the cunning of his brain and the skill of his sword, hurled back the Turks from Europe and raised Hungary to the pinnacle of glory. But a tragic night followed Hunyadi's blazing day. Seeming secured forever against their enemies, the Hungarians quarrelled—noble and burgher and peasant—among themselves, and in the height of their division the old enemy broke in again upon them. This time there were no wise and gallant Kings and no united people, and at the fatal battle of Mohacs the flag of Hungary went down for the first time in centuries.

For two hundred years thereafter Hungarian history was a humiliation and a tragedy. But at length the Turkish power in Europe was broken, under the walls of Vienna, by the Poles and the French, and the Hungarians with the Austrians, flung themselves upon their old enemy. Turkey was vanquished, and Hungary, in 1718, was again free— free, but desolated.

THE CONNECTION WITH AUSTRIA.

Began now the connection with Austria as a free and equal union of two independent nations. In time the fascinating Maria Theresa wept beauty's tears over her "chivalrous Hungarians," and drew the Hungarian magnates to the Austrian capital, where she smiled and gushed over them. In turn the flattered magnates could do no less than expend in Vienna the revenues of their estates and adopt the dress and manners, and finally the language, of the Austrians. In a space of time these Hungarian magnates, degenerated like the Irish peers, and—renegade to their manhood and nationality—became contemners of their own country, sycophants of Austria, and cultivators of Imperial souls. Josef II., Maria Theresa's son, carried on with greater vigour and less discretion his clever mother's de-nationalising policy. He ignored the rights of Hungary, refused to wear the crown of King Stephen, and schemed to suppress the national language. His vigour caused a national reaction, and his successor, Leopold, conformed outwardly to the Hungarian Constitution. But the monarch who followed Leopold reverted to the policy of Josef, and thus forced a section of the Hungarians into secret conspiracy to destroy the connection. The conspirators were detected and executed or imprisoned, and for a time Hungary became subservient to Austrian rule. But when, after the fall of Napoleon, Austria openly ignored the Constitution and governed Hungary at its will, there was virtue found in a few men to set out upon the seeming hopeless task of re-kindling national spirit in the listless land. For five years they cried aloud that Hungary was still Hungary, and that the King of Hungary must govern through the Hungarian Constitution. The people shook their heads—"Hungary was!" they said, and passed along. But after a while one mused, and a second paused, and another lingered; and the thought that, after all, Hungary was not dead, ripened in the land. Austria determined to put an end to the folly by conscripting the thinkers and the taught. So the Emperor of Austria ordered a levy of troops on Hungary, and an amazing thing happened. Hungary declined to recognise his authority and refused to obey his command.

"The King of Hungary is alone entitled to our allegiance while he governs through the Constitution. To the Emperor of Austria Hungary owes no allegiance. Convoke the Diet of Hungary and let the levy of troops be decided by it, or decided not at all." This was the reply of Hungary to the Emperor Franz. For five years the contest briskly waged— Franz seeking to impose Austria's will as the law in Hungary, and the awakened Hungarians resisting any will but the will of Hungary as **their law.** In the end Franz was beaten, and after the lapse of eleven years the Diet, in 1825, was convoked to discuss and settle the affairs of Hungary. It is from this date the history of Hungary that nearly concerns us begins.

COUNT SZECHENYI.

The opening of the Diet of 1825 was marked by an incident that created great excitement throughout the country and resentment in the highest circles. A member of the Upper House, rising from his seat, addressed the august assembly of Hungarians in the Hungarian tongue.

It was a daring act. Indignation prevailed amongst the members at this outrage on respectability. The insult was accentuated by the fact that it came from one of themselves, for Stephen Szechenyi was one of the greatest of the nobles. He was remonstrated with by the older magnates. They pointed out to him that the speaking of the Hungarian language was all very well for serfs and boors, but entirely unfit for gentlemen. They counselled him, being older and sager, not to excite the derision of enlightened Europe, and particularly of Vienna, the hub of the Universe, at the very outset of his career. He listened to them in silence—he was a man of great silences—and thanked them for the kindly interest they took in him. Then the old nobles went back to their fellows and comforted them, telling them all was set right. "Of course," said they, "he saw the absurdity of his position when we had it pointed out to him, and how irretrievably he would compromise himself if he continued this native language nonsense. After all, we must remember we were young like himself once, and apt to do foolish things. So let us say no more about it."

And when the forgiving nobles reassembled in the Upper Chamber, and Szechenyi arose again to address them, they received him with courteous applause. For they wished to encourage the repentant sinner lest he might falter in his apology.

For a moment the young noble stood silent in the centre of the House. Then fixing his eyes on the leader of his advisers, he opened his mouth, and lo! out of it slowly rolled Hungarian periods. As the astonished and deceived nobles sat spellbound, his voice rose and rang and swelled with passion and triumph and exultation through the Chamber, chanting, in the despised tongue of the nation, the story of Hungary's woe, and foretelling her resurrection. When he ceased, the old men sat dazed, but many of the younger nobles, stirred in their hearts, stricken in their consciences, set up a shout of applause.

The country was astounded and pleased, the denationalised nobles dumbfounded. They could find words scarce strong enough to express their indignation at Szechenyi. Szechenyi was immovable. One day he walked into the Lower House and sat listening to a discussion on the ways and means of fostering the national language. Paul Nagy rose and testily told his brother deputies that the discussion was mere babble. "You know," he said, "the Government is hostile to the language—and you know it will not permit us to levy taxes for the purpose of placing it in a position to compete with German. To enable our language to compete with that of our rulers—to enable us to stem the flood of denationalisation, the obvious course is to establish a Hungarian Academy of Sciences. Now that costs money—we have not got it—the Government will not provide it. The nobles should do so, but they are Germanicised, and will not do so. If by any miracle they set the example, others would follow, but why discuss impossibilities?" and Nagy, having silenced the babblers, sat down.

Szechenyi rose in the House, and begged its permission to hear him for one minute. The permission was accorded, and Szechenyi delivered a short speech in Hungarian. This was the whole of it: "I am a noble. I shall contribute the entire of one year's income from my estates to found a National Academy of Sciences." The House was moved to enthusiasm. "I will contribute a thousand florins," cried one member, "And I two thousand," "And I—and I," and soforth, and in a few minutes' time the respectable sum of 150,000 florins was guaranteed, and the Hungarian Academy of Sciences became a reality. At present it flourishes, famed through Europe, and its funds amount to some two and a-half million florins—result of a forty-word speech.

The country rang with the name of Szechenyi, and before peasant, burgher, or noble understood very well what had occurred, Szechenyi was leader of the nation. Nobody thought it strange. It seemed as if they had been waiting for him and he had arrived at the appointed time. The reason was simple enough. He was the one man in Hungary just then who knew his own mind and his country's needs, and was equipped by study, observation, and character to lead her. Szechenyi was at this period thirty-four years old. He was of an ancient family, ennobled for centuries, and for a Hungarian an extremely wealthy man. As a youth he had fought against Napoleon, and after the close of the Napoleonic wars he travelled over Europe, studying and noting the social and political conditions of each country. When he returned to Hungary his mind was shocked at the contrast it presented to most of the other countries of Europe. Its nobles, spiritless and corrupt, anxious only to retain their privileges and extort their rents—or the equivalent of rents—from the people; the people ignorant, the whole country decaying. Szechenyi dreamed of making Hungary happy and prosperous, and rendering the relations between Austria and his country amicable by other means than political agitation or armed insurrection. "Revive your language, educate yourselves, build up your agriculture and your industries," this was the basis of his teaching.* He taught rather by example than by precept that politics were of small account, and rarely interested himself in them, but he laboured unceasingly to implant love of country in his people's hearts—to improve their intellectual and industrial condition. His busy brain was ever devising new schemes to benefit the country, his iron will surmounting the obstacles that barred their path, his steady hand pointing the way to their realisation. He strove to unite the nation —peasant and noble—in a common brotherhood of affection and awaken them to a recognition that the interests of one

---

* The so-called National Education System in Ireland was suggested by the system established by Austria in Hungary, but was much better adapted to its primary purpose of denationalisation. The system under which "education" was administered in Hungary during the Austrian dominance was thus described: "In one word—Stultification. If a student obtains a first-class certificate, you may be sure he is a fool; if a second, he may not be more than ordinarily ignorant; but if he get only the lowest he runs a fair chance of being a clever fellow. The course of study is so laborious and at the same time the books to be read, the comments to be listened to, and all things to be learned, are so adapted to shut out every idea of what is good or great or beautiful that one who has followed out the system is not only less wise than before for what he has learned; but from the time that has been occupied it is impossible also that he should have devoted any attention to the acquisition of better things."

were the interests of all—to make them realise that whether they were gentle or simple, they were first of all Hungarians. The people followed him unquestioningly and enthusiastically. They witnessed the wonderful and beneficent changes this one man's genius was making in the land, and to them he seemed almost a god; but the nobles, save a small and enlightened minority gazed on him askance. Too stupid to understand he was their best friend, they regarded him as an enemy, a revolutionary, and when he published his famous work on Credit, which may be said to have thoroughly awakened Hungary to national consciousness, the stupid magnates could see in it, not their guide to salvation, but the subtle teachings of a ruthless Jacobin. " Do not," he exhorted the people in this work, " pass your time in lamentations over the glories of former days. Look forward and let your patriotism aim at restoring the prosperity of our fatherland. Do not say with the doubters, ' Hungary has Been '; say with me, ' Hungary shall Be !' " " Treason, revolution," muttered the denationalised nobles.

DEAK AND KOSSUTH.

The tireless patriotism of this remarkable man aroused in Hungary a real national life. The country became instinct with vitality, and those who visited it after a few years stood amazed at the change. The political Nationalists sought to persuade him to accept their leadership, but Szechenyi declined to place himself at the head of a political movement. Francis Deak, a Catholic country gentleman, and Louis Kossuth, a Protestant barrister, two younger men, became the political leaders. Deak was thirty years of age and Kossuth thirty-one when they met for the first time in the Diet of 1833, and were drawn together by a common patriotism and a common faith in the efficacy of political action. But they differed widely in many ways. Kossuth was imbued with French revolutionary principles, and dreamed of the Universal Republic. He hated Austria, and his secret ambition was to see Hungary an independent Republic. Deak did not share the principles of the French Revolution. Neither did he hate Austria, only Austrian oppression. He was willing to see Hungary linked with Austria, provided the link were one of friendship not of steel. Here is Deak's programme in Deak's own words :—

" Hungary is a free country, independent in its whole system of legislation and administration. It is subordinate to no other country. We have no wish to oppose the interests of our country to the unity of the Monarchy or the security of its existence; but we consider that it is contrary to law or justice that the interests of Hungary should be made subordinate to those of any country

whatsoever. . . . We will never consent that it shall
be sacrificed to the unity of the system of government.
. . . . Our Constitutional life is a treasure which we
cannot sacrifice either to foreign interests or to material
advantages, howsoever great. Our first duty is to preserve and strengthen it."

Deak stood on the Pragmatic Sanction. That is, very
much as if we in Ireland took our stand on the Settlement of
1782, and denied the validity of the Act of Union and of all
legislation made in England for this country. Kossuth
equally exhorted Hungary to uphold the Pragmatic Sanction
and insist on Austria doing likewise ; but to Kossuth this was
but a political weapon.

Again and again the voice of Deak thundered in the
Diet in denunciation of its subserviency to Austrian tyranny.
The slavish asked " What can we do? We cannot fight
Austria with the sword—what then is there left but to
submit and be silent?" " Your laws are violated, and you
shut your mouths," Deak responded, " Woe to the nation
which raises no protest when its law is outraged. It con-
tributes of itself to impair the respect due to its laws. The
nation which submits to injustice and oppression in cowardly
silence is doomed." He sometimes desponded, but he did
not because of his despondency cease to fight. " The feeling
of patriotism," he said in one of his speeches, " is not kept
alive in Hungarians to the same degree as it is in the men
of other nations, either by the inspiring memories of the
past or by sentiments of vanity and self-esteem. Our history
can look back to nothing but disastrous civil wars and bloody
struggles for the preservation of our very existence. Europe
scarce knows that we live. Alas, it looks upon our fatherland as but a fertile and uncultivated province of Austria.
Yet I hold him for no true Hungarian to whom this poor,
suffering country is not dearer than the most brilliant
Empire in Europe."

There spoke the true patriot, and in that spirit Deak
fought every abuse and every evil. He fought for the right
of the Hungarian's house to be his castle, for the right of
the tiller of the soil to own his land. And when he was
told that such a right was repugnant to the Constitution,
he withered up his opponents with the scornful words :
" Repugnant to the Constitution! What a thing is the
Constitution if it forbids us to seek the well-being of millions
of our countrymen—the strength of our nation. Justice
demands that we should do so—the law directs we should
do so. The Constitution cannot be opposed to justice and
law." And when the opponents of right solemnly laid it
down that all property in land belonged to the lords of
the soil, Deak pulverised the humbug with a sentence :

" The gods of old claimed but a share in the ownership of the woods and fields and hills and vales and streams—have ye grown greater than the gods?"

The fearless bearing and convincing logic of Deak, backed as he was by the County Councils, which sturdily refused to carry out the arbitrary ordinances of the Austrian Government, inspirited the Diet and even impelled the nobles to agree to agrarian reform. Then the Austrian Government intervened. It would permit no agrarian reform —not it.

Ferdinand IV. filled the throne, but Metternich was the real ruler of the Empire. His was the fatal mind that cannot distinguish between Reform and Revolution, and begets, according to circumstance and environment, the Reactionary or the Anarchist. Metternich would rebuild the Bastille, and on every road Deak advanced he spied the busy masons. Szechenyi saw and said: " The Nation must depend to some extent upon Vienna."

" The Nation must depend upon itself alone," answered Deak, marching forward. " Come back. Let us have peace and we shall have prosperity," Szechenyi called after him. " Can you not see," retorted Deak, as he grappled with the masons, " that it is dread of our prosperity impels the Austrian Government to seek to bar Hungary's progress?" and then the Tyrtæn Magyars twanged their harps and blew great trumpet-blasts that echoed around the Carpathians. So when the Diet of 1833 came to an end, there was a mighty hubbub in the land, the people noisily asking: " Who are these Austrians that they should rule us?" and " Why should we respect these nobles of ours since they are but the dogs of our enemies?" Intelligent village ruffians thumped the tables of the village inns to emphasise the fact that Hungary was a very great country, and the Magyars a very great people, and seditiously refused to doff their caubeens when the awful Austrian officials passed by. " Why should we take off our hats to the fellows who stole our Pragmatic Sanction?" they asked of the village fathers. " And what was our Pragmatic Sanction that they stole?" asked the village fathers. " What was our Pragmatic Sanction?" echoed the ruffians. " Why it was—it was—it was— our country and everything, don't you see!" The village ruffians were perfectly right, although they were not certain themselves on that point. Now all this was a great victory, since it gave the Magyars a good conceit of themselves— without which, until Tibb's Eve, Hungary would never have regained a doit of her stolen right.

THE DIET OF 1836.

The Diet of 1836 was the most unlike thing to a mothers' meeting that the finite mind of man could conceive. The patriots demanded that the people should be provided with a first-class education. The Government explained that to educate the people would inevitably lead to anarchy, communism, murder, rape, robbery, pillage, and atheism. Thereupon the patriots fell to debate the matter and incidentally express their views on Austria and things Austrian. The thoughtful Louis Kossuth wrote painfully accurate reports of (1) What the supporters of Austria in the Diet said about the people of Hungary, and (2) What the supporters of Hungary in the Diet said about Austria, the Austrian Government, the Austrian officials, and the Hungarian seoinini. These reports he lithographed and circulated through the country, at six florins a month. The country read them feverishly and began to roar out its indignation. So the Austrian Government thought it high time to square Kossuth. He was a poor man with a large family, and it suggested to him that it would be a good thing for him to employ his considerable talents in a quiet position at a handsome salary under the Empire. The offer was declined brusquely.

And so the Government "struck terror." Szechenyi, Kossuth, Wesselyeni, a noble who was one of his friends and sympathisers, and some others were arrested and indicted for treason, and they were condemned to several years' imprisonment.* The deputy, John Balogh, was arrested afterwards. John was a blunt man, and had spoken his mind of the " striking terror " policy with a frankness that left not a shred to the imagination. As a result of his arrest, his seat in the Diet was declared vacant, and a Government candidate full of smiles and promises issued his address to the electors. The electors promptly re-nominated John Balogh. And the Government thereupon instructed the Lord Lieutenant of the county to present each free and independent elector with a five-florin note and invite him to come up to the Government stores and choose such goods as he might yearn to possess—on the day of the poll. On the day of the poll the electors returned John Balogh by a sweeping majority, after which they hoisted him on their shoulders and carried him in triumph to the County Council

---

* Baron Wesselenyi was found guilty of treason for saying: "The Government sucks out the marrow of nine million peasants, and will not allow us nobles to better their condition by legislative means; but retaining them in their present state, it only awaits its time to exasperate them against us—then it will come forward to rescue us. But woe to us! From freemen we shall be degraded to the state of slaves." It is fair to the Austrian Government to add that it treated the Hungarian political prisoners as political prisoners, and not as felons.

Rooms, each elector bearing in his fist a stout stave on the top of which was stuck the generous Government's five-florin note. In the Council Chamber they found the Lord Lieutenant, and moved him to the chair. When he was in it, each free and independent elector advanced in turn and stated his opinion of the Lord Lieutenant's action. When the man sought to escape, he was held in the chair by main force, and for four hours compelled to listen to the condemnation by his countrymen of his treachery. At the end the five-florin notes were torn up and flung in his face. Though Kossuth was in prison, the " striking terror " policy had abjectly failed, and the Government abandoned its prosecution.

THE " PESTH GAZETTE."

Two years passed ere the Diet was convoked. It met again in 1840, and its first act was to demand the release of Kossuth and his companions. " Let us make a deal," said the Government ; " we release Kossuth—you moderate your opposition." " No," said Deak nobly, " our duty to our country is greater and holier than a sympathy for our friends. Liberty gained at such a price would be more painful to them than all their sufferings." The Government surrendered, and Kossuth was released.

Now, Kossuth was a journalist, and understood the power of the Press. Returned from prison, he founded the " Pesth Gazette," and taught a simple creed. Firstly—That Hungary was a very great nation ; secondly, that none but the Hungarian nation had right or claim to Hungary ; and thirdly, that Austria and Austrian institutions and language had no manner of right in Hungary. The " Pesth Gazette " became a dominant influence in Hungary. When in doubt the Hungarian began to ask, " What does Louis Kossuth say ? " and what Louis Kossuth said was what most of Hungary echoed. There were stormy times in the Diet. The patriots demanded equality of taxation and official recognition of the Hungarian language. They won the Language fight by two votes—they lost the Taxation battle. "This must not endure," said the "Pesth Gazette," and Louis Kossuth founded the Hungarian League of Industry and Commerce.*

* The Protective System advocated by Kossuth was based on Freidrich List's National System. List visited Hungary in 1844, where he was enthusiastically received by the Hungarian leaders, Kossuth hailing him as the " Economic Teacher of the Nations."
" The splendid natural advantages with which a benign Providence had so liberally endowed it," said a Hungarian writing in 1850 of Hungary, " were looked upon with hatred

This League came into collision with the Austrian Government. That was what Kossuth designed it to do. A glorious fight ensued. Kossuth pinned his faith on the County Councils, and he did not err. When the Hungarian League accepted the Government's challenge, and the Government came swooping down, the Government was tripped up, kicked, buffeted, and banged about the head by the fifty-five County Councils of Hungary. In its blind rage the Government did what Kossuth yearned it should do—deposed the nobles from their position as Chairmen of the County Councils, and appointed paid Austrian officials in their stead. "Now nobles of Hungary will ye be men?" asked Louis Kossuth. The Austrian insult proved too much for those nobles who had not ceased to remember they were also men. They came over to Kossuth by the score and consented to renounce their feudal privileges and bear their share of the burdens of their country.

The Diet of 1847 was convoked, while the land palpitated with excitement. The Government nominee issued his address to the electors of the " Loyal County of Pesth," and Louis Kossuth flung down the gauntlet to Metternich by entering the list against the Austrians' candidate for " The Loyal County." Metternich foresaw that the return of Kossuth for Pesth would make Kossuth master of the Diet, and then——. The end no man could foresee. So the full machinery of Austrian corruption and Austrian intimidation was turned upon the electors of Pesth. And in its teeth Kossuth was carried trimphantly into the Diet on the shoulders of nobles and peasants.

1848.

The Diet demanded the Restoration of Hungary's Independence. The people stood behind it, virile and determined; and in the early days of 1848 Austria yielded. The

---

and envy by its benighted rulers; they feared lest it should grow too strong for them, and therefore directed all their ingenuity to choke the springs of its industry; and to prevent the development of its commerce it was determined that Hungary should become a granary to Vienna, Bohemia, and Moravia, whose manufacturing population it was to supply with raw materials, and to pay double for the necessaries it received in return. A system of revenue regulations was also established between Austria and Hungary which prevented the transmission of any manufactures from the latter to the former, by a heavy prohibitive duty, and subjected all commercial transactions between the two countries to an oppressive taxation."

Emperor Ferdinand came to Hungary and agreed to the claim of the Nation. The Laws of 1848 were passed and sanctioned, and a Hungarian Government, sovereign in Hungary, and responsible to the Hungarian people, came into being, with Louis Batthyany as Premier, Szechenyi as Minister of Public Works, Francis Deak as Minister of Justice, and Kossuth as Minister of Finance. Kossuth was satisfied. He moved a loyal address to the Throne, and the Hungarian nation, freed from all foreign interference and empowered to form a national army, threw up its cap and huzza'd for the re-birth of Hungary.

But a Court Camarilla in Vienna had determined that there would be no free Hungary. Scarcely had the country started on its career of freedom when Wallach and Serb and Croatian swarmed over the borders, fed with stories of Hungarian designs to oppress and destroy them, and instigated to pillage and massacre. The Hungarian Government ordered the Austrian troops in garrison forward to repel the marauders, and the Austrian troops marched out and fraternised with the marauders. Then great men began to lose their heads in Budapest, and proposals of measures tending to Absolutism were made. Deak saw the danger to the newly-free State, and dryly reminded the Parliament that troops and artillery, not the hangman and the gallows, would repulse the marauders. Later Deak, with the Premier, Batthany, journeyed to Vienna, but the King received them coldly and dismissed them with evasion. The Lord Lieutenant of Croatia, secretly supported by the Vienna prototypes of the patrons of the Curragh mutineers, advanced into Hungary, but the improvised Hungarian militia defeated him with heavy loss, and the Austrian Lord Lieutenant of Hungary thereupon fled, leaving behind him proofs of his complicity in the treacherous attempt to again subjugate Hungary. Ferdinand nominated Count Lemberg as the new Viceroy, and attempted to revoke the Constitution of Hungary. But it takes two to revoke a Constitution. The Hungarian Parliament declined to recognise Lemberg, and declared any who gave him aid, comfort or advice enemies of the State. Nevertheless, Lemberg insisted on coming to Budapest, where the mob murdered him upon his arrival. Next the Emperor—or rather the camarilla in whose hands he was a tool—nominated Jellachich, Ban of Croatia, as Lord Lieutenant of Hungary, at the same time ordering the Austrian Grenadiers to march on Budapest. The moment was chosen by the Viennese Republicans for a revolt, in which the Grenadiers and the National Guard joined, and seized Vienna. Jellachich, Windischgratz and Ausperg assaulted the city, and the defenders appealed to the Hungarians for aid. Kossuth, who dominated in the Hungarian Parliament, induced it, after a prolonged discussion, to send the half-armed and undisciplined national army to the aid of the Austrian Revolutionaries. The city fell, and the Hungarians, badly defeated, were driven back towards Budapest, swiftly followed by Windischgratz at the head of his victorious army. Kossuth had made his first great political mistake, and committed a military blunder.

Deak and Batthyany had kept the Austrian Government deprived of any shadow of justification to plead to Europe for making open war upon Hungary, or for treating the Hungarians as rebels. "Defence and the Laws of 1848" was the motto inscribed upon the banner of the Hungarian army. The despatch of the army by Kossuth to the aid of the Austrian revolutionists and its invasion of Austrian soil gave the Austrian camarilla its first plausible pretext for use against Hungary abroad and at home. Windischgratz proclaimed the Hungarians "Rebels." He approached the capital of Hungary on the morning of the 2nd January, 1849, and Deak and Batthyany went forth to meet him. Kossuth and his other colleagues in the Government had crossed the Danube with the Great Seal and the Crown of St. Stephen, and proceeded to Debreczin. Said Deak to Windischgratz, "Hungary seeks nothing which is not hers by law." "I make no terms with rebels," quoth Windischgratz. Vainly Deak strove for terms of peace which would ensure Hungary her Constitution. "I make no terms with rebels," was the triumphant reply. Then Deak declined to use his influence to persuade Kossuth and his colleagues to unconditional surrender, and, with Batthyany, was placed under arrest. The Austrian forces entered the Hungarian capital, and Windischgratz wrote to his master, now Francis Josef—"I have conquered."

Francis Josef was the nephew of Ferdinand, who, after the Vienna Insurrection, abdicated without troubling to obey the Constitution by seeking the consent of the Hungarian Parliament. The Parliament pointed this out, and pointed out, moreover, that the monarch must come to Budapest and be crowned there, and swear to protect the Constitution before Hungary would owe him allegiance. The new monarch curtly declined, and Kossuth retrieved his political mistake. "We have rebelled against no Government," he wrote; "we have broken no allegiance; we have no desire to separate from the Austrian Empire; we desired no concessions and no innovations; we are satisfied with what is ours by law." The Catholic Bishops of Hungary hurried to the monarch and entreated him to remember his Coronation Oath. But they appealed in vain. The Austrian army was in Budapest, and all looked dark for Hungary.

KOSSUTH AND GORGEI.

Then the fortunes of war turned. Arthur Gorgei, a young Hungarian who had been a junior officer in the Austrian army, evinced a surpassing military genius. Out of a more or less armed mob he made an army, with which he fell upon the Austrians and smote them. Before his brilliant strategy the Generals of the Empire failed. Gorgei's name rang round the world, and to his soldiers he became almost a demigod. There are no demigods. All men are human. For all time the names of Szechenyi, Kossuth, Deak and Gorgei will be associated with the struggle of Hungary for her freedom. Impartial History will record that Szechenyi relaid the foundations of the nation; that Kossuth inspired the enthusiasm without which no nation can be rebuilded; that Gorgei gave the war the measure of military success that made Hungary's name respected and implanted the feeling of national superiority in the Hungarian heart; and that Deak, steadfast and wise, out of the ashes of defeat kindled the fire of victory. But that same impartial history will record that, while patriotism was the animating motive of the four men, vanity was present in two—Kossuth and Gorgei. Kossuth beheld Gorgei's dazzling victories and rise into popular idolatry with some jealousy. Gorgei, on his side, irritated by Kossuth's interference in matters of military strategy, spoke lightly of Kossuth. The collision might have had no serious consequences for Hungary had it not been for Kossuth's mistake in decreeing the deposition of the House of Hapsburg, and raising the flag of a Republic.

This time Kossuth's political blunder was fatal. Gorgei had brought the war to the point of success, but the war that Hungary waged up to the 14th of April was a War of National Defence. Hungary had taken up arms not to dethrone the King, but to defend the Constitution. Kossuth's action changed its character into a revolution. The step was taken without consultation with Gorgei, and was bitterly resented by him and the bulk of the army. The Hungarians are Royalist, not Republican, by instinct. The English Premier's confidential agent at Vienna—Magenis—wrote to him at the time that Kossuth's action had lost him the confidence of the army. But a graver consequence followed—the intervention of Russia. Gorgei had Austria beaten. Austria now appealed to Russia on the ground that the movement was merely revolutionary; and Russia, apprehensive of what might happen in Poland —or professing so much, with an eye on Transylvania—crossed the Carpathians to Austria's assistance. Gorgei, in the circumstances, accepted the Republic, and for a space the world was thrilled by the gallant fight the Hungarians, under Gorgei's brilliant leadership, put up against two Great

Powers. But it was obvious there could be only one result in arms. Kossuth, realising his blunder, submerged his Republicanism and planned to offer the crown of Hungary to one of the Russian Imperial House. But this time he was too late to retrieve his error. When all hope was gone Kossuth renounced the dictatorship to Gorgei, who surrendered three days later, with his army, to the Russians at Vilagos. Klapka, in the fortress of Komorn, held out for a space, seeking for terms involving amnesty and the restoration of the 1848 Constitution, but it was in vain. Kossuth and some of the other leaders escaped to Turkey; many fell into Austrian hands, and were executed or imprisoned. There was sympathy for Hungary among the Nations—sympathy without works being cheap. Freedom-loving England, through the mouth of her Premier, declared that the hearts and souls of the English people were with the Hungarians; but their bodies and purses were, as usual in such cases, absent. The Heart-and-Soul Premier of England wrote to Austria, in the friendliest fashion, that it would be most desirable if Austria ceased to oppress Hungary and restored her her Constitution. Whereupon Austria replied to England, without any pretence of friendliness whatever, that England knew how to play the tyrant better than any Power in the world, and instanced the case of "unhappy Ireland." After which Old England dropped the correspondence.

Thus it was that, 68 years ago, the flag of Austria was raised above the land, and the Austrian Dragoon was the law in Hungary—her Constitution trampled, her Parliament closed, her institutions uprooted, her lands confiscated, her language banned, her affairs administered by Austrian officials, her country parcelled out into "military districts," and her name erased from the map of Europe. "Hungary is dead," said Europe. But we shall see how, by the steadfast patriotism and genius of Francis Deak, she was brought to a glorious resurrection.

NOTE.—General Gorgei surrendered with 22,000 men—the main body of the Hungarian army—to the Russians at Vilagos. Kossuth stigmatised Gorgei's surrender as treason, and for many years Gorgei's name was execrated by most of his countrymen. When in 1904 I wrote the "Resurrection of Hungary" I accepted the Kossuth view of Georgei's action as true. Since then I have had opportunity of studying the anti and pro-Gorgei literature which grew up in Hungary. It is sufficient to say that the majority of Hungarians do not now believe that Gorgei was guilty of treachery; but many hold that Gorgei could have insisted on terms of capitulation. The Hungarian army, however, was outnumbered 7 to 1, and, militarily, the position of Hungary was hopeless. Had Kossuth resigned the dictatorship to Gorgei after Russia joined forces with Austria, it is possible that Gorgei, as an opponent of Kossuth's mistaken proclamation, could have made terms. But Kossuth, great and patriotic man as he was, had not mastered the art of self-renunciation, and only resigned the dictatorship to Gorgei when the country was **in extremis.** It is due to General Gorgei —or rather to his memory, for he died in 1916, at the age of 98—that I should insert this note.—**A. G.**

Resurrection of Hungary:

A Parallel for Ireland.

I.—The Migration of Deak.

Francis Deak had been placed under arrest by the
Austrians in an early stage of the war for declining
to advise Kossuth and the members of the Hungarian Diet to unconditionally surrender. In the
latter stage he had resided on his estate at Kehida.
When the Hungarian flag had been trampled in
the blood of its soldiers and Hungary lay prostrate,
all her other leaders dead or in exile, Deak
bethought himself it was time to sell his estate and
move into town. So he sold his estate and moved
up to town—to Pesth—and hired a bedroom and a
sittingroom at the Queen of England Hotel, and
walked about the streets, playing with children,
giving alms to beggars, and conversing with all
sorts and conditions of men. The Austrians regarded
him doubtfully. "What did Deak sell his estate
and come to Pesth for?" they asked each other.
"Keep your eyes on him, my children," said the
Austrian Prefect to the Austrian police.

But although they kept as many eyes on him as
Argus had, still they could find nothing in Deak's
conduct to warrant his arrest. They had taken
away Hungary's Constitution, they had taken away
even Hungary's name, yet they could not construe
playing with children, giving to beggars, and talk-

D

ing with men and women, into treason, and that was all Deak did. Still the uneasiness and mistrist of the Austrians grew. "It would be a good thing," at length said one brilliant Austrian statesman, "to make Deak a Grand Justiciary.* This would console the Hungarian people." And they made the offer to Deak. "When my country's Constitution is acknowledged I shall consider your offer," replied Deak. "What Constitution?" asked the Austrians. "The Constitution of 1848," said Deak. "Why, my dear Deak," said the Austrians, "have you forgotten that we have crushed your Hungarian revolution?" "The Constitution still remains," said Deak. "The Constitution of 1848 was a quite impossible affair," began the Austrians. "The Constitution still remains," repeated Deak. "Let us point out to you——" began the Austrians. "It is useless, gentlemen," said Deak; "it is not a matter for argument. The Constitution still remains." Then a conciliatory Austrian statesman put his arm beneath Deak's, and said, coaxingly, "Surely, Deak, you don't demand that after such a series of accomplished facts we should begin affairs with Hungary over again?" "I do," said Deak. "Why?" asked the Austrian. "Because," said Deak, "if a man has buttoned one button of his coat wrong, it must be undone from the top." "Ah, ha," said the Austrian, "but the button might be cut off. "Then, friend," said Deak, "the coat could never be buttoned properly at all. Good afternoon."

"Deak wants the Constitution back," said the Austrians; "children cry for the moon." "Repeal the Union—restore the Heptarchy," said the English statesman, scoffingly, but Ireland had no Deak. In Deak's little room in the Pesth hotel every night a few friends gathered who puffed tobacco and drank moderately of wine. They had no passwords and no

* Judex Curiæ.

secrecy—they discoursed of Hungarian history, Hungarian literature, Hungarian industries, Hungarian economics, and the Hungarian Constitution, which they obstinately declined to oblige the Austrians by believing to be dead. "It is not dead, but sleepeth—owing to the illegal administering of a drug." Deak, who was a cheerful man, talked of the day when it would awaken, and made jokes. Visitors to Pesth from the country districts came to visit Deak. They stopped an evening, smoked a pipe and drank a glass of wine with him and with those who gathered in his sitting-room, and as they talked despair fell from them. Deak's sanguine spirit crept into their hearts, and they left convinced that Hungary was not dead. Then they returned to their districts and said to the people: "Though our Parliament has been abolished— though our County Councils have been suppressed, though martial law reigns throughout the land, though our language is banned and our Press muzzled, though Batthany is dead, Szechenyi in a madhouse, and Kossuth in exile, countrymen, all is not lost. Francis Deak has re-arisen in Pesth. We have seen him, we have spoken with him, and he charges us to say to you, 'Lift your hearts up, people of Hungary. Justice and Right shall prevail. Hungary shall rise again!'" Tyranny walked the land and crushed with iron hand every manifestation of nationality; but hope, rekindled by Deak, it could not crush out. The light that shone nightly from the window of Francis Deak's room lit up Hungary —the conversations and witty sayings of the men of all shades of opinion who gathered around his fireplace were repeated and passed from mouth to mouth throughout Hungary. The figure of Deak impressed itself stronger than the State of Siege on the Magyar. Deak grew and grew in his imagination till he grew into a Colossus—in his shadow protection, in his hands strength. "Hungary shall arise," said the Magyars, "for the great Francis

Deak—Deak the Unswerving, Deak the Farseeing,. has told us so.''

Now the strength of Francis Deak in 1850 lay mainly in the fact that Hungary was united. Hungary before 1848 had been aristocratic and democratic, republican, royalist, revolutionary, reactionary—all sorts and conditions of things. Hungary emerged from the war united—class distinctions had faded, party distinctions as they had been understood had vanished. Some men blamed the revolutionists, some men blamed the reactionaries, but all were agreed that Hungary must govern itself for the future or perish, and to Deak the whole nation looked to show them how the national existence could be preserved. Those who had been the West-Britons of Hungary, the Austrian Garrison, had learned wisdom and patriotism from the terror that had devastated the land, and with "all due reverence and loyalty,'' they forwarded a memorial to the Emperor of Austria, telling him in plain words that dragooning the people and blotting out the name of Hungary was not the way to win the hearts of their countrymen.'' ''Hungary is, indeed, indissolubly connected with Austria,'' said the erstwhile Garrison, ''but Hungary has rights which Austria cannot deny or take away— she has a right to free municipal institutions and a free constitution. We are loyal subjects of your Majesty, but it is not incompatible with our loyalty to demand the restoration of our rights.'' ''That is quite enough,'' said the Emperor, ''have the fellows who signed this memorial placed under police surveillance.'' ''And let them thank God that your Majesty is merciful enough not to chop off their rebelly heads,'' said Bach.

Buch was an Austrian Lloyd-George. In his early days he had been possessed of a thirst for aristocratic gore and a habit of shrieking ''Liberty, Equality, and Fraternity,'' wherever he went. He hated tyranny and kings and lords and loved

the labouring poor. He shouted so loudly that the
Government, becoming moidhered, took him by the
hand and introduced him to polite society and a
number of duchesses. In a short time Bach learned
to shout the other way round, and damned all and
sundry who would dare gainsay whatever the Lord's
Anointed—Francis Josef—decreed. Like his English copy, Bach was blessed by nature with a cheek
of brass, and by its aid he soon became the Emperor's right-hand man. Said the Emperor to Bach:
"This Francis Deak is giving us some trouble in
Hungary; better conciliate him." "It shall be
done, sire," said Bach; and then he smilingly turned
to Deak and said: "It appears, Deak, you are not
satisfied with the manner in which Austria governs
Hungary. Now, let us discuss the matter in a
reasonable and statesmanlike spirit. Let Hungary
appoint you her representative, and you can open
negotiations with me here in Vienna." "I must
beg you to excuse me," replied Deak, "but I cannot negotiate with Vienna while the Hungarian
Constitution is illegally suspended. As you see,
Herr Bach, while Hungary has no Constitution I
can have no political existence."

So far to hint at the policy Deak had conceived,
a policy of Passive Resistance, which in eighteen
years beat the Austrian Government to its knees.
Deak stood by the Constitution of **Hungary.** He
declined to argue or debate the merits of that Constitution or the "fitness" of his countrymen for
it—good or bad, fit or unfit, it was Hungary's property and Hungary alone could relinquish it. He
refused to go to Vienna or to go to Canossa. Pesth
was the capital of his nation, and in Pesth he planted his flag. "Keep your eyes on your own country," he said to the people, from which it may be in-
ferred that a policy of Passive Resistance and a
policy of Parliamentarianism are very different
things, although the people of Ireland have been
drugged into believing that the only alternative to

armed resistance is speech-making in the British
Parliament. Deak wrote on his banner: "No compromise on the Constitution," and he never swerved
a hair's breadth during his struggle from that
motto, as we shall see in following the development
and triumph of his policy.

II.—How Francis Josef Visited Pesth.

The light from the window of Francis Deak's
room in the Pesth hotel irritated and alarmed the
ministers of darkness. An Austrian garrison, politely
called a police force, even as is the Royal Irish
Constabulary, occupied Hungary. Its duties were
very similar—to keep the movements of Hungarian Nationalists under surveillance by day, to
pay them domiciliary visits by night, to report or
disperse any assembly of Hungarians whereat
the National feeling was fearlessly voiced, to super-
intend with their bayonets the confiscation of the
soil, and to seize and destroy Hungarian newspapers
or prints which had courage enough to beard and
denounce the Tyranny. An Austrian Lord Lieutenant sat in Pesth and erased the historic territorial
divisions of Hungary, the Hungarian Parliament
was declared dead as Cæsar, and a swarm of hungry
Austrian bureaucrats ruled the land. Trial by jury
was abolished, and Austrian removables, at 4,000
roubles per annum, manned the Bench; the Hungarian language was officially prohibited   in   the
transaction of public business, and fired neck-and-
crop out of the schools; and even as animosity and
distrust are sought to be kindled and kept alive between Irish Catholic and Irish Protestant by the
English Government, so the Austrian Government
sought to kindle and keep alive race-hatred in Hungary.

And yet Francis Deak, sitting on the Bridge of
Buda-Pesth on a sunny afternoon, encouraging little

boys to throw hand-springs and telling little girls stories of gnomes and ogres and beautiful princesses rescued by gallant cavaliers—who always bore good Hungarian names—Francis Deak sauntering along to Parade chatting to the disengaged, and Francis Deak by night in his hotel discussing the history, literature, and general position of Hungary, with men of different callings, violently disturbed the equanimity of the bureaucrats in Pesth—yet why they could not say. The wave of disturbance rolled on to Vienna, and the statesmen there hit upon a subtle plan for the extinction of Hungarian Nationality beyond the power of all the Kossuths and the Deaks in the world to revive. This was to incorporate Hungary in the Germanic Confederation, so that if at any time Hungary again attempted to raise her head, not only Austria, but Prussia, Saxony, Bavaria and all the other countries of Germany would be bound to swoop down on her. But France intervened. Austria bluffed, but France remained firm. "We shall treat the attempt to obliterate Hungary as a casus belli," said the French Government, whereupon Austria caved in, and furthermore the State of Siege was abolished.

The abolition of the State of Siege was little change in one way—the bureaucracy still ruled the land, and the Constitution was still in abeyance—but it permitted Deak to carry out one side of his policy with greater freedom. The Kostelek or Agricultural Union which he had founded set itself to compete with Austrian farm produce and wipe it out of the home and foreign market; the Vedegylet or National Protective Union which Kossuth had founded was freer now to wage war on the Austrian manufacturer, and the National Academy was freer to preach love of Hungary's literature and Hungary's language, than hitherto. The Hungarian exiles co-operated with the people at home—they sought support in the countries where they dwelt for Hungarian products and aroused sympathy and appreciation for Hungarian literature. It was in 1854 the State of Siege was abolished—in 1857 the progress of Hungary was a "cause of serious apprehension to the Court of Vienna."

And all this time Francis Deak, the guiding and directing mind, never appeared on a public platform, never made a single speech, never moved a resolution solemnly protesting against Austrian despotism.

Bach in Vienna was alarmed and disconcerted. He felt it necessary that Deak's influence should be destroyed, but how to destroy it puzzled him. At last he hit on an idea as brilliant and original as a modern Englishman himself could conceive—the idea of "a Royal Visit." "You must visit Pesth, sire," said he to Francis Josef. And Francis Josef prepared to visit Pesth. The Pesth newspapers were instructed to announce that a new era was about to dawn. Francis Josef was coming to Pesth —he was coming to restore the confiscated estates of the political offenders, and shower blessings on the people, and, therefore, he should be accorded a loyal and enthusiastic reception. Francis Deak would, of course, welcome him with open arms, for Deak was a loyal man. "I am," said Deak, "to the King of Hungary." "And, of course, the Emperor of Austria is King of Hungary," suggested the reptile Press. "He is entitled to be," said Deak, "when he complies with the law, swears to uphold the Constitution of Hungary, and is crowned with the crown of St. Stephen in Buda. I am a Hungarian—I owe allegiance to the King of Hungary—I owe none to the Emperor of Austria."

The Emperor of Austria arrived in Pesth on the 4th.of May, 1857, and was received with prolonged and enthusiastic cheers by the Viennese imported into Pesth for the occasion, by the plain-clothes policemen, the Austrian officials and the members of their families, and by the lion-and-unicorn shopkeepers. The people looked on at the magnificent procession, which entered the city under a triumphal arch—erected by public subscription of the Austrian bureaucrats and their hangers-on in Pesth—bearing the inscription "God has sent You." But it was really Bach. The procession paraded the city in the following order:—

A Band of Austrian Lancers.
A Detachment of Lancers.
A Detachment of the Rifle Brigade.
A Band of Court Trumpeters.
Police Officials.
Carriages of Loyal Nobles.
Prince Paul Esterhazy in his State Carriage, with twenty-five Running Footmen.
Prince Nicholas Esterhazy in a Carriage-and-Six, with twenty-two Running Footmen.
The Cardinal Archbishop in a Carriage-and-Six.
A Brass Band.
Twelve Bishops in Carriages-and-Four.
A Bishop on Horseback with a Silver Cross.
The Emperor on Horseback.
The Empress in a Carriage, wearing a Hungarian Hat.
Six Gingerbread Coaches with the Ladies of the Court.
A Brass Band.

The Emperor was received at the triumphal arch by the Mayor of the town—one Von Connrad—who assured him of his own loyalty and that of the people of Pesth—after which Von Connrad had to be protected by the police from his loyal fellow-citizens.

A Te Deum was sung in the Castle, and a great display of fireworks was given that night at a cost of 5,000 roubles, subscribed "on behalf of the people of Pesth" by the Austrian officials. "It was money well spent," said the Austrian newspapers. "The people remained out till after midnight viewing the illuminations, on both sides of the bridge, which were simply superb. The spirit of loyalty was everywhere enthusiastically manifested—and none who witnessed the glorious scene could feel other than convinced that the visit of His Majesty the Emperor has completely annihilated the schemes of those wicked men who would seek to lead a naturally loyal people like the Hungarians away from their duty and their own best interests—which are inseparably connected with the maintenance of the Empire.''

It was a great time for the officials and seoinini of Pesth. There were levees and balls and banquets and loyal speeches go leor, and the Emperor bubbled over with love for his Hungarian subjects. '' I have come to examine into the wishes and necessities of my beloved Hungary,'' he said in reply to the address of the Catholic Hierarchy. '' It affords me a deep pleasure to be again among my Hungarian people and to show this beautiful land to my dear wife, the Empress. It shall be my continual effort to promote the well-being of my faithful Hungarian people.''

Her Majesty the Empress visited the convent schools with her Hungarian hat on, and insisted on only Hungarian dances being danced before her.* His Majesty the Emperor went to the Academy and expressed his admiration for the Hungarian language. '' It is surely a New Era,'' said the Hungarian jellyfish; '' let us present him with an address, Deak.'' '' No,'' said Deak. '' Not a grovelling address,'' urged the jellyfish; '' an address pointing out the grievances under which we labour, and demanding their removal.'' Said Deak : ''While Francis Josef violates the law and arbitrarily abrogates the Constitution Hungary cannot recognise him.'' But the loyal-addressers determined to present an address, and they did. Desewffy drew it up, and in it he said :—

'' We do not doubt that your Majesty will in the course of your inquiries arrive at the conviction

---

* The Empress Elizabeth later became truly friendly to the Hungarian nation, and her influence was exerted in support of Deak. After the Ausgleich and her Coronation as Queen of Hungary she resided much of her time in Hungary, where she is remembered with affection and esteem.

that it will be possible to bring into harmony those historic institutions which are bound up with the life of the nation, and to which the people are devoutly attached, with the requirements of the age, the necessity for the unity of the monarchy, and the conditions of a strong government. We will readily co-operate with the other subjects of your Majesty in everything that may be needful to maintain the security of the monarchy, to heighten its prestige, and to increase its power. In the greatness of your Majesty and the strength of the Empire lie our own security, and in the general welfare of the monarchy our own prosperity. The unity of the monarchy is the result of centuries; it comes from the co-operation of all the national forces of the Empire. A people which has had a past is never able to forget its history. This country has learned the lessons which history teaches, and the interest of your Majesty demands that it should not forget them. Our Fatherland feels and acknowledges the obligations it is under to your Majesty and to the common monarchy; it is ready to discharge these obligations—to do everything but this—to be untrue to itself, to renounce its individual existence, and abjure the creed which is itself founded upon its dynastic feelings and its devotion to the dynasty.''

Cardinal Szilowsky went to the Emperor to present this loyal address, and the Emperor bowed him out. After which the Emperor returned direct to Vienna instead of visiting Keckesmet, where his faithful people had set fire to the triumphal arch under which he was to enter. But the Vienna newspapers proclaimed that the Emperor's visit had been a marvellous success and that all Hungary was now loyal. Some Hungarians even desponded and remarked to Deak that the Austrian regime in Hungary seemed certain to endure. "One day," replied Deak, "I consulted my gardener, who also knew something about architecture, as to the solidity of a vinedresser's hut which had been erected on my estate. Said the gardener: 'The building may stand for a long time if the wind does not blow hard.' 'Yes,' said I, 'but suppose it does blow hard—and often?'"

A few months after the Deak-destroying visit of the Emperor Francis Josef, Bach realised that his grand scheme had been a fiasco—Hungary was as strong and as anti-Austrian as ever. "I must fix up Deak," said Bach, and he again invited him to come to Vienna to discuss the Constitution. "I know nothing of any Constitution, except the Hungarian Constitution; I can only treat on the basis of the Hungarian Constitution," replied Deak. "Come and let us discuss matters," urged Bach. "There can be no discussion, no argument, no compromise on the Hungarian Constitution. It still remains—and I remain in Pesth," said Deak. And so the year of Our Lord 1859 dawned for Hungary.

III.—The Fall of Bach.

In the spring of 1859 all Europe saw that war between France and Austria was imminent. Louis Napoleon engaged with the Hungarian exiles to make the Independence of Hungary one of the conditions of peace if he won the war—they in turn engaged to induce the Hungarian troops in the Austrian service to desert, and offered to make Napoleon's brother King of Hungary. But the French Emperor, after defeating Austria, broke his engagement on a plea of "the exigencies of the European situation."

Francis Josef came back from the wars in a chastened spirit. "My beloved subjects," he said to his people, "truth compels me to proclaim that we have been whipped," and, therefore, he announced he

would devote his whole and uninterrupted attention
to establish the "internal welfare and external
power of Austria by a judicious development of its
rich, moral, and material strength, and by
making such improvements in the Legislature and
Administration as are in accord with the spirit of
the age." Next he fired out Bach. Thirdly, he invited Baron Josika, a Hungarian, to become Minister of the Interior. "Your Majesty," said Josika,
"I am a Hungarian. I understand Hungarians. I
do not understand Austrians. If you appointed an
Austrian to govern us Hungarians, he could not
govern us well because he is alien to us. Neither
could I govern well your Austrians, since I am of a
different race. I assure your Majesty that the man
who pretends he can govern a people well, who does
not belong to that people, or else who has not spent
his lifetime among them, is a humbug." Josika's
reason for refusing office we commend to English
statesmen as an excellent jest. Golouchowski, a
Pole, was then offered and accepted the office declined by Josika. He and the Emperor put their
heads together, and finally decided to increase the
number of members in the Reichsrath—which then
was the equivalent of what we know as the Privy
Council—that they might better confer and consult
with it as to how to fix up matters. Six members
were summoned from Hungary. "What shall we
do?" asked the summoned of Deak. "Don't go,"
said Deak. "If Francis Josef wants to consult Hungary, let him come to Pesth and consult her through
her Parliament." Whereupon three of them refused
to go, and three went and made eloquent speeches
on the floor of the House, incited thereto by Count
Desewffy, the loyal-addresser of 1857, who through
attending tea-parties and things organised by Rech-
berg and Von Hubner, two Austrian Union-of-
Hearts statesmen, came to the conclusion that Deak
was really the obstacle to the better understanding
of two peoples whom God had created as the com-

plement of each other, and Francis Deak, instigated by the devil, kept asunder. Poor Von Hubner, however, was an honest fellow, and in the exuberance of his New Eraian enthusiasm he grew quite sentimental about Hungary, with the result that the Emperor dismissed him from office. The Hungarian County Councils had been abolished in defiance of the Constitution, and the Emperor and Golouchowski concluded their first step in the Conciliation game should be to revive these Councils in defiance of the Constitution, since they dared not admit the right of the Hungarian Parliament. If they acted honestly, the thing was simple enough. The Hungarian Parliament need only be convoked, and the County Councils would be brought again into being by the command of that Parliament. But it was the last thing the Emperor or Golouchowski intended to do at this period. They had set out with the object of killing off the demand for an autonomous Hungary and drawing the fangs of Hungarian disloyalty by restoring her a strictly limited district control over her gas-and-water, and by saying kind things of the Hungarian people and offering jobs and titles to influential Hungarians. "Let the dead past bury its dead," said Golouchowski—among the dead which it would bury being the Hungarian Constitution of 1848, a fact of which Golouchowski forgot to remind Hungary, but which Hungary did not forget. There were, of course, wise men in Hungary who saw quite plainly that Deak was entirely wrong in his policy, and who resented the fun he made of the conciliators. "Let us first arrive at a reconciliation with Austria, and then we shall be able to get justice done to the claims of Hungary and get our Parliament back," said the Wise Men to Deak. "Let Austria first recognise the lawful status and authority of the Hungarian Parliament, and then by all means let the Parliament recognise the necessity for harmonising the distinctive rights of Hungary with the recognition of the common monarchy,'' Deak replied to the Wise Men. ''Expediency,'' whispered the Wise Men to Deak. ''Principle, Principle, Principle!'' Deak shouted back, and his voice echoed through Hungary.

The Emperor and Golouchowski, to avoid ''recognising the lawful status and authority of the Hungarian Parliament,'' appointed a Hungarian Royal Commission to inquire into the working of Bach's Municipal Law—that is, to re-create the County Councils. The country looked to Deak. It wanted its County Councils back badly, and it hoped he might find some means of accepting the Commission. But Deak was inexorable. ''Return the Emperor of Austria your patents,'' he said to the Commissioners. ''None but the King of Hungary can appoint a Royal Hungarian Commission.'' So the Royal Commissioners returned their patents with a polite note, in which they informed the Emperor of Austria and his Ministers that the work they were asked to do was work for the Hungarian Parliament, and the Hungarian Parliament alone. ''See,'' said the Wise Men, reproachfully, ''Deak's absurd and quixotic notions have prevented Hungary from having her County Councils restored.'' But the reproach fell on deaf ears. Hungary was grieved, but unshaken. ''Whatever it may seem on the outside, we feel that Deak is right,'' said the people. ''To Hungary Deak can do no wrong.''

The splendid allegiance of the people to Deak saved the Hungarians. Had they listened to the voices of the weaklings and the teachings of expediency, they would have got their County Councils—in exchange for their principle—and there was an end of Hungary. But Hungary had a statesman, not a politician, at her head. Deak's immobility and Hungary's solidity baffled Austria. Austria could not recede—her Imperial existence depended on reversing Bach's Absolutist policy. She could not advance—unless she paid Hungary toll. Deak had foreseen and knew—and smoking his pipe, waited. And the result was that Austria offered toll. By Royal Ordinance the County Councils were restored—Austria must needs save its face by making the restoration on the outside an Imperial affair—but at the same time the Hungarian Parliament was convoked. The wisdom of Deak was demonstrated even to the Wise Men, and Hungary not unnaturally was going to cheer when Deak told it not to. "Wait, my countrymen," said he, "until the Parliament opens, and we see what we shall see. There is abundant time to cheer afterwards." Deak knew his Austria, and Hungary sobered up, and in a calm and critical spirit awaited the now famous "Meeting of the Hungarian Diet of 1861."

IV.—How the Hungarians Refused to Send Representatives to the "Imperial Parliament."

The County Councils were re-established. Their first action was to dismiss the Austrian officials who had been planted on the counties during the Ten Years' Tyranny, their second to strike out the rate for supporting the Austrian Army, their third to order the tax-collectors to collect no taxes unless levied by authority of the Hungarian Parliament. "What is the object sought after by the Hungarian County Councils?" asked a Vienna journal indignantly. Its answer to its own question did not convey the truth half so well as the prompt reply of the County Council of Pesth: "To sweep away every trace of Austrian rule, and hold Hungary for the Hungarians." Francis Josef was disconcerted. He invited Deak to come and discuss matters with him, and Deak went. Francis Josef promised Deak that he would satisfactorily settle the Hungarian question, and assured Deak he might banish all suspicion from his mind as to Francis Josef's bona-fides. Deak was not bamboozled, but he decided to remove all pretext for breaking faith from Francis Josef's grasp. Therefore Deak advised the County Councils to a less strenuous policy until the Parliament met and they saw what kind of a Parliament it was to be, and the County Councils bowed to Deak's statesmanship, and tamed their hearts of fire. Suddenly the news came to Pesth that Golouchowski had resigned and that Von Schmerling had succeeded him, and then came the news that Schmerling had a policy which was infallibly to settle the Hungarian question and the Bohemian question and the Croatian question and the other questions that disturbed the Austrian Empire. Forty years later certain English staesmen rediscovered Schmerling's profound policy and labelled it "Home Rule All Round." Schmerling proposed to establish, or re-establish, local Parliaments in the different countries of the Empire, these Parliaments having control over internal affairs, but no control over Imperial taxation, military matters, foreign affairs. and soforth. An Imperial Parliament in Vienna was to control all such things. This Imperial Parliament was to consist of 343 members, of whom Hungary was to have 85, Bohemia 56, Transylvania 20, Moravia 22, Upper and Lower Austria 28, Croatia and Slavonia 9, Styria 13, the Tyrol 12, and the smaller States smaller numbers. Hungary received the Schmerling policy with a cry of derision. "Do you think Hungarians are going to discuss the affairs of their country with foreigners in a foreign city?" they asked. "You are mad, or else you seek to insult us." Excitement grew in Pesth, and Deak had to use all his influence to restrain the people from proceeding to acts of violence against the Home-Rule-cum-Empire Party, which was almost wholly composed of Austrians or the sons of Austrians. "Be calm," said he to the people; "await the meeting of the Diet. A single false step and all may be ruined." The Emperor's warrant for the

E

convening of the Diet was received, and Deak was
immediately elected for Pesth.   Three hundred
representatives in all were elected that March
of 1861, two hundred and seventy of them
being avowedly anti-Austrian, and the handful
hurlers on the ditch. When they had been elected
they refused to meet in the Castle of Buda, whither
they had been summoned. " The Constitution of
1848 fixed our meeting place in Pesth," they said,
" and in Pesth we meet or not at all." The Austrians fought, cajoled, and gave way. The result
was hailed as a great national victory, since in her
despite Austria had been forced to recognise the
Laws of '48. On the 6th of April, 1861, the Hungarian Parliament was opened by the Royal Com-
missioner, Count George Apponyi. The deputies went dressed in the national costume of
Hungary, and when gathered in the hall
they, with a simultaneous impulse, shouted
the dying words of Count Louis Batthyany, the
Premier of Hungary, as he fell in 1849, beneath the
bullets of his Austrian executioners, " Eljen a
haza !" " My country for ever !" Then Francis
Josef's message was read by Francis Josef's Com-
missioner. His Majesty felt deeply, he said, that
mistrust and misunderstanding had arisen between
Austrians and Hungarians, and he wished to restore
peace and harmony. To that end he invited the
Hungarian Legislature to meet, look after Hungary's gas-and-water, and send representatives to
the Imperial Parliament in Vienna. The hall resounded with the scornful laughter of the deputies
of the Hungarian people. Francis Deak calmed the
tumult. It was sought, he said, to have them transfer
to a foreign assembly sitting in the capital of a
foreign country, and calling itself an Imperial
Parliament, the right of making laws for
themselves and their children. Who would acquiesce ?" " None !" shouted the representatives
of Hungary with one voice. " None, indeed," said

Deak, "and let us in terms consonant with the dignity of our nation tell him so who has proposed it." Whereupon Deak drew up and the Hungarian Parliament adopted the famous "First Address of the Hungarian Diet of 1861 to His Imperial Majesty Francis Josef, Emperor of Austria, in reply to his Speech to the Parliament of the Free Kingdom of Hungary." In this great document, every line breathing manliness, patriotism, and resolution, Deak stated the case of Hungary, not for Francis Josef only, but for all the world. The Loyal-Addresser, as we know him in Ireland, had ceased to exist in the Hungary of 1861:

"The twelve years which have just elapsed," said the Address, "have been to us a period of severe suffering. Our ancient Constitution has been suspended. We have been grievously oppressed by a system of power hitherto unknown to us. The burden of this crushing system has been exercised by Imperial agents, who have carried it out with vindictive feelings, with narrow powers of apprehension, and often with evil intent. In their eyes the feeling of liberty was a crime; fond attachment to our nationality and the purest patriotism were not less so. These men have exhausted the strength of our land, have converted the property of the nation to illegal purposes, and have made our nationality an object of persecution. Each day brought new sufferings; each suffering tore from our bosom another fibre of faith and confidence." "We suffered," continued the Address, but in manly triumph added, "we were not untrue to ourselves" —hence Austria is forced to abandon Absolutism, and "We, the representatives of Hungary, assemble to recommence our constitutional activity." The first step we are called on to take, say the addressers bluntly, is a painful one—because it is to send **you,** Francis Josef, an address, while still illegalities and tyranny exist; but our first duty we know—it is " to devote our united strength and all our capa-

bilities that Hungary may remain Hungary. If
the independence of our country be menaced, it is
our duty as men to raise our common voice against
the attack.'' And it **is** threatened, continue the
addressers—threatened by the very first step which
you, Francis Josef, have taken in a Constitutional
direction. It has been violated in that the Hungarian Constitution has been only re-established
conditionally, deprived of its most essential attributes.   It has been violated by the Diploma of
October.

"That Diploma would rob Hungary for ever of
the ancient provisions of her Constitution, which
subject all questions concerning public taxation and
the levying of troops throughout Hungary solely
to Hungary's Parliament; it would deprive the
nation of the right of passing, in concurrence with
the King, its own laws on subjects affecting the
most important material interests of the land.   All
matters relating to money, credit, the military
establishments, customs, and commerce of Hungary
—these essential questions of a political national
existence—are placed under the control of an Imperial Parliament, the majority of whose members
will be foreigners.   There these subjects will be discussed from other than Hungarian points of view,
with regard to other than Hungarian interests.   Nor
is that all—in the field of administration this
Diploma makes the Hungarian Government dependent on the Austrian—on a Government which is
not even responsible, and in the event of its becoming so would render an account not to Hungary,
but to the Imperial Parliament, who would give us
no guarantee for our interests where they should
come into collision with those of Austria.   Were
this idea to be realised Hungary would remain
Hungary only in name, whilst in reality she would
become   an   Austrian   province.   This   forcible
attempt directed, in defiance of right against us and
our constitutional independence is not only in oppo-

sition to our laws, but is an attack on the Pragmatic Sanction—on that fundamental State compact concluded in the year 1723 between Hungary and the reigning House."

The Address then recites the history and provisions of the Pragmatic Sanction, and asks what surety could Hungary have that in an Imperial Parliament overwhelmingly foreign in race and divergent in interest, Hungarian rights and interests would be respected. Such a Parliament would necessarily place Hungarian affairs under the control of an Austrian majority—"It would make our interests dependent on an entirely foreign policy." Further on the Address continues: "We cannot consent to the withdrawal from the province of the Hungarian Diet of the right to decide **all** and **every** matter concerning public taxation and the raising of military forces. As we entertain no wish to exercise the right of legislation over any other country, so we can divide with none but the King of Hungary the right of legislation over Hungary; we can make the Government and administration of Hungary depend on none other than its king, and cannot unite the same with the Government of any other country—**therefore, we declare that we will take part neither in the Imperial Parliament nor in any other assembly whatsoever of the representatives of the Empire; and, further, that we cannot recognise the right of the said Imperial Parliament to legislate on the affairs of Hungary,** and are only prepared to enter on special occasions into deliberation with the constitutional peoples of the hereditary States as one independent nation with another."

"Do you want to be crowned King of Hungary?" continued the Address in effect. "Very well; first comply with the law—cease to illegally suspend our Constitution, and then we shall arrange about your coronation." And the Address concluded: "Neither might nor power is the end of government; might is only the means—the end is the happiness of the people. . . . The King of Hungary becomes only by virtue of the act of coronation legal King of Hungary; but the coronation is coupled with certain conditions prescribed by law, the previous fulfilment of which is indispensably necessary. The maintenance of our constitutional independence and of the territorial and political integrity of the country inviolate, the completion of the Diet, the complete restoration of our fundamental laws, the reinstitution of our Parliamentary Government and our responsible Ministry, and the setting aside of all the still surviving consequences of the Absolute System are the preliminary conditions which must be carried into effect before deliberation and conciliation are possible."

On the 5th of July a messenger sped from Pesth to Vienna with the Address of the Hungarian Parliament to Francis Josef. A day or two later and all the world heard of it. The Press of Vienna exploded with indignation. "Here," said they, "we have offered the right hand of friendship to the Hungarians, and the lazy, good-for-nothing, ungrateful scoundrels spit upon it, because, forsooth, we don't offer and give them full permission to disrupt the Empire." The English Parliament was highly indignant. England was aiming to get Austria and Prussia into war at that time in the hope that Prussia's growing commerce might be destroyed. "This fellow, Deak," said the liberty-loving legislators of London, " is really no better than a Red Republican. He rejects the generous offer of the estimable Emperor Francis Josef, and cunningly blinds the fatuous mob to the great superiority of the Imperial-Parliament-plus-Home-Rule-All-Round policy to his own, which is nothing more nor less than to make Hungary absolutely independent of Austria, acknowledging only the Emperor as King. It is patent to any ordinary intelligence that it would be wholly impossible for

Austria and Hungary to subsist under such an
arrangement for a year.''* '' For a year,'' wrote an
English follower of Lord Macaulay—'' nay, not for
six months. If Deak's scheme were put into operation, Hungary would be crushed in six months'
time.'' However, the Hungarians declined to be
instructed either by Vienna or by London, and
awaited calmly the reply of Francis Josef to their
Loyal Address.

V.—And How the Emperor of Austria Lost His Temper.

On the 21st of July the Emperor Francis Josef
replied to the Address of the Hungarian Diet.
'' Faithful subjects,'' said he, '' you are acting in
an extremely silly manner. You want the right to
decide on taxation and other matters for Hungary
—why, I offer you the privilege of coming into our
Imperial Parliament here in Vienna and deciding,
in conjunction with my other faithful subjects, the
taxation for the whole Empire. Your Little Hungary ideas are neither patriotic nor wise. Develop
an Imperial soul, and get out of your parochial rut.
Reflect how much finer it is to be a citizen of the
Empire than the beadle of a parish. Besides, your
law, history, and facts are altogether wrong. Hungary is subordinate to Austria. God and Nature
intended her to be so. Set to at once and elect your
representatives to the Imperial Parliament, and

* The Right Hon. Mr. Peacocke and Lord John Russell declared in the English Parliament that if Austria yielded to
Hungary's claims, Austria '' might as well dismember the
Empire.'' '' If we made such a concession '' [to Ireland],
said Peacocke, '' We should not only Repeal the Union—we
should restore the Heptarchy.'' Lord Bloomfield, the English Ambassador in Vienna, urged the Emperor to refuse to
accept the Hungarian Address.

remain assured of our Imperial Royal grace and favour.''

These words were not the Emperor's exact words, but they give the true spirit of the reply. It was read to the Parliament at Pesth amid cries of anger. But Deak, cool and far-seeing, held the fiercer spirits in check, and on the 12th of August the Deputies, on his motion, adopted the celebrated '' Second Address of the Parliament of Hungary to Francis Josef.'' Deak was its author, of course, as he was the author of the preceding one. Calmly he examined each claim put forward on behalf of Austrian control of Hungary, and calmly he disproved each claim. He exhibited Francis Josef and his Ministers to the world as Violaters of the Law, Rebels to the Constitution. '' We asked not for concessions,'' says the Second Address, '' we proposed no new laws for the further security of our rights. We demanded only that the Law be observed—we asked that legality and constitutional procedure should entirely, not partially, take the place of absolute force. The Rescript which your Majesty sent us positively refused to satisfy our rightful wishes. From its contents and spirit we have come to the painful conviction that your Majesty does not wish to reign over Hungary in the spirit of the Constitution !''

'' Your Majesty,'' the Address continues, '' has, in violation of the Pragmatic Sanction, suspended our Constitution and our laws by the force of absolue power, and even now will not cause this arbitrary suspension to cease. You promise to restore us fragments of our Constitution, whilst withdrawing from us its most essential rights. By arbitrary authority you suppress our fundamental laws, and set in their stead an Imperial Diploma and Patent which you wish us to regard as fundamental laws. You require that we should send representatives to an Imperial Parliament, which has been created by arbitrary decree without our concurrence, and that with regard to our most important interests we should transfer to that Parliament the right of legislation which our nation has always exercised in its own Parliament, and that we should surrender the rights of our country by virtue of which it has always determined its own taxation and the levies of troops, and that we should submit ourselves in these matters to the Imperial Parliament. You set aside the fundamental principle of every constitutional government that sanctioned laws can only be repealed by the collective legislative factors. Your steps throughout are so unconstitutional as to menace the very existence of the Pragmatic Sanction—to set aside all that is contained in it as a fundamental contract in the shape of conditions for the security of the nation. . . . The Constitutional Independence of the country is seriously infringed by the very fact that, without the previous consent of the Hungarian Parliament, you ordain laws and command us to send representatives to the Imperial Parliament. Thus, you act as if the Hungarian Parliament were a body bound to accept the commands emanating from the sole will of the sovereign as law—nay, as if it were bound to inscribe them in the statute-book, even though they were in opposition to the Constitution and the sanctioned statutes of the realm. In what, then, would the constitutional independence of Hungary consist, and where would be the guarantee of this independence if at a future period a successor of your Majesty, appealing to this precedent, should act in the same manner with our other laws and rights, and should, by a command of his own power and authority, suppress or modify them without the previous consent of the nation, and then instruct the Diet to complete these mandates in the field of legislation ?"

The Address then deals with the consequences of sending members to the Imperial Parliament—it means, it says, that " the disposition over the property and blood of the nation would pass into the hands of a body, the considerable majority of whom would be foreigners—the greater part of them Austrians—and it might easily happen that they would impose burdens upon us in support of interests and in compliance with obligations which are not our interests nor our obligations."

The Address, in dealing with the Financial Relations of Hungary and Austria, repudiates any liability on the part of Hungary for State Debts contracted without Hungary's consent. While repudiating them, however, it declares that in order to ensure that the "heavy burdens which the reckless conduct of the Absolute System has heaped upon us may not involve us all in a common ruin" it is willing to go further than its legal duties require. But it adds, "We will only deal with the matter as a free, independent, separate country, and if our independence is menaced we shall be justified before God and the world in refusing to undertake burdens and obligations which neither law nor equity can claim from us."

"We could not send deputies to the Imperial Parliament," says the 66th paragraph of the Address, "without sacrificing our most essential rights and our constitutional independence. That Parliament Hungary could not enter without the anxious fear that, despite all verbal assurances, she would be considered an Austrian province—that under the mask of constitutionalism the attempt at incorporation which the Absolute Power has so often and unsuccessfully attempted was to be renewed." "A forced unity," the Address continues, "can never make an Empire strong. The outraged feeling of the individual States and the bitterness arising from the pressure of force awaken the desire for separation, therefore the Empire would be the weakest just at the moment when it would be in want of its united strength and the full enthusiasm of its peoples. The position of an Empire as a Great Power whose unity can only be maintained by force of arms is precarious and least safe in the moment of danger. The mutilation of the political rights of a country is an injustice, and will always give rise to feelings of bitterness and discontent. A State which by its well-ordered relations can offer its citizens material prosperity can for a time venture upon such a step with comparative impunity, **for with many the satisfaction of material interests diminishes the feeling of the loss,** although it can never be a politic measure even in such a State to deprive a nation of its rights. But if a State, whether through errors or through misfortune, can do very little for the increase of material prosperity—nay, is compelled for self-support to impose fresh burdens on its nearly exhausted citizens, to call again and again for new sacrifices— such a State is acting in opposition in abridging the political rights of a nation, and thus outraging its feelings. The heavy burdens press more heavily as the conviction gains ground that the political rights are menaced; the just feeling of bitterness undermines every willingness to sacrifice, and extinguishes all confidence in a Power which **cannot** aid the material interests of its citizens and will not spare their political rights."

The Second Address reiterated the fearless and manly declaration of the first one. "With the most profound respect, and at the same time with the sincerity we owe to your Majesty, our country and ourselves, we declare that we hold fast to the Pragmatic Sanction, and to all the conditions contained in it without exception, and that we cannot regard or recognise as constitutional anything which is in contradiction of it . . . . We protest against the exercise, on the part of the Imperial Parliament, of any legislative or other power over Hungary in any relation whatsoever. **We declare that we will not send any Representatives to the Imperial Parliament, and further, that any election by other instrumentality will be an attack on our Constitution,**

and we declare that any person elected by such means cannot in any respect represent Hungary.[*]
Whereas, no one has a right to regulate the affairs of Hungary, except by authority of the lawful king, and of the constitutionally-expressed will of the nation, we hereby declare that we must regard as unconstitutional and non-binding all Acts or ordinances of the Imperial Parliament referring to Hungary or its annexed parts. We further declare that we cannot regard as constitutional with reference to Hungary, and therefore as binding, any State burden or obligation founded by the Imperial Parliament, any loan contracted by its authority, or the sale of any Crown property sanctioned by it, and that we shall regard such as having taken place unlawfully and without the consent of the land. We declare that we will maintain unimpaired the right of the nation to vote its supplies and regulate its taxes and military levies in its own Parliament, and will never agree to the transfer of these rights to the Imperial Parliament. . . . We declare finally, that we are compelled to regard the present administration of the country, especially the despotic conduct of unconstitutional officials, as illegal and subject to punishment according to the laws of the country; and the direct and indirect taxes imposed in violation of the law and levied by military force as unconstitutional. . . . Your Majesty by your Royal Rescript has rendered common understanding impossible, and has broken off the thread of negotiations. The Royal Rescript does not stand on the footing of the Hungarian Constitution, but it establishes as fundamental laws the Imperial Diploma and Patent which emanated from absolute power and are in opposition to our Constitution. We are bound by our duty to our

---

[*] " The Hungarians perceive very plainly that this one point involves **all,** and though they would yield a little on other matters they are unanimous in resisting the summons."—London " Times," August 13, 1861.

country, by our position as representatives, and by our convictions, to the Hungarian Constitution, and on this footing alone our deliberations must take place. These two directions deviating from, nay, opposed to one another, cannot lead to the wished-for union. Our most holy duty has pointed out the direction we must take. We must therefore declare with the greatest sorrow that in consequence of the Royal Rescript we are also compelled to regard the thread of negotiations through the Diet as broken up."

"It is possible," the Address concludes, "that over our country will again pass hard times; we cannot avert them at the sacrifice of our duties as citizens. The Constitutional freedom of the land is not our possession in such a sense that we can freely deal with it; the nation has with faith entrusted it to our keeping, and we are answerable to our country and to our conscience. **If it be necessary to suffer, the Nation will submit to suffering in order to preserve and hand down to future generations that Constitutional Liberty it has inherited from its forefathers.** It will suffer without losing courage, as its ancestors have endured and suffered, to be able to defend the rights of the country; **for what might and power take away time and favourable circumstances may restore, but the recovery of what a nation renounces of its own accord through fear of suffering is a matter of difficulty and uncertainty.** Hungary will suffer, hoping for a great future and trusting in the justice of its cause."

On the 12th of August the Second Address of the fearless Hungarian Parliament was despatched to Francis Josef at Vienna. On the 21st Francis Josef replied by dissolving the Parliament.* The Deputies declined to acknowledge his act as legal, and in solemn procession marched to the House, which was occupied by Austrian soldiers, who at the bayonet's point kept them out. Deak, turning from the House, lit a cigar and walked back to his hotel,

where he joined in a game of bowls. "What is the
news?" asked his landlord. "Austria," said Deak,
as he knocked down the ninepins, "has declared
war."

VI.—The Bloodless War.

The Pesth County Council protested against the
illegal dissolution of the Hungarian Parliament. The
Emperor replied by ordering the Pesth County
Council to be itself dissolved. The County Council
disregarded the Emperor's order and continued to
hold its meetings, until the Austrian soldiery entered the Council Chamber and turned them out
by force. As the Councillors emerged into the
streets they shouted with one voice: "Eljen a
Magyar Huza!" "God save Hungary!" The shout
was re-echoed by the people who had congregated
outside, and who, raising the Councillors on their
shoulders, carried them through the streets, singing the Hungarian National Anthem. From the

---

* "The Hungarian Diet has been invited to do at this
time," wrote the London "Times" in August, 1861, "precisely what the Irish Parliament did at the end of the last
century, and by a fictitious extension of the parallel we can
understand exactly what is now occurring at Pesth. The
Irish Parliament assented, as everybody is aware, after some
vehement debating, to the proposed Union, and the incorporation of the two States was lawfully and peaceably con-
summated. Let us suppose, however, for illustration sake,
that the Irish Parliament had refused its assent and had
claimed to stand on its own rights and privileges in pre-
ference to amalgamating with the Parliament of the Empire.
Now if under such circumstances we can conceive that
George III. had dissolved the refractory Assembly with
threats of military force, had declared that Ireland possessed no valid privileges, having forfeited them all in the
recent rebellion, had left the Irish to return members to
Westminster as soon as they thought better of their duties,
and in the meantime had sent troops to live at free quarters
on the Irish people—if we can imagine an English monarch
adopting a policy such as this, we shall get an exact idea
of the course pursued by the Austrian Government at the
present day."

windows of his house the Chairman of the County Council addressed his fellow-citizens: "We have been dispersed by tyrannic force—but force shall never overawe us," he said. "Austrians violate Justice and the Law, and then tell us we are disloyal subjects. When they restore what they have taken from us, then let them talk of loyalty. Until then, countrymen, let us make ourselves as disagreeable to them as we can. To-day the soldiers of the Emperor of Austria have driven the representatives of the people of the capital of Hungary from their assembly-house, and the representatives of the people answer Francis Josef that never shall he pervert Hungary into Austria—never subdue the Hungarian spirit—never live to see our noble nation an Austrian province. Hungary for ever! Hungary for the Hungarians!"

Every County Council throughout the land followed the example of the County Council of Pesth and shared its fate. The officials of the County Councils patriotically refused to transfer their services to the Austrians, and for a little time something like anarchy prevailed in the land. Francis Josef appointed a Hungarian renegado named Palffy military governor, and proclaimed a coercion regime. A Press censorship was established, all local governing bodies were superseded by Austrian officials, and trial by Removables instituted. "The disloyalty of the Hungarian local bodies pains my paternal heart," said Francis Josef. "I come here," said Palffy, "as a good chief and a kind friend." "Behold the good chief and kind friend," said a Pesth newspaper, "Palffy—the renegado. Judas, we salute thee." Palffy suppressed the newspaper and resumed: "The welfare of Hungary has always been and always will be proportioned to the loyalty of its people to the Emperor. See? Those who preach otherwise are seditious, blasphemous, or harebrained persons. Be loyal and you will be happy." Whereupon a Hungarian humorist wrote a rude rhyme which he entitled "The Austrian Thieves." "The Austrian Thieves" became a popular song in Hungary, and the tune to which it was sung was heard one day by Palffy played by a military band. Thereupon he summoned all the military bandmasters before him. "In future," said he, "observe that no revolutionary tunes are played by your bands, and above all, take care not to play that seditious new song, 'The Austrian Thieves.'" "Your Excellency," said one bandmaster, gravely, "it is not a new song—it is a very old tune."

Deak admonished the people not to be betrayed into acts of violence nor to abandon the ground of legality. "This is the safe ground," he said, "on which, unarmed ourselves, we can hold our own against armed force. If suffering be necessary, suffer with dignity." Meantime Deak walked about Pesth smoking his pipe, and gathered his friends around him each night in the Queen of England Hotel, discussing affairs. He had given the order to the country—Passive Resistance—and the order was obeyed. When the Austrian tax-collector came to gather the taxes the people did not beat him or hoot him—they declined to pay him, assuring him he was a wholly illegal person. The tax-collector thereupon called in the police and the police seized the man's goods. Then the Hungarian auctioneer declined to auction them, and an Austrian of his profession had to be brought down. When he arrived he discovered he would have to bring bidders from Austria, also. The Austrian Government found in time that it was costing more to fail to collect the taxes than the taxes, if they were collected, would realise. In the hope of breaking the spirit of the Hungarians, the Austrians decreed that soldiers should be billeted upon them. The Hungarians did not resist the decree—but the Austrian soldier, after a little experience of the misery of living in the house of a man who despises you, very strongly resisted it. And the Hungarians asserted that from their enforced close acquaintance with the Austrian army they found it to be an institution they could not permit their sons, for their souls' sake, to enter, wherefore they proposed that enlistment in the Austrian army was treason to Hungary, and it was carried unanimously.

The eyes of Europe became centered on the struggle, and when the "Imperial Parliament" met in Vienna without the Hungarian representatives turning up to its deliberations, the Prussian and French Press poked such fun at it that it became a topic for laughter throughout Europe. So within nine months of the illegal dissolution of the Hungarian Parliament of 1861, Hungary, without striking a blow, had forced Austria into the humiliating position of a butt for Europe's jests. "Austria can wait and win," said Schmerling. "She can't wait half so long as we can," replied Deak.

It is always a pleasure to turn to the liberty-loving Press of England for its contemporary criticism on European affairs. The "Times" of 1861 was very sad. It hoped Austria would have been freed to fight Prussia for England's good, and the Hungarians spoiled the game of the English diplomats. "We would have been pleased," said the "Times," "if the Hungarians had united with the Austrians." "But," it added, shrewdly, foreseeing the triumph of Hungary, "the Emperor has gone the wrong way to do the right thing."* "The right thing," in

---

* "The London "Times,' censuring the Austrian Government for mismanagement, explained the art of deluding nations and seducing their leaders as practised by England. In the present day the Irish people have seen the process successfully worked on the leaders of the Irish Parliamentary Party. On August 29, 1861, the "Times" wrote in its leading article :—

"An English Premier, under the circumstances, would have sent for M. Deak ; in old times the Sovereign would have 'closeted' him. The leader of the Hungarian Diet would have been reasoned with if he was sensible, **flattered if he was vain, cajoled if he was weak**. . . . That may seem

English opinion, in 1861, was to deprive Hungary of her Constitution—" Unite " her—but it should have been done in the English New Eraian fashion. " Why does not," said the " Times," on the 24th of August, 1861, " Austria follow **our** example ?" It was because the Austrians, while as tyrannical, were not so hypocritical. They were honest enough to admit that it was not the salvation of Hungarian souls but the nourishing of Austrian bodies that was their prime consideration. The " Times " warned the Emperor of the danger that Deak's policy foreshadowed for him. " Passive Resistance," it wrote, " can be so organised as to become more troublesome than armed rebellion." Fortunately for England, Ireland has seldom resorted to passive resistance to her rule in this country, the Irish having been led by their eloquent leaders to believe that Parliamentarianism and Public Meeting are the interpretation of the phrase Moral Force.

VII.—The Failure of Force and " Conciliation."

Austria strove to encounter the Passive Resistance of Hungary by ordaining, as England did in Ireland a generation later, " exclusive trading " illegal. The Hungarians despised the ordinance and pursued their policy, occasioning much filling of jails with " village ruffians," " demagogues," and other disreputable people who disturb the peace of

---

a shabby and undignified way of proceeding, but it is the way in which such things are done. The history of our own Unions is full of crudities which detract rather largely from the grandeur of the transactions We hardly know any cases in which it is so unsafe to look behind the scenes. But the Acts were accomplished—accomplished without illegality or violence, and perhaps by the best means available at the time. At anyrate, the end was ensured, and we are now reaping the benefit of the measures But how different has been the course of the Austrian Minister !"

a country which a stronger country desires to rob. Yet a few months of the jail-filling process and Austria found herself in another cul-de-sac. "The Hungarians are an emotional and generous people," thought Francis Josef; "I shall try the friendly monarch policy." And he amnestied all those whom but a few months before he had thrust into prison. But the Hungarians did not respond to the dodge and sing Alleluia for the generosity of the royal gentleman in Vienna. They had sucked wisdom from experience, and did not feel in the slightest grateful for having the lash lifted an inch off their backs to prevent them kicking too hard. And when the excellent monarch, like the gentleman who, out of his bounty, built a big bridge at the expense of the county, was generously pleased to grant a subvention to the Hungarian National Museum and the Hungarian National Theatre at Pesth—out of the Hungarian funds—the Hungarians, far from being impressed by the royal generosity, added another satirical stanza to "The Austrian Thieves."

In the meantime the Hungarian Deputies continued to meet, not indeed as the Parliament of Hungary, but as the Hungarian Agricultural Union, The Hungarian Industrial League, the Hungarian Archaeological and Literary Association, and soforth, and through their debates and discussions kept the people of the country in the right road of National policy. There was no law, for instance, to compel Hungarians to support Hungarian manufactures to the exclusion of Austrian ones, but the economic wisdom of doing such a thing was emphasised in discussions at the admirable associations which we have named, and the results of these discussions had a force as binding as law upon the people. A succession of Hungarian gentlemen travelled Europe, seeking new fields for an Hungarian export trade, and keeping the Continental Press au courant with Hungarian affairs. At home, the Press was utilised to produce works of educational value to the Hungarian people—works National in tone and spirit, and the Hungarian historical novel became a feature of the time. A scarcity fell on the land in 1863, but the spirit of the Hungarian people tided them over what in Ireland's case in 1847 became an appalling disaster, and at the end of the year of famine, Francis Josef, baffled by the manly policy of a spirited people, attempted overtures for a reconciliation, and announced that it was his wish to satisfy Hungary " not only in material respects, but in other respects." But the Hungarians suspected him of insincerity and ignored his overtures—still continuing to refuse to recognise his kingship or his law, or his officials, or to pay his taxes, unless under compulsion. The benevolent Emperor then sought to delude the Hungarians by putting up Lustkandl, a jurist, to prove beyond all doubt that the Hungarians were a subject race, and not at all entitled to govern themselves as an independent people. Deak smashed up Lustkandl in an article, after which Austria and Prussia went to war with Denmark.

It was not as a consequence of Deak's demolition of Lustkandl that Austria went to war with Denmark—it was only in sequence of time. Denmark owned the Duchy of Schleswig-Holstein, which both Austria and Prussia lusted after and claimed they were entitled to by right. Meanwhile Europe was scoffing at Austria's Imperial Parliament. The Bohemians, after spending two years in it, grew disgusted, recalled their representatives to Bohemia, and declined to recognise any laws passed in Vienna affecting Bohemia as binding. Thus repudiated and boycotted by the two chief countries of the Empire— Hungary and Bohemia—the "Imperial Parliament" became a standing jest for the politicians of the Continent. Francis Josef came back from the wars to find the name of Austria sinking lower day by day, and once again he caused overtures to be made to Hungary for reconciliation. Hungary's answer was the same—when she got what she demanded she would talk of friendship.

The friendship of Hungary had, however, become of urgent necessity to Austria, for Prussia was already quarrelling with Austria over the spoil of the Danish war. Bismarck had marked the deficiencies of the Austrian army and the internal weakness of the Austrian Empire, and decided the time was favourable to dethrone Austria from the headship of the Germanic Confederation and exalt Prussia in her stead. The statesmen of Vienna, viewing with alarm the prospect of war with Prussia, with a "disloyal" Hungary on their flank, endeavoured to placate Bismarck and conciliate Hungary. Deak was asked the price of Hungary's "friendship." He answered in the Easter of 1865 in the columns of the "Pesth Napolo"—The restoration of Hungary's Free and National Constitution. "The Hungarian Nation will never give up its Constitution," he wrote. "It is prepared when that independence has been restored to take the legal measures necessary to bring its laws into harmony with the stability of the monarchy." Rumours of a change of policy spread through the land and at the end of May an official announcement reached Pesth that his Majesty was about to visit his beloved subjects in Pesth and inaugurate another New Era. Meantime the statesmen of Vienna staved off Prussia, while they anxiously awaited a success for the Royal Visit to the Hungarians in securing for them, if not the active assistance, at least the benevolent neutrality of Hungary in the impending war.

VIII.—The Royal Visit of 1865.

It is to be clearly understood that the visit of his Imperial Majesty, the Emperor Francis Josef, to Pesth, the capital of disloyal Hungary, on the 6th of June, 1865, was wholly unconnected with politics, and was in no wise prompted by the fact that war between Austria and Prussia appeared inevitable. His Majesty went to Pesth for the purpose of seeing the races. So the journals of Vienna officially announced, and so the Austrian Governor of Hungary informed the Hungarians. "His Majesty," ran the semi-official announcement, issued at the end of May, "journeys to Pesth to see the races, and his visit is to be regarded as semi-private." At the same time, however, it was thought well, in order to cut the claws of seditious and noisy persons, to insert paragraphs in the newspapers recalling to the recollection of the Hungarians the kind words His Majesty had on more than one occasion used about Hungary, and the chief journal in Vienna even went so far as to say that His Majesty was so fond of the Hungarians that, but for certain ministers, he would long since have abolished military law and settled the Hungarian question satisfactorily. "The monarch," remarked this Vienna journal profoundly, "is equally the monarch of Hungarians and Austrians, and loyalty to the sovereign is as incumbent on the Hungarian as on the Austrian. Hungary can have no grievances against the sovereign, whatever faults she may find with his ministers." "The Emperor," said the London "Times" of June 10th, 1865, "is inclined to make great concessions." It was an observant man who first wrote that history repeats itself.

His Majesty arrived in the capital of his disloyal kingdom at nine o'clock in the morning of Tuesday, June 6th, 1865. He was accompanied by several persons of rank and by his Governor of Hungary, Palffy. He drove through the streets in an open carriage, being cheered here and there by small knots of people, but the bulk of the inhabitants neither stood in the streets to watch him pass nor heeded his presence. The business of Pesth, except amongst the garrison and the royal warrant-holders, went on as if His Majesty had not come to see the races. His Majesty pulled up at the Palace of Buda, where the chiefs of the garrison and a number of titled sycophants received him. The Cardinal Primate, Szilowsky, read an address of welcome. We give an exact translation, since it may serve as a model for some of our fellow-countrymen:

Your Imperial Royal Apostolic Majesty—Most Gracious Lord! It is with feelings of infinite affection and joy that we now humbly do homage to your sacred person. The appearance of your Majesty in our dear country is now as always beneficial to us. At present it inspires us with hope, and we are, therefore, the more bound to be eternally grateful to your Majesty whose love for and graciousness towards us has been invariable. We entreat you to believe that the Hungarian people are truly faithful to the Throne and cheerfully prepared to lay down their lives for your Majesty. We daily beseech God to protect you and crown your exertions in our behalf with success, and while humbly rendering our homage, we fervently pray your Majesty may live long and be ever happy.

His Majesty in reply read from a sheet of paper a few sentences—in Hungarian—in which he hinted that he meditated convening the Hungarian Diet— at a future date—if his Hungarian subjects backed up the Empire. The language and the graciousness so pleased the addressers that we read " the walls trembled " to their " hurrahs." After which his Majesty visited the Agricultural Exhibition, and expressed his deep interest in Hungarian agriculture and his heartfelt wishes for abundant Hungarian harvests. Governor Palffy was meanwhile busy in stirring up the latent loyalty of the people of Pesth. In the morning, when his Majesty arrived, there had been very few flags exhibited on the houses, whereupon Palffy set about persuading the people to hang flags out, and succeeded admirably. When his Majesty left the Agricultural Exhibition his eyes lighted up with pleasure, for he beheld the bare city of the morning beflagged all over. A little later, however, his Majesty discovered that the newly-erected flags were green-white-and-red tricolours—the official ensign of Independent Hungary. Palffy was indignant and bent upon making an example of some of the people who had thus tricked him, but his Majesty ordered Palffy to forbear lest he might make matters worse. His Majesty, however, avenged himself when he got back to Vienna by firing Palffy out.

In the evening his Majesty presided at a banquet, and drank the toast of " Prosperity to Hungary," amidst much enthusiasm from the Austrian placemen and the Royal warrant-holders. Next day he presented a gift of a few hundred pounds to the Hungarian Academy of Science, and conversed affably with Deak, who was one of the heads of the Academy.   His Majesty also drove constantly through the streets, and saluted every man who saluted him—among whom, as the "Times" correspondent remarked, there were no young men, and he talked on no less than three occasions in forty-eight hours of the " gallant and chivalrous Hungarian people " whom he was quite sure would support the Throne were it assailed. Palffy organised a torchlight procession and ran a regatta in his honour. but the enthusiasm failed to flow. At the races his Majesty condescended to leave his royal box and mingle familiarly with the people, smoking a cigar, but the people were not impressed.   So after a command night at the National Theatre, where "God Save the Emperor" was played and loudly applauded by his Majesty's faithful garrison, his Majesty quitted Pesth on the 9th of June, leaving behind him the following proclamation :—

To My Hungarian Subjects—During my stay in the heart of my kingdom of Hungary I have continually received from the different ranks and classes of society, as well in the cities as in the country at large, unmistakable proofs of loyalty and attachment. Being moved by their hearty confidence in my paternal intentions, I desire to give all the expression of my thanks and the assurance of my full favour. In quitting my beloved Hungary, in which I should much like to remain longer, I take with me the agreeable hope of being able—in some time—to return, in order, as I declared on the day of my arrival, to complete the work which all of us have so much at heart. In the meantime, I depend on the protection of God, and confidently count on the energetic support of every true Hungarian.

Francis Josef.

His Majesty returned from his trip to the Pesth Races with the conviction that it would be decidedly dangerous to go to war with Prussia just then, and to buy peace he handed over one-half of the spoil he took in the Danish war—the Duchy of Lauenberg —to Prussia for the nominal sum of £500,000, or less than £5 18s. per head of the inhabitants, throwing in the soil and the cities for nothing. This eased the strain, for Prussia affected to be contented, and the danger of war seemed to have passed. Whereupon Austria turned to resume the coercing of the Hungarians.

IX.—Austria's Last Card.

Scarcely had the Treaty of Gastein, by which Austria ceded Lauenberg to Prussia, been formally signed, than the Austrians found reason to suspect that Prussia desired more than that Duchy as the price of peace. Accordingly, coercion was suspended, soft words were spoken of the Hungarians, and an amazing amount of virtue and innate loyalty to the Emperor Francis Josef were discovered by the journalists of Austria to exist in the souls of the countrymen of Deak and Kossuth. The doubt of the Austrians as to Prussia's designs became a certainty after Lauenberg had been handed over, for when that had been done the Prussians immediately asked for the remainder—Holstein—to surrender which to Prussia, under the circumstances, would have been tantamount to Austria resigning the headship of the German Empire.

It was clearly no time for coercing the Hungarians—Prussia was making friendly references through her Press both to that country and to Bohemia, and was seeking to conclude an offensive alliance with Italy. As against an allied Prussia and Italy and an insurgent Hungary and Bohemia, Austria could count only on Saxony, Bavaria, Hanover, and a few minor German States for support, and defeat under these circumstances appeared inevitable. With Hungary on her side, however, the matter would be very different, indeed with the active support of Hungary the Austrian Emperor believed he could march to Berlin and dictate the terms of peace to King Wilhelm. But before any hope of Hungarian support could be reasonably held, it was patent that there must be "concessions," and Austria was reluctant to make concessions. There was one alternative to yielding to Hungary, it seemed to the Austrian statesmen—and it they sought—an alliance with France against Prussia. Napoleon, it was known, regarded with apprehension the growing power of the Prussian kingdom, and to Napoleon the Emperor Francis Josef turned, but a little too late. Bismarck's piercing eye had read the mind of Francis Josef, and when the Austrians approached the French Emperor, they found that Bismarck had squared him into neutrality.

There was clearly nothing for it but to "conciliate" Hungary. "Something must be done," said the Emperor. "Something must be done," his statesmen echoed. In view of the possibilities he had got rid of Schmerling, who made his exit on the Budget of 1865, and Count Pouilly, somewhat of a figurehead, took his place, but the real force in the new Cabinet was the Moravian, Belcredi, whose infallible plan for patching up the Empire was the Home-Rule-all-Round specific, although, being naturally an opportunist he was not prepared to limit himself too much. When the news came that France would not join Austria against Prussia

in the event of war, the Emperor assembled his
sages, and the result was the Manifesto of the 20th
September.

The Manifesto of the 20th of September, 1865,
was a franker document than State documents
usually are. First, it abolished the Imperial Parliament, because as it admitted very frankly, the
machinery of the Imperial Parliament had been
upset since Hungary refused to send her representatives to Vienna, and kept them at home instructing the people to ignore the laws made by the
Imperial Parliament. The manifesto then acknowledged the right of Hungary, Bohemia, and the
other countries to manage their own affairs and
conserve their separate nationalities, and it wound
up by declaring the authority of the Hungarian
Parliament and the other countries' Parliaments
restored. And the Emperor added he would do
himself the honour of visiting Pesth in December
to open the Parliament of Hungary.

"So far, so good," said Deak, "but this must
not be a mock Parliament." The former Deputies
of Hungary met under Deak's presidency in Pesth
to consider the Manifesto, and they unanimously
resolved to accept nothing less than the restoration
of the Constitution of 1848, and the establishment
of a separate Hungarian Ministry, responsible only
to the legally-crowned King of Hungary, and the
elected representatives of the Hungarian people in
the Parliament of Hungary. The election of the
members of the new Parliament gave Deak, who was
himself elected for Pesth, 200 followers out of 333.
The remainder comprised the Conservative or
former Austrian party, but who were now pledged
to Deak's policy on the question of the status of the
Parliament, and the Separatists, who, while they
supported Deak's demands, declared nevertheless
for separation and a Republic. On the 6th of December the Parliament of Hungary was elected.
On the 12th the Emperor Francis Josef left for

Pesth to open it. All Europe waited expectantly the result. Prussia suspended for a while her war preparations to see what Hungary's action would be, and Hungary herself waited quietly and calmly to know whether this meant the restoration of her liberties, or whether it was merely another Austrian dodge to secure Hungarian aid in her hour of need —which, indeed, it was. But, unlike Ireland, Hungary had learned from her frequent betrayals not to trust the oppressors when they came bearing gifts, and it was in no mood of loyal enthusiasm, but in a critical and perhaps cynical spirit Hungary awaited the speech of Francis Josef to the representatives of the Hungarian nation.

X.—The Meeting of the Hungarian Diet of 1865.

On the 14th December, 1865, the Emperor Francis Josef opened the Parliament of Hungary in state. His Majesty was dressed in Hungarian costume. He read his speech in the Hungarian language. The Hungarian Members of Parliament, clad also in the national costume, listened to it politely, and some cheered when he remarked that he came to talk to them with the "frank candour" that befitted a monarch discussing the commonweal with his people. Deak sat silent throughout. "There shall be no compromise," he had promised the people, and Deak knew his Austrian.

The Emperor's speech was much better written than anything Mr. Duke could do in the way of speech-writing. It is true it contained a number of venerable sentences which have done duty for Giant Humbug in many generations—"Spirit of mutual concession," "great work of conciliation," "prosperity of Hungary," but it was distinctly cunning and plausible. It pretended to give everything while in reality it gave little. It rallied the patriotic drum so much that a Hungarian Deputy

drily observed that for using the expressions
his Majesty used—and meaning them—five years
before, his Majesty would have thrust a Hungarian
into jail. At the end of the speech the deputies
applauded, and when the Press of Vienna next day
exultantly proclaimed that Hungary had been
appeased—and now—God be praised!—was with the
Emperor—the Deputies politely explained that what
they applauded was not the speech, but the admirable pronunciation of the Hungarian language
the Emperor Francis Josef possessed—for a
foreigner. The Emperor's speech was delivered
from a dais, above which hung a painting of Hungary, symbolised as a woman bearing in one hand
a naked sword, and in the other a tablet inscribed

"1848!"

a quiet reminder from the fearless Magyars that
the Law and the principles of 1848 were the Law
and the principles that stood for Hungary.
As he read, he glanced occasionally from the corner
of his eyes at Deak, who sat silent and outwardly
impassive, and did not move an inch even when
the speech ceased. Stripped of its casing, the
speech of the Emperor meant that Austria was
willing to erect a subordinate Parliament in Hungary with a limited control over home affairs, and
to confer with Hungary on common affairs—in the
Imperial Parliament—but the Constitution was not
to be restored; the Laws of '48 were not to be
recognised; the municipal institutions of the
country were not to be re-erected. But so plausibly
was the new Austrian scheme for the humbugging
of Hungary put by the Emperor, such a glamour
did he invest it with, so touching were his appeals
to and eulogies of Hungary and the Hungarians that
had Francis Josef been on the throne of England,
and had the people he had to deal with been Irish
instead of Hungarian, he would infallibly have
been proclaimed the greatest man since Agammenon

and the very best. As for the Hungarians, they only said " Francis Josef plays the trickster." *

The Emperor saw from his failure to deceive Deak that he could scarcely hope to humbug Hungary on this occasion. But, nevertheless, he felt bound to neglect no means to weaken the national spirit, wherefore he fixed his headquarters at Buda, and displayed an enthusiastic interest in all that patriotic Hungarians took interest in. He mixed affably with the people, and assured them confidentially that he really considered himself more of a Hungarian than an Austrian—he wore a Hungarian tricolour tie of Hungarian manufacture. He told them he would bring the Empress down to see them —the Hungarian is nothing if not chivalrous. He gave dinner-parties every night in the Palace of Buda, and invited every patriot whose name he could find on the Police Shadowers' List to attend them. In fact the number of dinner-parties he gave laid him up with indigestion in Vienna for three days after his return. And firework displays became so common that the people ceased to take interest in them. Notwithstanding, Hungary continued to whistle " The Austrian Thieves," and the Parliament, after duly considering his speech, adopted an address in reply on the motion of Deak, who warned them "never to give up principle for expediency," which in courteous but firm language informed his Majesty that Hungary declined all compromise, and was neither to be intimidated nor cajoled into the surrender of her rights. The address was presented to Francis Josef on the 24th of February. In the course of it, the Parliament of Hungary said:

The advocates of a policy of expediency need not be astonished if, after having been the victims

---

* Mr. Gladstone's second Home Rule Bill (1893) was mainly modelled on this Austrian proposal which the Hungarians unanimously rejected.

of many deceptions, Hungary has learned caution, and declines to enter on the path they invite and follow. It was by standing fast to principle our ancestors saved the Fatherland, and compelled the restoration of our Constitution in its integrity. Esau when in want sold his birthright for a mess of pottage—he got the pottage—but there was strife ever after. To such a pass would the apostles of expediency bring our land—to such straits, your Majesty, would pseudo-friendliness and pseudo-concession-making reduce us.

The address was presented to the Emperor at Buda. The Emperor, in a temper, replied that what he had said he had said, and he issued a rescript, to make an end of the matter, assuring his beloved Hungarians that he would firmly uphold the principles he had enunciated in his speech. The Vienna Press warmly supported him. They assured him that it was quite impossible for Hungary to continue the struggle, and that, anyway, Hungary did not want to continue it, as her people were at heart loyal and were totally misrepresented by Deak and the other political agitators who were raising the ructions. All parties in the Parliament debated the Royal Rescript with commendable frankness. "It is not our interest to strengthen Austria in any way," said Baron Eotvos, the Moderate. "There must be absolute equality and parity of rights between Hungary and Austria," said Apponyi, the Conservative. With a unanimous voice the Parliament presented a second Address to the Emperor Francis Josef, which they sent him within twenty-four hours of receiving his Rescript. The second Address left nothing to be desired on the score of frankness. It told him that Hungary demanded the complete restoration of her Constitution, the recognition of her independence as a kingdom, the reconstitution of her municipalities, the acknowledgment of her territorial and political integrity,

the acceptance of the Laws of 1848, and the absolute
amnesty and compensation of every person who had
been imprisoned or injured in consequence of the
illegal government Austria had maintained in the
land since 1848. And, it added, until Hungary got
those things she declined to regard the Emperor
Francis Josef as King of Hungary, or Austria as
other than her enemy. The Emperor merely replied
by exhorting Hungary to be loyal, and the deputation which presented the Address thereupon
turned upon its heel and left his presence. A few
hours later Francis Josef quitted Pesth baffled and
agitated. Not a cheer was heard, not a hat was
raised as he left the railway station. The Hungarian Parliament continued to meet as if nothing
had occurred, and by the direction of Deak acted
as if the Laws of '48 and the Constitution had never
been suspended. And Austria was impotent, even
if she had been strong enough to intervene, for
Bismarck's   subtle   policy   had   succeeded:
Prussia and Italy had formed an alliance. Austria knew it was no longer possible to avert war,
and was feverishly arming to fight for the hegemony
of the German Empire. In this dire strait Francis
Josef swallowed his big words, and again made
overtures to Deak. Deak's reply was concise and
decisive. All the demands formulated by the Hungarian Parliament must be conceded before Hungary would consider any other question. "Under
no circumstances," added Deak, "shall Hungary
send members to an Imperial Parliament or anything on the plan of an Imperial Parliament." * It

---

* "Hungary inhabited by men who did not speak Hungarian, who set no store on preserving the political identity
of the Hungarian kingdom, would be no Hungary for them.
And this is the terrible picture which they always keep before their eyes when judging of the probable consequences
of any change or reform. They do not ask: ' Will this make
me or my fellow-citizens richer ?' But ' Will this leave us
as good Hungarians as we were ?' . . . . Mr. Mocsáry,
in   a   pamphlet entitled ' A Kérdések Kérdése '—' The

was no time for Austria to attempt to bully or humbug Hungary. The Hungarian Parliament proceeded to discharge its business as if no Austria existed, and Bismarck, satisfied that Hungary would not rally to Austria's aid, caused war to be declared on the 18th of June, 1866.

XI.—The Austro-Prussian War.

The Prussian army, within a few days of the declaration of war against Austria, overcame the resistance offered by the small German States which had thrown in their lot with the latter and advanced into Bohemia, where the Austrians under Marshal

Question of Questions "—which appeared in 1866, has stated with remarkable clearness the terrible consequences which, in his opinion, would result from Hungarians sitting at Vienna in a legislature common to the whole Austro-Hungarian Empire. He asks, in the first place: Who would be sent to represent the nation in such an assembly? Naturally, such Hungarian politicians as could express themselves in German, not only with fluency, but with elegance. As Mr. Mocsáry truly observes but few men are gifted by nature with the faculty of making themselves complete masters of two languages. But few are born orators even in their mother-tongue. The consequence would be that Hungary would be represented at Vienna by the least Hungarian of Hungarians, by men to whom not Hungarian, but German, was their mother-tongue. In every country it is the upper classes of society who are the least national. Of no country, perhaps, is this more true than of Hungary. Every ambitious father's principal care would be to make his son a complete German. With the German language would come German ideas, German modes of thought, German feelings; and thus Hungarians would be divided into two unequal classes—the denationalised and ambitious few whose talents would no longer serve the cause of their country, and, on the other hand, the Abdiels of patriotism, who, spurning civilisation as the wages of treason, would retire to their lonely farms, would deny their children the advantages of education, lest they, too, might be infected by the example of triumphant apostasy, and would gradually die out 'the Indians of the Old World at once pitied and extirpated.' "—Patterson, " The Magyars."

Von Benedek, an Hungarian Imperialist, were assembled. Simultaneously the Italians attacked the Austrian army in Italy, and the Italian fleet sailed into the Adriatic. The Austrian army in Italy and the Austrian fleet in the Adriatic proved, however, too much for the Italians. The Archduke Albrecht defeated the Italian army at Custozza, and the Austrian fleet under Tegethoff disposed of Italy's navy at Lissa. But these were the only victories Austria achieved. On the 3rd of July the Prussian army utterly defeated Benedek in the Battle of Sadowa, and compelled the Austrians to flee across the Elbe, leaving 40,000 men and 160 cannon behind them. The victors immediately occupied Prague, the capital of Bohemia.

The occupation of Prague opened the road to Vienna, and the Prussians prepared to march on the Austrian capital. In this desperate strait, the Austrian Emperor purchased peace from Italy by retroceding Venice, and the Austrian army which had been engaged there under the Archduke Albrecht hastened back to defend Vienna. Francis Josef then sent to Pesth for Deak, and Deak on arriving at midnight in Vienna was received by the Emperor, pale and haggard, in the palace. "What am I to do now, Deak?" the monarch asked of his opponent. Deak's laconic reply is celebrated in Austrian history, "Make peace, and restore Hungary her rights." "If I restore Hungary her Constitution now, will Hungary help me to carry on the war?" the Emperor inquired. The reply of Deak exhibits the fearless and uncompromising character of the great Magyar. It was in one word, "No." He would not make the restoration of his country's rights a matter of barter. The Emperor turned sadly away and Deak left the palace. He had not gone six hours when Francis Josef issued a piteous appeal for help in his dire extremity to the people whom he had for years dragooned and cajoled. This is a translation of the

Emperor's last effort to hoodwink the Hungarian people into acting against their own national interests:

To My Faithful People of Hungary.

The hand of Providence weighs heavily upon us. In the conflict into which I have been drawn, not voluntarily, but through the force of circumstances, every human calculation has been frustrated, save only the confidence I have placed in the heroic bravery of my valiant army. The more grievous are the heavy losses by which the ranks of those brave men have been smitten; and my paternal heart feels the bitterness of that grief with all the families affected. To put an end to the unequal contest—to gain time and opportunity to fill up the voids occasioned by the campaign, and to concentrate my forces against the hostile troops occupying the northern portion of my Empire, I have consented with great sacrifices, to negotiations for an armistice with Italy.

I now turn confidently to the faithful people of my Kingdom of Hungary, and to that readiness to make sacrifices so repeatedly displayed in trying times.

The united exertions of my entire Empire must be set in motion that the conclusion of the wished-for peace may be secured upon fair conditions.

It is my profound belief that the warlike sons of Hungary, actuated by the feeling of hereditary fidelity, will voluntarily hasten under my banners, to the assistance of their kindred, and for the protection of their country, also immediately threatened by the events of the war.

Rally, therefore, in force to the defence of the invaded Empire! Be worthy sons of your valiant forefathers, whose heroic deeds gained never-ending laurels for the glory of the Hungarian name.

Francis Josef.

The Austrian Emperor's "profound belief" that "the warlike sons of Hungary," whom Austria had so long and so cruelly oppressed, were willing to fight to perpetuate the power that enslaved them, was quite unfounded. The Hungarians possessed both spirit and intelligence, and openly rejoiced in the success of the Prussians. The only Hungarians who voluntarily rallied to the fight were the Hungarian exiles, who formed a legion under General Klapka and proffered their services to Prussia, "to help in the overthrow of the accursed Austrian tyranny.'' The Prussians, having completed their arrangements, marched on Vienna, and on the 20th July their outposts were in sight of the Austrian capital. Realising that all hope of succour from his "faithful Hungarian subjects" was gone, the Emperor begged the Prussians to grant him an armistice with a view to making peace proposals. Owing to the attitude of France, which had become alarmed at the rapid success of the Prussian arms and considered the dismemberment of the Austrian Empire would seriously affect its position, the Prussians reluctantly conceded the armistice. They did not feel themselves strong enough at the time to face France allied with Austria. Four years later they wreaked a bloody revenge on Napoleon III. for his intervention. Four days after the granting of the armistice the Austrians accepted the conditions imposed by the victors, and in the following month the treaty of peace was definitively signed at Prague. By the Peace of Prague Austria surrendered the hegemony of the German Empire and gave up her rights as a member of the Germanic Confederation. She agreed to pay Prussia a war indemnity of forty million thalers, and to permit portion of her territory to be occupied by Prussian troops until the money had been paid. She consented to Prussia joining a new Germanic Confederation and assuming the headship of it, and annexing the North German States of which heretofore she had been the suzerain power. In Italy she gave up all her possessions save Trieste, and thus after thirty-two days' war she was hurled from the position she had held for centuries in Europe. On the 1st of June, 1866, Austria was at the head of all Teutondom—on the 1st of August she was at the tail. And on the morrow of the signing of the Peace of Prague the humbled tyranny found itself face to face with the country it had oppressed, as England oppresses Ireland, demanding reparation for the wrongs that had been done and full restoration of the rights that had been stolen away; and almost as impotent to resist the demands of Hungary in 1866 as England was to resist the demands of Ireland in 1782, when, returning beaten from America, she found herself confronted in Ireland by 200,000 armed and disciplined men, who, unfortunately for their descendants, were led not by a farseeing and steadfast statesman like Francis Deak, but by an eloquent and emotional orator, Henry Grattan.

XII.—Count Beust.

The Austrian Empire seemed doomed. The Imperialists were demoralised—the oppressed exultant. Francis Josef turned to his ministers and begged them to show him how he could continue to wear the Imperial diadem. "Play the despot," advised Belcredi and Esterhazy and Pouilly—the Old Guard had lived but never learned, but Francis Josef had. It was at last clear to him that if the Empire were to be saved from disruption, freedom and fairplay must be accorded its constituent nationalities—that it must no longer be ruled in the interests of Austria alone. Wherefore the Emperor fired out Pouilly, and looking round for a serviceable man to patch up things, fixed on Baron Beust, a foreigner of some small reputation, to act as Austrian Foreign Minister—or in plain English, to keep the concern from falling to pieces.

Now Beust was not a great man, nor was he a particularly good one. He was no enthusiast for liberty—no idealist—no ardent lover of mankind. He was a mediocre man, very fond of admiring the smallness of his feet, and devoted to a good dinner, but he had an excellent understanding of the value of keeping the peace when unable to fight, and as he never permitted his prejudices or temper to betray him into a quarrel where he believed the chances were against him, Francis Josef felt that Buest was just the man to fix up the Hungarian question.

Buest was born in Saxony in 1809, and his early life was spent in the minor branches of the diplomatic service. So far as he had any convictions, he was a believer in autocracy, and when he attained high rank in the Saxon diplomatic service, he became intensely unpopular with the people. "Be moderate in all things" was one of his favourite maxims, and when his unpopularity grew to a point at which it became dangerous to the stability of the State, Beust jumped jim-crow and saved the Saxon throne by becoming something of a Radical. Thenceforward he enjoyed popularity in his own country, and if he did not secure its greatness, he at least did it no harm. In his new role, he appeared as the defender of the small German States against Prussian aggression, and thus secured for himself the hostility of Bismarck who, while despising his intellect, was not free from apprehension of his bourgeoise cunning. When the Austro-Prussian war broke out, Beust blundered by taking the wrong side, and after Sadowa resigned his office in Saxony to escape the vengeance he felt Bismarck would wreak upon him. This was the man whom, with a clearer insight into character than could have been expected, Francis Josef invited to save the distraught Empire from dismemberment. Beust replied he would. on one condition—that he should never be asked to get up earlier than nine o'clock in the morning, as he went to bed late, and to this the Emperor, who himself rose with the lark, complied. Beust's first step was to demand an agreement with the Hungarians. "On that," he said, "the continued existence of the Empire depends," and even bigoted opponents of Hungarian claims admitted, albeit reluctantly, that this was the case. "Peace with Hungary means the existence or non-existence of Austria, and it must be concluded without delay," said one Austrian statesman publicly and frankly. "We must choose between two evils," said the "Times" of Vienna—the "Nieue Freie Presse"—"capitulation to Hungary is the lesser one." "Hungary," said Beust, "is an ancient monarchy, more ancient as such than Austria proper. The Kingdom of St. Stephen has a pedigree of centuries, and its constitutional principle was asserted in the earliest times. Its race and language are entirely different from those of the other peoples which constitute the monarchy. Its people are powerful, brave, united." But it was no consideration of justice that moved Beust to settle the Hungarian question. The consideration that moved him was that if the Hungarian question were not settled to the liking of the Hungarians, the Hungarians would settle it for themselves by disrupting the Empire. Twenty years later he frankly stated the position: "Austria had been beaten after a short but most disastrous war; Prussia had forbidden her any further interference in German affairs; the country was almost in a state of latent revolution; and an outbreak in Hungary, promoted by foreign agents and foreign gold, with Klapka doing Bismarck's bidding, was in the highest degree probable, and would, had it occurred, have led to almost overwhelming disaster. Knowing this, I felt bound to advise the Emperor to accede to the views of the Deak party." Such was the man with whom Francis Deak had now to deal, and with whom he eventually concluded the Ausgleich, or Agreement, by which Hungary was freed from foreign dominion.

XIII.—The Surrender of Austria.

On the 19th of November, 1866, the Hungarian Parliament met, and received a rescript from the Emperor Francis Josef, in which he declared he had

resolved to give due "consideration to its demands
and claims," and hinted at the appointment of a
responsible ministry and the introduction of responsible government in all parts of the Empire. Deak
mistrusted the tone of the rescript. In it he dis-
cerned the voice of Belcredi rather than the voice
of Beust, and reflecting his mistrust, excitement
reigned in Pesth. In the midst of it Beust hurried
to the Hungarian capital to the house of the
National leader. It was the first meeting of the two
men, and Beust, had he any intention of playing a
game against Deak, abandoned it after the inter-
view. He found Deak ironwilled and impenetrable
—not discourteous, as Beust wrote half-complain-
ingly years afterwards, but shortspoken and abrupt.
Beust gave Deak an assurance that he would not
rest until the Hungarian Constitution was restored,
and Deak felt that Beust, though his motives were
not of the highest, was sincere. An unspoken—an
unwritten—agreement was made between the two
men. Beust had to fight and overthrow Belcredi,
who was still Prime Minister, before he could restore
the Hungarian Constitution. Deak had to prevent
the excitement of Hungary playing into Belcredi's
hands, while at the same time maintaining the
unyielding attitude of the nation. But Deak was
too skilful a politician to involve himself with Beust,
whose defeat was possible. After his meeting with
the Saxon statesman in Pesth, he avoided any further direct conference with him, but by secondary
channels the two men kept in touch.

  While the struggle between Belcredi and Beust was
proceeding in Vienna, Deak kept the Hungarian
Parliament as calm as the excitement of the times
would permit. Every deputy was ready with a
scheme for the final settlement of the Hungarian
question, and with a speech upon it, and between
the Republicans, Radicals, and Conservatives—all
agreed that the status quo was impossible, but all
differing as to what New Hungary should be—only

Deak could have saved Hungary from playing into Belcredi's hands. The result would probably have been another effort to enforce arbitrary rule upon Hungary, and a consequent insurrection, in which the Austrian Empire might have disappeared; but Hungary, weak and exhausted after the struggle, would not unlikely have fallen into the hands of Russia in the partition of the Empire, for the Hungary of 1866 was not the strong Hungary of to-day. This was the danger Deak foresaw, and desired to avert; but he was too great a man to desert a principle because of possible danger in its enforcement. Therefore, even while he felt that if Beust failed, his uncompromising attitude might involve war, Deak did not waver. In the address which he drafted in reply to Francis Josef on the 15th December, 1866, he spoke on behalf of Hungary in straightforward terms: "None of your Majesty's proposals," he said, "will be taken into consideration by the Parliament of Hungary until all the demands made by the Parliament of Hungary are conceded, and a ministry responsible to it alone assumes power. . . . Between Absolutism and a nation deprived of its constitutional liberties, no compromise is possible."

This was the firm language of a patriot statesman speaking on behalf of his nation to the head of a power which oppressed it. Deak's firm reply evoked a despotic rejoinder. In the beginning of 1867, the Emperor issued a decree making military service compulsory on the Hungarians. Belcredi was on top. A shout of rage and defiance rang through all Hungary, and for a moment it seemed as if insurrection would break out. Only the strenuous efforts of Deak saved the situation. He saw that the crisis had come, but the last moves in the game had not been played. His voice was heard above the tumult and the Parliament, swayed by him, sent a deputation to the Emperor with "Hungary's Last Word," as it has been called—the reply to the Em-

peror's conscription decree—which had been drawn
up by Deak himself, and in which he said, speaking
in the name of the Parliament of Hungary—" Let
your Majesty cancel the decree and all other measures sanctioned by Absolute power in defiance of
our Constitution, let your Majesty restore our Constitution in its integrity, and that as speedily as
may be." It is reminiscent of the stern addresses
of the Volunteers of 1782 to the British representative in this country.

The deputation bearing the ultimatum went to
Vienna and presented it to the Emperor, who, to
their delight and surprise, replied that he was ready
to cancel the army law and accede to all the wishes
of his beloved Hungarians " when the obstacles
which hindered the formation of a responsible Hungarian Ministry were removed."   The Council of
Sixty-seven, which had been appointed by the Hungarian Parliament to investigate into these obstacles, thereupon addressed his Majesty on the
subject, and after a severe struggle between Belcredi and Beust the former went down.   Deak's
unyielding policy had killed him. On the 7th of
February, 1867, the Emperor dismissed Count Belcredi from the Premiership and appointed Count
Beust his successor. On the same day he summoned Deak to Vienna, and in the Imperial Palace
pledged his word to his old antagonist to concede all
that had been demanded. Four days later, Julius
Andrassy, who had fought in 1848 for Hungarian
freedom, and for whose apprehension his Majesty
had been pleased to offer a reward of several thousand crowns, was summoned also to Vienna.
Andrassy, after the defeat of 1849, escaped
to France, where he lived for years in exile,
returning to Hungary on the proclamation of the
amnesty. When, in response to the Emperor's tele-
gram, he went to Vienna, it was to be informed by
the Emperor that he desired him to undertake the
formation of a National Ministry for Hungary,

responsible to the Hungarian Parliament, with Andrassy himself as Premier.

On the 18th of February, 1867, the Hungarian Parliament reassembled in Pesth to hear the reply to the "Last Word." It came in the form of a Royal rescript suspending the Conscription law and all other obnoxious laws until such time as the Hungarian Parliament declared itself willing to adopt them, and restoring the Constitution of Hungary. The reading of the rescript was followed by prolonged cheering from the Deputies, which, taken up by the waiting crowds outside, rolled and echoed through the streets like the roar of artillery. The appearance in the street of the hunted patriot of eighteen years before—Julius Andrassy, now Prime Minister of a freed Hungary—was signalised by the continuous shouting of "Eljen a haza!"— "My Country for Ever," the words with which the previous Prime Minister of a free Hungary—Count Batthyany—went to his death at the hands of the Austrians. At night Buda-Pesth flamed with bonfires and shone with illuminations—and next day its citizens—and the people elsewhere—busied themselves tearing down all Austrian flags, ensigns and devices—particularly the double-headed eagle— brother to the lion-and-unicorn—and burning them in the streets to the chant of the Marseillaise or Petofi's National Anthem. The proceedings, however, being likely to lead to great boisterousness, the National Government issued a proclamation— it was its very first—to the people, ordering them not to tear down any more of the Austrian ensigns —as the officers of the National Government would remove them themselves.

What the Ausgleich or Agreement between Austria and Hungary consisted in, how the Emperor Francis Josef went to Pesth and was crowned King of Hungary, and how Hungary, who won her independence by refusing to send members to the Imperial Parliament or to admit any right in that

Parliament to legislate for her, has prospered and grown giant-like in her strength since she became mistress of her own household we shall relate, after which we hope to convince some very practical people that the fight for Ireland's independence, when circumstances do not permit it to be waged with sword and gun, is nevertheless not in the alternative to be fought out on the floor of the British House of Commons.

XIV.—The Ausgleich.

Under the Ausgleich or Agreement between Deak on the part of the Hungarian Parliament and Beust on the part of the Austrians, ratified by the Emperor as King of Hungary, the relation of Hungary to Austria is definitively laid down. By it the King pledges himself to uphold in all respects the Constitution, privileges, and territorial independence of Hungary, to convoke within the year another Parliament, if one Hungarian Parliament be dissolved, to recognise the right of Hungary alone to decide on what her contribution to the military forces of the common army shall be. Under the Ausgleich Hungary does not recognise any authority in the Parliament of Vienna, and is free to conclude treaties and arrangements with other nations, on the footing of a free independent nation without consultation with Austria except in certain specified circumstances. Hungary also retains her national army—the Honveds, which she herself raises and pays, her national flag and national ensigns, supreme power over all her territory, her own mint and her own language, none other being legal in public offices, courts of law and in the State Documents.

In Pesth a ministry comprising a Premier, a Minister of Education and Public Worship, a Minister of Finance, a Minister of Justice, a Minister of

Agriculture, a Minister of National Defence, and a Minister of the Court sits and is responsible only to the Hungarian Parliament. A similar ministry, save that the Minister of the Court is the Emperor himself, sits at Vienna, responsible to the Austrian Parliament. The Parliament of Vienna consists of 353 members, that in Pesth of 444—we speak of the elective houses—the Houses of Magnates are hereditary or nominative, somewhat like the English House of Lords—but the power rests finally in the hands of the Lower House, which can compel the House of Magnates to assent to any measure it affirms three times. The rights and powers of both the Austrian and Hungarian Parliaments are equal, and although Austria pays 68 per cent. of the common expenditure, whilst Hungary pays only 32, Hungary has an absolutely equal vote in the expenditure of the money. The Austrian and Hungarian Parliaments annually elect a delegation of sixty members each, who assemble alternately in Vienna and Pesth, and deliberate separately—communicating with each other by written messages, the Hungarian delegates. writing in Hungarian, the Austrians in German. The deliberations are on the common affairs of the Empire, and these delegates elect what is styled the "Common Ministry"—a Minister of Foreign Affairs, a Minister of War, and a Minister of Common Finance. These three Ministers are charged with the conduct of the affairs of the Empire in its relations with the outer world only, and they are responsible not to the Parliament of Hungary nor the Parliament of Austria, but to the delegates elected from each of these. Either Hungarian or Austrian delegates possess the right of initiation. Under no circumstances can any debt be contracted in the name of the Empire or for any Imperial purpose without the consent of Hungary. The name Austro-Hungary is substituted for Austria in all official documents. In a word it may be said that

the Ausgleich is a compact between two independent
nations, agreeing for their better security and territorial integrity to have a common sovereign and
to act in concert in regard to foreign affairs.*

Not all in Hungary considered the Ausgleich
satisfactory. The Republicans adhered to the belief
that any connection with Austria was a source of
weakness, not strength to Hungary. And when
Francis Josef came to Pesth for his crowning, the
Republican Deputies, who numbered thirteen, held
aloof from participation in the ceremonies. But they
freely and frankly admitted that Deak had done
magnificently for Hungary, and they discountenanced any display of hostility to Francis Josef on the
occasion. Francis Josef, who was a tactful man,
appreciated   this   attitude of the Extreme Left,

---

* "Though the Emperor of Austria and the King of Hungary happens to be the same physical person, he is juridically
two persons, his prerogative in the one case being entirely
different from his prerogative in the other. For instance,
while in Austria the people have only such rights as the
Emperor has allowed them, in Hungary the position is reversed, and the King has only such rights as the people have
allowed him in the Constitution. In Austria the Emperor
may issue ordinances which have the force of law, even to
collect taxes and levy recruits; in Hungary the King may
do nothing of the kind. If he should attempt to do so any
officials that dared to assist him would be guilty of high
treason, and dealt with for that capital crime. As in the laws
of all civilised nations, it is an act of treason for a subject to
appeal to a foreign sovereign, so it is treason for a subject of
the King of Hungary to appeal to the Emperor of Austria.
All Hungarian institutions are based on the firm bedrock
fact of an independent Hungarian Kingdom. There is an
Austrian Parliament and a Hungarian Parliament, but there
is no such thing as an Austro-Hungarian Parliament; consequently there are no Austro-Hungarian M.P.'s; neither are
there any Austro-Hungarian subjects. They may belong to
either the one State or the other, but not to both.   The
actual true significance of the term Austro-Hungary . . . .
is that two independent nations, called respectively Austria
and Hungary, have become united for certain definite purposes to their material advantage. Simply that and nothing
more nor less than that."—De Lisle's "Hungary of the
Hungarians" (1914).

and marked his appreciation by the issue of a proclamation which caused him to be personally esteemed by those who were his political antagonists. It was a proclamation removing every disability and every penalty inflicted for opposition to Austrian rule and an invitation to all Hungarian exiles to return and share in the new freedom of their country. In this proclamation Francis Josef used no word that might hurt the feelings of any of his antagonists—he did not call it "an amnesty" nor a "pardon." He wrote: "I, Francis Josef, hereby annul all decrees and penalties inflicted upon my Hungarian subjects for any political causes up to this date and restore all lands forfeited, fines exacted," etc. It was a kingly proclamation, and the exiles said so, while some of them refused to take advantage of it.* Francis Josef followed this up by allocating a presentation made him in Pesth of 100,000 ducats to the widows and orphans of the Hungarians who had been slain in the War of Independence—a presentation which greatly added to his popularity.

On the 8th of June, 1867—eighteen years after the armed effort of Hungary to maintain her Constitution had been crushed in the blood of her people—Francis Josef was in Pesth to formally restore the Constitution of 1848, and pledge himself as King of Hungary to defend it with his life. At seven o'clock in the morning of the happy day, his Majesty, accompanied by his nobles, rode from the palace to the parish church of Buda, above which floated the tricolour of the Hungarian Patriots of 1848, and reaching its door knelt down, until the Primate

---

* Kossuth, who was averse from the Ausgleich, declined to take advantage of the Emperor's proclamation, holding that Austria was not to be trusted; but seventeen years later—in 1884—he declared his re-acceptance of the House of Hapsburg, convinced the Ausgleich was honestly upheld. His son, Francis Kossuth, is one of Hungary's present political leaders.

of Hungary sprinkled him with holy water and touched him with the crucifix, whereupon trumpets and drums sounded, and Francis Josef arose and entered the church, on the high altar of which the crown jewels of Hungary were placed. Approaching the altar, he turned and, facing the congregation, took the oath of allegiance to Hungary in a loud firm voice. "I, Francis Josef," he cried, "by God's grace Apostolic King of Hungary, swear by the Living God, by the Blessed Virgin Mary, and by all the saints that I will uphold the liberty of Hungary and the rights, privileges, customs, and liberties of the Hungarian people of every creed and every station, and inviolably maintain the Constitution, privileges, and territorial integrity of Hungary, and do all that may be righteously done to spread the renown and increase the prosperity of this my kingdom. So help me God." After which the king descended from the altar and bowed down before it, while the Primate and Bishops made the sign of the cross above his head, and the Litany was chanted. Then the monarch was anointed, the royal mantle of St. Stephen placed upon his shoulders, the iron crown placed upon his head, the sword of St. Stephen placed in his hands, which drawing from its sheath, and standing in front of the altar, he flashed before him, then to left and then to right, while outside the cannon thundered the news that the King of Hungary had sworn the oath of allegiance to the Nation.

The sceptre and globe were next handed to the King by the Primate, and he was conducted to the throne by the nobles and the bishops, bearing the insignia of all the nations of the Austro-Hungarian Empire. The Primate, standing before the altar, lifted up his hands and prayed for the strength of God to maintain the King while he maintained his oath, and at the end of the prayer bishops, nobles, and congregation joined in three cheers for the King of Hungary. Again the cannon thundered out, and simultaneously all the bells in Buda-Pesth were tolled joyfully.

The procession moved from the church—the fifty-two counties of Hungary, each represented by its nobles, its professional men, merchants, artisans, and farmers, all clad in national costume, and all carrying arms, led the way, with the tricolour flag of Hungary waving in the front, after which came the Church dignitaries, then Count Beust, and behind him in the faded green mantle of St. Stephen, with the iron crown on his head, the King of Hungary—after him a long line of notables and regiments of Hungarian Hussars, with their bands playing Hungarian music. Arrived in front of the parish church of Pesth, the King rode his horse up the mound there, and facing the north, drew the sword of St. Stephen from its sheath and cut with it northward, then turning his horse to the south, to the east, to the west in rapid succession, he cut with the sword in each direction—this ceremony signifying that the King called God to witness that come the enemies of Hungary from any quarter of the world, he would defend his kingdom with his life. At the conclusion of this ceremony the people, whose enthusiasm had been wrought up to the highest pitch, burst through the guards like a torrent, and crowded round Francis Josef with a mighty shout of "Long live the King!"

In the evening a great banquet was held in the palace, and Buda-Pesth was illuminated, so that, to use the description of a perhaps excited chronicler, it looked brighter than in the glare of the midday sun. Bands played throughout the city, and rockets burst all through the night over it. In the meadows along the river bank the people were entertained at a great feast, at which the oxen were roasted whole and the wine supplied in hogsheads. They spent the night in dancing, singing, and generally acting with so much unrestrained enthusiasm that a scandalised English journalist of the time wrote that their con-

duct was quite Irish! Beust, in his memoirs, tells
how, as he was going to the banquet, a white-haired
old man, at least eighty years of age, fell on his
knees before him as he stepped from the carriage,
and clasping his hand, kissed it again and again,
passionately exclaiming: "My father, my father!"
Count Beust speaks of this incident as a
humorous occurrence. Beust's inability to understand the Magyar mind afterwards led to trouble
and his fall from power.*

For three days Pesth and all Hungary abandoned
itself to feasting and merriment, and then resumed

---

* The London "Times" special correspondent, in a series
of supercilious but well-written articles, wrote on the
occasion:—

"Such a sight as Pesth now presents will probably never
be shown again. It is quite impossible to give an idea of
the splendour of some of the dresses in which, however, the
servants vie with their masters in all except buckles, buttons
and clasps of precious stones. . . . Under all their loyalty to
the King of Hungary there is a feeling that they have
won a victory over the Emperor of Austria. He is vanquished, and in his triumph as a King he acknowledges
his submission as the Kaiser of the adjacent Empire with
which they are allied. . . . To-night there will be another
people's feast, and more oxen will be roasted or
put on the spit entire, and more wine drunk, and
more boors get drunk, and dance and sing and
fight each other à la Irlandaise. Within a four days'
journey of our shores there is now in progress a scene such
as might have been witnessed in the old barbaric world,
when Kings were crowned with strange magnificence. . . .
The proceedings were in Hungarian, and among the many
phenomena connected with the present position of the
Kingdom none is more remarkable than the fact that the
Magyar language has been raised almost from the dead
within the memory of man. It owes its present use to
Count Szechenyi, for up to his time it was scarcely known,
or, if known, was never used in society by the Magyar
nobles, and was restricted to the peasantry. When he
began to speak it he was scarcely understood by his class;
he was almost laughed at for his persistence in adopting it
in every-day life. Now it is indeed as much national as is
our own speech, although Hungarians have not lost their
polyglot powers, and all Magyar gentlemen speak German
and French, and many of them English."

its business with seriousness and energy. But Deak did not participate in the feasting and merrymaking. He was a quiet man and disliked fuss. The Parliament of Hungary—Royalists and Republicans—voted that he should act as Palatine of Hungary—that is Protector—and crown Francis Josef. He declined to do so. Francis Josef anxiously asked Andrassy how he could honour Deak. "Sire," said Andrassy, "you have wealth, titles, offices, and decorations at your disposal; you can honour other men with one or all of them—but with them you cannot honour Deak." The King then sent Deak a photograph of himself and the Queen in a diamond-mounted frame. Deak declined to accept it, but when the King pressed him anxiously to know some way in which he could express the esteem and gratitude he felt for one who so long had been his resolute antagonist, "Sire," Deak replied, "when I am dead, you can say 'Francis Deak was an honest man.'"

Deak had declined to be Prime Minister, declined to be a member of the Cabinet. He wished to retire to his little home at Kehida—his whole fortune amounted to just £300 a year—and finish his life in the calm happiness of rural retirement, but his countrymen appealed to him to remain in Parliament, and he did so, with a sigh. For nine years he remained a simple member of the House, but stronger than any minister in it, and when he died—in 1876—his death was the occasion of an unprecedented outburst of grief. Hungary bowed herself in mourning. As his funeral passed through the streets the people knelt and wept on the pavements. By his own request his grave was made a plain one. A truly great man, he was like all the truly great ones of the world, simple and unostentatious to the end. The Queen of Hungary wept tears of genuine sorrow above his coffin. The King of Hungary, whom for years he had fought foot to foot, whom he neither flattered nor failed to sternly condemn when

occasion demanded, mourned with the Hungarian
people when Deak died. "In him," said Francis
Josef, "we have lost our noblest and our greatest
man."

XV.—Present and Past Hungary.

Since the conclusion of the Ausgleich and the
restoration of the Hungarian Constitution Hungary
has outstripped many of the European countries in
material progress. Like a strong man long bound
who regains his freedom, exulting in his re-
awakened strength, Hungary has used its strength
to the full and with enthusiasm.

The latest full official statistics of Austria and
Hungary available are those dealing with the year
1910. In that year the population of Austria was
28,324,940, and the population of Hungary
20,886,847. Hungary's progress not only in agriculture, but in mining and manufacturing industries
since the restoration of her national Constitution,
might be, with small exaggeration, called marvellous. Her output of iron before she regained her
freedom was infinitesimal—like our own. She is
now turning out half-a-million tons yearly. Her
output of coal before she regained her freedom
amounted to a couple of hundred thousand tons
annually. It is now 7,000,000 tons per annum. But
one single fact will suffice to give the reader some
conception of the giant strides Hungary has made
in her liberty. In Austria, to-day, there are thirty
thousand steam-boilers—in Hungary there are
twenty-nine millions. And forty years ago the Austrian Press and the Austrian statesmen assured the
world, as the English Press and the English statesmen assure it now about Ireland—that the people of
Hungary were a very interesting people, brave
enough and with some rude notion of the arts, but
fickle, inconstant, lacking in application—in a word,

devoid of the great Teutonic virtues of sobriety, patience, and industry. Hungary has shown the world how Austria lied. In Ireland, Irishmen have been found to believe the libel and to agree with England that fine fellows though we be in many ways, we yet lack the staying power of the Saxon. So men have risen to tell us, as Belcredi told the Hungarians fifty years ago, that our own defects of character, not the government of our country by foreigners, is the root-cause of our misery. However, Belcredi found few Hungarians base enough or foolish enough to credit him. Hungary believed in itself and relied on itself, Ireland did neither, and of the two nations both seemingly helpless and utterly crushed in 1849—the one that believed in itself has since become a nation among the nations of the world—the one that sought succour from its masters is still the most oppressed in Europe. The difficulties the Hungarians had to overcome were little less than those which confront the Irish in Ireland. Ireland was several times "planted" with English and Scotch families. Hungary was again and again "planted" with Austrians. As in Ireland, the bulk of the descendants of these Austrians became in time at one with those among whom they dwelt, but a minority remained unabsorbed. As in Ireland, there were diverse creeds in Hungary. As in Ireland the bulk of the people were Catholic, but there was a strong Presbyterian or Calvinist minority, and a considerable number of Lutherans and Greek Catholics. As in Ireland, while a proportion of the Nationalist leaders came from the non-Catholic ranks, the bulk of the Nationalists were the Catholics. The Calvinist, Lutheran, and Greek Catholic Hungarians were long apprehensive—an apprehension the Viennese Government lost no opportunity of exciting—that in an independent Hungary where a majority of the voting power would necessarily belong to the Catholics, they would be intolerantly treated. The history of inde-

pendent Hungary has proved how baseless the apprehension was. From the day the Constitution of
Hungary was restored, the fullest equality has
reigned, and sectarian intolerance is utterly
unknown in the kingdom. But Hungary had to contend with difficulties which Ireland can never have
to overcome. Hungary was surrounded on all sides
by people hostile or inimical to her—not alone Austrians and Russians, but the Slav hordes who had
been taught by unscrupulous and cunning statesmen
to regard Hungary as an enemy to them. These
" hordes " were used again and again to raise frontier questions which however settled, injured Hungary. If settled in her favour, the hatred of the
" hordes " for the Hungarians was increased; if
settled against her, she lost part of her territory.
The frontier of Ireland has been fixed by nature.
Whatever British statesmen may do, they can never
use the frontier question to raise up enemies for
this country other than Great Britain itself.

Nor were the potent weapons of calumny neglected
by Austria. Austria, like England, had the ear of
the world, and into it for generations she poured
what tale she pleased about the Hungarians. In
her Press, in her theatre, in her society, the Magyar
was ever held up to ridicule. His history was
declared to be invention, useful only to burlesque,
his traditions formed material for the wits of
Vienna to exercise their humour on, his character
was drawn in the grossest colours—he was a drun-
kard, a lazy ne'er-do-well, a blundering ignoramus,
an ingrate who bit the hand of his Austrian would-
be benefactor. In the Austrian beer-gardens—the
equivalent of the English music-halls—vulgar
beings, clad in grotesque imitation of the Hungarian costume, who sang songs reflecting on
the Hungarian character, were the popular buffoons.
The Austrians called them " Magyar Miska," or
" Hungarian Michaels "—Michael being the popular
peasant-name in Hungary—as the English call their

music-hall Irishmen "Irish Micks" or "Irish Pad-
dies." Nor was there at one time wanting in Hun-
guary the equivalent of the Irish seoinini—debased
Hungarians who, anxious to conciliate the strong
ones, applauded the libels on their race, affected to
despise the customs, traditions, history and language of their country, to consider everything Hungarian vulgar and all things Austrian polite.
"Fertaly-magnas" Kossuth called them in bitter
satire—"quarter-gentlemen." The English language cannot quite convey the significance, but at
all events, it was the Hungarian nickname for what
we call the seonini.

The Magyar peasant, when he rendered the soil he
laboured at more productive and thus increased its
value, was rewarded by an addition of taxation—
in bitterness then he let his land go wild—and
"See," said the Austrians, "what a villainously
lazy lot these Hungarians are!" In Ireland, in our
time, the peasant who reclaimed the waste was rewarded by having his rent increased and was evicted
from his home when unable to pay it. His neigh-
bours, warned by his fate, let the waste lie waste.
"See," said the English, "what a lazy lot these
Irish are!" The Magyar peasant who kept his
house decent and trim and brightened it as far as
in him lay, was assessed for heavier taxation. Then,
when he let his house go half to ruin, the Austrian
called the attention of the world to the uncleanly
and slovenly Magyar. So the English have held us
up to the world as "the dirty Irish," so, too, they,
having made education among us penal for generations, deplore to Europe our ignorance. So did the
Austrians when they had denied Hungary a
National system of education or a university—
though, indeed, unlike the English, they never put
a price on the head of a teacher—lament to Europe
the trouble they had in dealing with so barbarous
and ignorant a people. And for generations Europe
believed that one of the most gallant, interesting,

and gifted people of the world were, indeed, nothing
better than ignorant boors, drunken, immoral, and
intractable, whom Austria was compelled to occasionally punish in the best interests of civilisation.

The world has forgotten the Austrian calumnies
since Hungary has become free. It half, where it
does not wholly believe the charges made against
Ireland and the Irish. England has poisoned the
world's ear against us, and we have allowed the
world to drink in the poison, because we have raised
up as our leaders in these latter times, not
Szechenyis and Kossuths and Deaks, but men of
mean mind to whom notoriety was dearer than truth
and honour and gold or title or social recognition
of value exceeding principle—compromisers, when
they were not corrupt, timid in action and boastful
in words. In Mitchel—a better man—Ireland had a
half parallel to Kossuth—she never had a Deak.

To-day we are fighting precisely the same fight in
Ireland as the Hungarians did in the early Forties.
As it was in Hungary when Szechenyi, and Deak.
and Kossuth were beginning, so it is in Ireland
to-day. Our rich men are pro-English as the rich
Hungarians were pro-Austrian—our people are
divided as the people of Hungary were divided.* As
Szechenyi, a non-Hungarian-speaking Hungarian,
realised the value of the language which had become
in Hungary in those days, as it is in Ireland in
modern times, to be deemed a lingua rustica—so
non-Irish-speaking Irishmen in our time have
realised the value of the Irish language and thrilled
it again with life. Szechenyi throughout his life
could never speak Hungarian without effort or without an Austrian accent—some of his lieutenants in
the revival could never speak three sentences of it—
but they taught all Hungary to be proud of it, and
taught all young Hungary to speak it, so that to-day
the Hungarian language is the only language of

---

* Since this was written in 1904 matters have improved.

millions in Hungary whose grandfathers spoke no word of it. Public spirit, enterprise, and national self-consciousness were the outcomes of the language revival in Hungary, and these in time made Hungary free. Hungary built a National University herself, and in it educated her most brilliant sons to teach her people in the arts of peace and war, and train them in the virtues. But first of all she trained them in patriotism—trained them to see in Austria the enemy. Out of the university came the "Redcaps," who fought Austria on the battlefield, and the political leaders, thinkers, artists, scientists, and captains of industry who fought Hungary's battle in other spheres. Her literary men made Buda-Pesth her literary capital. They did not go to Vienna. Her people bought books and papers printed in Hungarian, which thousands of them could not read, because they were printed in Hungarian. Her journalists drove out the Austrian beer-garden, with its stage-Magyar, from Hungary, and in its place created a National Theatre, where the past glories and future greatness of Hungary were made familiar and prophesied to the eyes and ears of the people. Greater than all the patriotic resolutions of Ireland are the monuments of Hungary's patriotism that to-day stand in the capital of Free Hungary—the National University, the National Museum, and the National Theatre, built in despite of Austria, by the pence, shillings, and pounds of the people of Hungary.

In the same spirit of patriotism the Hungarians cast from them the garb they wore, since it was similar to the garb worn by the Austrians, and clad themselves after the fashion of their ancestors, thus stamping their individuality upon the foreigner—in the same spirit, they banished the dances of Austria, the songs of Austria, and the amusements of Austria from their social entertainments and refused to sit in the same restaurant or wineshop with a soldier wearing the Austrian uniform. It was in this spirit that the inhabitants of Pesth, most of whom were descended from Austrians, answered when twitted by the Austrians with that fact—" What our ancestors were in ages past is not to the purpose. We are Hungarians now." A French writer tells us of a peasant who when answering the interrogatories of an Austrian official stated his nationality to be Hungarian, but stated it in the German language. " How can you call yourself a Hungarian when you speak German?" said the official sneeringly. "If your master declines to register me as a Hungarian because I do not speak Hungarian," replied the peasant promptly, " tell him that although I am ninety years old, I am not too old to learn."

The temptation to dwell upon the striking parallel which the Hungary of the early decades of the nineteenth century affords to the Ireland of to-day, has led us into being discursive, but the " Visionaries " who look forward to an Irish-speaking Ireland in the near future will be comforted by this passage from the book of Patterson on the Magyars, written in 1869, two years after the restoration of Hungary's independence:

Few travellers who are now whirled by the railway or the steamboat to Pesth, where they find a gay modern capital, with its large booksellers' shops full of Hungarian books, with its National Museum, and its Palace of the Academy, suspect how new all this is. In 1820 there was no museum, there was no Academy, nay, there was not even a capital. The idea that Hungary ought to have a capital had not yet arisen, or was as yet confined to the brains of a few poetical visionaries. There was then scarcely any Hungarian literature, much less any booksellers' shops for its sale. The very language in which the present literature is written was then in the process of making.

And the same author, speaking of the early days of the language revival, writes:

The establishment of a sporting newspaper was regarded as a matter of almost national interest, and its editor, in consideration of the services he thus rendered to the literature of his country, was made a member of the Hungarian

Academy. In a similar spirit to subscribe to a journal of fashions, written in the Hungarian language, is spoken of as an act of patriotism. All this seems to us very absurd, but from the standpoint of the Hungarians themselves it is quite intelligible. The most mindless and frivolous of women, even if she have neither husband nor child, has still some influence in society. Why, then, should she be left uncared-for by the literary patriots? Why should she be left to perpetuate the traditions of tne days when as yet Hungarian journalism was not? Refusing to consider the question: "Of what use are the perfumed flâneurs of the Vaczi Utcza?"—it is thought better that they should make their bets in Magyar, rather than in German or French.

There is in this a hint for the Gaelic League. The Hungarian Gaelic Leaguers cast their net broadly, and if they could not turn sinners from their pet sin, they saw to it that the sin did not help the foreigner.

XVI.—Hungary and Ireland.

When Hungary was in the vortex of her struggle for national existence, one Charles Boner, English diplomat, visited the country, and wrote a book in which he gave the Hungarians the benefit of his superior British wisdom. Gently but firmly he chided their errors and pointed them out the way they should go. His book, which was published in the year 1865, possesses much interest for reflective Irish readers, for other Boners have been generous enough to give similar advice to us, and Irish people have been found to receive it with respect. The first fact that pained the good Englishman was that the Hungarians insisted on remembering the wrongs that had been inflicted on themselves and on their ancestors. "A Hungarian," wrote Boner, "always dwells on and cherishes his wrongs, and like the Irish, never loses an opportunity of putting them forward prominently." Even after Boner's reproach appeared in print, the Hungarians remained intractable, hating their oppressors and

venting their hatred in words and action. The next
fact that pained Boner was the uncompromising
attitude the Hungarians had taken up. They will
have no compromise, he writes. "They say, 'He
who is not with us is against us.'" They will not,
the Englishman complains, accept assurances, repre-
sentations, or even proofs that they are in the wrong.
They do not want proofs. "They assume as incon-
trovertible truths, particular views of their own with
regard to their grievances." "In every step taken
by Government, the animus which is invariably
shown to be inimical is affirmed beforehand, and by
their assertion all abide." The Hungarians truly
enough refused to see in the Austrian Government
aught but an enemy, which caused the Englishman
to complain that they were "wilful," "devoid of
political sagacity," "self-blinded," "inordinately
proud," and lacking "in the faculty of clear-sighted
deliberation, in the power to discriminate between
the desirable and attainable, in that wisdom which
inclines to compromise rather than to haughty anta-
gonism, where nothing is to be gained by it." Now,
if the Hungarians had hearkened to Boner—their
disinterested friend Boner, as he styled himself—if
they had compromised, doffed their caubeens, to the
Austrian garrison, presented loyal addresses to
Francis Josef, and sang "God Bless the Emperor,"
there would have been no Hungary to-day, great,
free, and prosperous, but in its stead an Austrian
province peopled by serfs and forgotten by the
world.

Hungary did not hearken to Boner. It derided
that "wisdom which inclines to compromise," and
remained defiant, immovable, and deaf to all blan-
dishments, and it won its game. It refused to see
the reasonableness of Boner when he chided it for
its foolish declaration that it would prefer a bad
native Government to a good foreign one. "It is
all very well," wrote Boner, in his Epistle to the
Hungarians, "to cherish old customs and privi-

leges," but he added, it would be much wiser to let the past be past and join in the great March of Progress. Boner was also compelled to point out to the Hungarians, as his countrymen have been compelled to point out to us, that they were sub-conscious liars while their oppressors were monuments of truth. "The Hungarians are continually being led by the predominance of the imaginative faculty," he wrote. "They are so accustomed to take what they fancy to be fact, and which should be so, for truth, that it is necessary to test carefully all statements in which national and political feeling is likely to bias them. Herein, as in numerous other cases, they are the very opposite of the German. He is slow to assert and scrupulous in examining. The Hungarian, borne away by imagination and his hot passions, boldly asserts as fact the promptings of his ardent temperament, and he will often lavish forth assertions as recklessly as he has always hurled defiance against his opponent." Is there a reader to whom this is not familiar, who, substituting "Irishmen" for "Hungarians," and "Englishmen" for "Germans," cannot recall having read in the books of the English the same passage? Nor is there a country in civilised Europe into the ear of which England has not poured the same story of the Irish that Boner poured into the ear of the world about the Hungarians when Hungary was down—that our grievances are imaginary, our charges against the English false—that, in short, we are liars and the English true-begotten children of Truth.

We shall journey some distance with Boner. He is instructive company. His British rectitude was shocked at the "moral terrorism" which restrained respectable Hungarians who desired to compromise and conciliate from doing either. "Fear of the others deter them," wrote Boner. "The Hungarians exercise a greater tyranny than any Government—for they morally stigmatise a man and brand him ruthlessly should he not act with them." Thus possible Hungarian Dillons and T. P. O'Connors blushed unseen, and men who would gladly have sold their country were constrained by the force of public opinion to remain honest.

Boner was concerned that the Hungarians should cut themselves off from the world by reviving their own language. He appealed to them for their own welfare to stick to German. Hear him on the Hungarian language and literature : " Hungarian literature cannot supply the place of that which Germany offers in such rich abundance. German is a language which associates the Hungarians with the civilised world—the language of a literature that has remodified Europe. This ignoring of a literature is part of a system "—Boner had discovered the dark plot—" and does not arise from an imperfect acquaintance with the language in which it is written, for every Hungarian of education speaks German well. It is like the present strict adherence to the national costume on the part of the men, a demonstration of political feeling rather than anything else." The " system " triumphed, and now the Hungarian language is the language of all Hungary, and the literature of Hungary is one of the great modern literatures. Again and again the benevolent Englishman deplored the uncharitableness and mental and moral defects of the Hungarians. " The bitter feeling existing among the Hungarians against the German population," he writes, " is so intense that in all concerning the latter it utterly blinds and deprives them of the capacity to form a reasonable judgment. . . . With the Hungarian every question becomes crystallised into one of nationality; this warps his judgment, for he thus regards even those which are most diverging from one sole special point of view. Argument is then at an end, and a rabid state begins. . . . He loves especially to take his stand on history. Against this nothing is allowed to have weight. . . . He can neither comprehend nor will tolerate that petty personal considerations should stand in the way of action that has once been resolved on; being himself ready to make any sacrifice for his convictions, he expects the same willingness in another who, up to a certain point, has marched along with him. Having also in a high degree what in German is called selbstgefuhl or feeling of his own personality, he has no exaggerated respect for or servile fear of mere authority or its representatives in office. . . . They [the Hungarians and Austrians] are as different as possible in nature, education, aims and political views. In character they are as unlike as the Irish and Scotch—indeed, I have often thought the buoyant Hungarian, swayed easily by passion resembled the former, while the Austrian, thrifty and methodical, reminded me of him of the north country."

Boner further pointed out to the Hungarian that the self-esteem and exclusiveness which forbade him to associate with the Austrian must lead to his undoing. "His contempt for the Austrian is nearly as great as his hate," wrote Boner. ". . . In every explanation given on political questions it is inevitably as a perfectly innocent victim that the Hungarian appears; not a shade of wrong appertains to him, nor is he answerable for one of his misfortunes. All is the work of others—he is merely the sufferer, a sort of modern Prometheus, whose gigantic unmerited suffering appeals, not in silence, but loudly to humanity and heaven." Where is the Irishman who does not recognise this English sarcasm as an old acquaintance; and who does not recognise himself in the following as painted to Europe by his enemy: "The Hungarian exhibits exactly the same fault which he attributes to his rulers—a dislike to hear the truth. . . . In the discourse of the Hungarians about themselves and their nationality there is not the remotest approach to anything like logical reasoning. . . .

Not to march with the Hungarians is in their eyes proof sufficient of rascality. . . . The Hungarian is always goading himself on by brooding over or recapitulating his wrongs, not only of to-day, but of the past as well. . . . For everything unfavourable that happens or has happened to them the Hungarians make the Government answerable . . . ; they have a dogma to which they cling as though salvation depended on it—that Government desires to ruin them financially . . . In every enactment, no matter what it be, the Hungarian discovers a plan, direct or indirect, for doing him some harm. . . . I have pointed to these things because no well-wisher to the Hungarians can observe them without regret."

Benevolent Boner! If the Hungarians had but taken his advice, forgotten their past, surrendered their language, assimilated themselves and learned the "wisdom of compromise," they would to-day be in the enjoyment of blessings similar to those which England showers on this country. But our primary purpose in resurrecting Boner is to exhibit him as a strenuous advocate of the policy of Parliamentarianism, which for years has been adored as the Only Policy For Ireland. The Hungarians rejected that policy and refused to permit their representatives to appear in the Imperial Parliament. Six years of persistence in this attitude reduced the Imperial Parliament to impotence, but Boner, like our wise men, perceived the folly of the Hungarian attitude and the immense advantage Hungary would derive from maintaining a party to fight the battle of Hungary on the Floor of the House—in Vienna. "It would be far wiser," wrote Boner, "if the Hungarians, instead of each one laying down his mandate, had entered the assembly and there fought their battle. They would have found among the German members faithful allies. . . . Their eminent qualifications for political life would soon have given them the ascendancy.

. . . The Government, even had it opposed good measures, would have been forced to give way. I cannot but deeply regret the determination of the Hungarians to have nothing to do with Parliament or office. . . . They, after all, are the greatest sufferers by it. . . . In no way do they more injure themselves and act against their own interests than by abstaining from all share in the Government and in declining to hold any office, for by their refusal men are placed in authority who are unfit for it. Yet, while the Hungarians suffer by the want of trust and incompetency of such officers, they chuckle at the abuses and imperfections to which their nomination leads." Worse still, Boner asserts, the Hungarians who refused to enter the Imperial Parliament "chuckled" at the Saxons who did, when these same Saxons were outvoted on every question where their interests collided with those of the Austrians.

Boner was not a fool. He was a shrewd Englishman, employed in the British Diplomatic Service. He wished for the defeat of the Hungarians, because he apprehended that if they succeeded in beating down Austria, **Ireland would imitate the Hungarian tactics and paralyse England.** "What I saw and heard," he wrote, "continually reminded me of Ireland . . . it is exactly the same . . . even as regards the rallying-cry 'Ireland for the Irish,' 'Hungary for the Hungarians,' . . . Pitt saw . . . that if matters were to mend, others besides Irishmen must legislate for Ireland. **This was essential.** He also saw that the Dublin Parliament must be under the influence of the Imperial Parliament. . . Of all the difficulties an Austrian minister has to encounter, the opposition of the Hungarians is undoubtedly the greatest, because of their intelligence, their boldness, their perseverance, and their **implacability.** But there are many others of minor importance. Supremacy of language is one of them. . . . Let us fancy to ourselves the Irish peasant speaking only his own native Irish and demanding equal rights for his tongue! . . ."

Boner was needlessly alarmed.   Hungary won, but Ireland did not know what her victory meant. All Ireland knows about European politics is what the British Press, having first coloured to suit British interests, permits her to know.   One strong, able, honest man in Ireland in 1867, after the failure of the Fenian insurrection, apprehending the significance of the coronation of Francis Josef at Pesth, could have rallied and led the country to victory. Ireland did not produce him.   Ireland produced Isaac Butt, who substituted for the claim of a nation the appeal of a province.

And now we have sufficiently outlined the history of the struggle in Hungary, and brought home the parallel to apply the lesson.   We must consider how the existing relations, apart from the actual connection which has subsisted, unwillingly on the one part, since the twelfth century, have been brought about. Six hundred years after the English invasion of this country, the English Parliament renounced all claim or title to govern this country.   Its Renunciation is still inscribed on the British Statute-book, and, nevertheless, the English Parliament governs us.   The discovery to be made is, How this illegality originated, and how it has been perpetuated.

The Parliament of Ireland, prior to the last quarter of the eighteenth century, despite the efforts of men such as William Molyneux, Dean Swift, and Charles Lucas, was almost a Parliament pour rire. It had little more real power than the statutory Parliament Mr. Gladstone proposed to establish in Dublin in 1886.   But it, however, served a useful purpose in keeping Dublin, to some extent, a National capital.   Men resorted to Dublin because of this even shadowy Parliament, and those who were honest and courageous among them sought to make the shadow substance.   In time they succeeded.

When Molyneux wrote his famous book asserting the independence of the kingdom of Ireland and the responsibility to the Irish people alone of the Irish Parliament, he was boycotted by the respectable people, and the hangman publicly burned his seditious book, but his ideas no hangman could burn, and they remained secretly working in the minds of the English-speaking Irish. Then came Swift—and shrewdly seeing that the independence of his country could only be achieved by uniting the old Irish and the new, he sought for years an issue to unite them on, and found it at length in Woods' halfpence. By his giant genius he united all Ireland, peer and peasant, Catholic, Protestant, and Dissenter, Norman, Cromwellian, and Gael in opposition to England, and when he had it united launched his thunderbolt in the famous "Fourth Letter of M. B. Drapier to the Whole People of Ireland"—his declaration that by the law of God, of nature, and of nations, the Irish people were as free a people as the people of England—and that no power other than the King of Ireland and the Parliament of Ireland had the right or authority to make laws to bind them. The English Government replied by offering a reward for Swift's discovery and apprehension, but they found none to earn it. As Swift himself wrote afterwards: "Not a traitor could be found, To sell me for six hundred pound."

Swift died without seeing the independence of his country achieved, but his spirit lived. He had implanted in the breasts of the descendants of the English Colonists in Ireland a feeling of resentment against England, and a feeling of kinship to a degree with the sons of men whose fathers died on the beaten side at Aughrim and the Boyne. Then came Lucas, lacking the genius of Swift and the scholarship of Molyneux, but bluntly honest, fearless, and incorruptible—inveighing against the English dominance in Irish affairs and lashing with a vigorous tongue the corruption and slavishness of the Irish Parliament. The mob of Dublin cheered to the echo the anti-English harangues of the honest demagogue, and the English Government in Ireland, fearing a weakening of its usurped power, proscribed him. On the younger generation the propaganda of Molyneux, Swift, and Lucas was not lost. Langrishe, Grattan, Flood, and others now appeared, and the War of American Independence placed the game in Ireland's hands. The country was denuded of troops, even as it was during the late Boer War, and "the loyal inhabitants" apprehensive of a French invasion, banded themselves together for common protection, procured arms, learned to use them, and then reflected that it was not the French who had imposed restrictions on their commerce and freedom of action. "England," as a contemporary writer says, "notwithstanding she had in some instances suspended, and in others prohibited the exportation of Irish manufactures, inundated the Irish markets with every species of her own, and with a view to effectually destroy all power of competition in Ireland, the great capitalists of England determined at any loss to undersell the Irish in their own markets—a loss, however, which they thought would be amply repaired by the monopoly which must necessarily succeed the utter destruction of the Irish manufacture. This system it was impossible for the Irish manufacturer to resist or counteract; his capital was too small to bear the losses of competition; resistance would have been vain; he had therefore no alternative but to change his trade or submit and famish." The Volunteers observed this, came to understand that it was not France who was the enemy, and accordingly, drafted and adopted the famous "Non-Importation and Non-Consumption Agreement." By this patriotic agreement the Irish Volunteers bound themselves not to import any goods of English manufacture which goods Ireland manufactured, or was competent to manufacture, and not to consume such English goods. The Irish merchants, the Irish shopkeepers, and the Irish people generally, enthusiastically followed the Volunteers in adopting the agreement. The English conspiracy was smashed and Irish manufactures revived to an unprecedented degree. For the first time for generations prosperity began to smile upon the land, and the national victory was celebrated in the Marching Song of the Volunteers:

> Wasn't John Bull a fool,
> When he took off our wool
> To leave us so much of
>   The leather, the leather!
> It ne'er entered his pate
> That a sheep-skin well-beat
> **Will draw a whole nation**
>   **Together, together!**

The whole nation had been drawn together by the "Non-Importation Agreement," and now demanded its freedom. The Volunteers originally all Protestant, threw open their ranks and invited their Catholic fellow-countrymen to come in—which they did—and when the delegation of the Irish Parliament walked to the Castle to demand the renunciation of England's claim to govern this country, it passed through streets lined by the armed grandchildren of the men who fought under opposing flags at Limerick, Derry, Aughrim, and the Boyne, now united in defence of their common country.

England renounced her claim to govern this country, awed by the bayonets of 200,000 Irish Volunteers. Though her divide-et-impera policy subsequently succeeded in riving the union of the people of Ireland, the memory of Dungannon she can never eradicate—the memory of that day when 300 Irish Protestants, representing the 200,000 armed defenders of the country, resolved in the Church of Dungannon that the independence of their country must ever be maintained, and that the Catholics of Ireland were their brethren.

England yielded to the Volunteers. She had no alternative. But secretly she planned their destruction and the destruction of our country. Suspicious of her acknowledgment of Irish independence, the Volunteers demanded that she should **expressly** renounce for ever all pretension to rule this country. In the English Parliament, a peer—Abingdon—opposed the Renunciation vehemently. Ireland, he declared, must be kept subordinate. The news came to Ireland, and 120,000 armed and disciplined men prepared to take the field. England threw up the sponge, and rushed the Renunciation Act through her Senate. If she had not done so, the Duke of Leinster would have been crowned King of Ireland by the Volunteers, and the countries for ever separated. This Renunciation Act—by it England renounces for ever all pretension to govern this country—remains inscribed on the British Statute Book. Under the Constitution no power exists or has existed since the year 1783 in the British Parliament to legislate for this country.

Grattan, unconsciously, was used by the English Government as an instrument to disband the Volunteers. When Sir Lucius O'Brien moved in the Irish House of Commons to call on the King of **Ireland** to declare war against Portugal, which was conspiring with the **English** Government against Irish trade, Grattan was silent; when Montgomery suggested Ireland should proceed to build a fleet to defend her coasts and commerce, Grattan was not his supporter; had he been, we to-day would be the free citizens of an independent and prosperous nation. When the Volunteers had been disbanded, the Castle raised a paid force, the militia, to help its scheme. Then when its preparations were completed it introduced the "Bill of Union." We need not call in question the validity of the " Act " of Union on the ground that it was carried by corruption and intimidation of the vilest type, or on the ground that what were declared to be fundamental provisions have since been violated by the English Government. The "Act" of Union was never valid. It does not and cannot exist as a law under the Constitution. The members of the Irish Parliament had no legal power to terminate the existence of that Parliament. They were, in law, simply trustees for the time being of a power proceeding from the people, and they were bound in law to deliver that trust back into the hands of its owners. Instead they sold it. "The Legislature," as Locke says, "cannot transfer the making of laws into other hands, for it is merely a delegated power from the people." Every great Irish lawyer pointed out at the time that the "Act" of Union could not be legal or binding—Saurin, Plunkett, Ponsonby, Ball, Bushe, Curran, Burrowes, Moore, Fitzgerald, and a score others; and no lapse of time, no ignorant acquiescence, can render legal an illegal act. No legal authority exists or can exist in the English Parliament to legislate for Ireland. If Ireland had adopted in 1800 towards the illegal Act of Union with England the attitude Hungary adopted in 1849 towards the illegal Union with Austria, England could not have sustained the "Act" of Union for ten years. Had Henry Flood lived she might have done so. Grattan was incompetent. He was an excellent orator, sincerely patriotic, but he was neither a statesman nor a leader of men. Plainly enough, like Saurin and Plunkett and Bushe and the other Irish legists he saw that the "Act" of Union was unconstitutional, but having salved his conscience by saying so, he considered he had done his duty to his country and returned to his favourite occupation of making eloquent speeches. All of the miscalled "constitutional" leaders who followed him worked on the assumption that the Act of Union was legal and binding. O'Connell asked for an impossibliity when he asked for Repeal of the Union—there can be no legal repeal of an illegality.

Count Beust, the Austrian statesman, who arranged the Ausgleich with Hungary, had, twenty years later, much adverse criticism to offer on Gladstone's attempt to "settle the Irish question." The man who "settled the Hungarian question" pointed out that the legislature Gladstone proposed to erect in Dublin, and which the Irish Parliamentary Party declared itself willing to accept in "final" settlement of Ireland's claim, conferred no real power on the Irish people, and even degraded Ireland to a lower position than she at present occupies, as in exchange for an illusory "Parliament," she was required to give up her claim to distinct nationhood. Gladstone, in introducing his Home Rule Bill, had the audacity to compare it with the Ausgleich carried out by Beust and Deak. Beust pointed out in his criticism of Gladstone that the Ausgleich rendered the Hungarian Parliament co-ordinate with the Austrian Parliament, rendered Hungary absolute mistress of her own affairs, and gave her the status in international law of a sovereign State. In Hungary the Austrian is as much a foreigner as he is in France or England, and, as in those countries, must be naturalised before he can claim the rights of citizenship. Gladstone's Bill proposed to erect a legislature in Dublin, subordinate to the Parliament of London—a legislature whose existence could be terminated in forty-eight hours if a majority of the British members of the British Parliament so desired, and this legislature was to be excluded from having any voice in questions of war and peace, foreign affairs, the army and navy, international treaties, customs dues, matters of currency, indirect taxation, etc. In return, Ireland was to resign for ever her status as a separate nationality and become a province of the Empire. There was scarce a province of the Austrian Empire whose petty Diet did not possess greater powers than Gladstone proposed to give his "Irish Legislature," and the proposal in 1861 of the Austrians to give

Hungary a Legislature with absolute power over the internal affairs of Hungary, but yet terminable in certain circumstances by the Act of the Viennese Parliament, was unanimously and contemptuously rejected by the Hungarian people. Beust, in continuing the analogy between the Hungarian and Irish questions, frankly admitted that Austria would never have conceded Hungary's demand had Hungary not made it impossible for her to refuse it by the policy she adopted and persisted in for eighteen years. England, the statesman showed, would, similarly, never concede Ireland's demands unless Ireland made it impossible for her to refuse them. There was no question of generosity or desire to do right in Austria's action. She had sworn again and again that she never would and never could admit Hungary's claims, as England has sworn again and again that it is mere midsummer madness for the Irish people to imagine she could assent to Irish independence. Swearing she would never consent, Austria consented—and England, like Austria, will consent when the Irish make it as impossible for her to combine dishonesty with profit as the Hungarians did in the case of Austria.

Count Beust admitted that the geographical position of Ireland was more favourable than the geographical position of Hungary, but he argued it as a serious weakness of her claim, that, unlike Hungary, Ireland had not a separate language and literature, and that she had, unlike Hungary, **given her case away by sending members to the British Parliament, thus recognising its authority.** The first of Beust's objections was made in ignorance of Ireland, and would not, of course, be urged by him if he lived to-day. Ireland has a distinct language and literature of its own. The second is more serious, but not fatal. From the inception of " The United Irishman "* we have opposed the sending of

---

* It will be remembered that the foregoing and all that follows was written in 1904.

Irishmen to sit in the British Parliament on two grounds (1) That it is a recognition of the usurped authority of a foreign assembly to make laws to bind the people of Ireland, and (2) That the policy of Parliamentarianism has been materially and morally disastrous to the country. We need not labour the latter point. No measure of a beneficial nature for this country has ever been passed by the British Parliament as a result of the presence, speeches, and action of the delegation from Ireland. The five measures which are usually accepted as beneficial, passed for Ireland by that Parliament—the Catholic Emancipation Act, the Tithes Act, the Church Disestablishment Act, the Land Act of 1881—with the supplementary Ashbourne Act—and the Local Government Act, were passed as a result of the unconscious carrying out by the people of the Hungarian policy—the policy of Passive Resistance—with occasional excursions into the domain of Active Resistance at strategic points. In one sentence the impotence of the Irish Parliamentary Party in Westminster can be exhibited. It has been there for thirty-three years—a generation—to keep it there Ireland has expended over £600,000—and during the period of its existence the population of Ireland has decreased by 20 per cent., and the taxation of Ireland for British purposes has increased by 70 per cent. No condemnation is further needed than these figures. A man who runs his business on such lines ends in the Bankruptcy Court. A nation which persists in running its business on such lines must inevitably go smash.*

The recognition of the competency of a British Parliament to make laws to bind this country, which the attendance of the Parliamentary Party at West-

---

* The decrease in Ireland's population since the inception of the Parliamentarian movement is now (1918) 23 per cent., and taxation of Ireland for English purposes has risen 300 per cent.

minster implies, is, of course, a great political mistake; but Count Beust's contention that Ireland surrendered her case when she returned men to sit in the British Parliament, goes too far. The Act of Union is illegal and unconstitutional. Acceptance of seats in the British Parliament by Irishmen cannot render this illegal enactment legal. The temporary acceptance of the Act of Union as binding has had the unfortunate result of misrepresenting the position of Ireland to the world, and of confusing the minds of her people. It has led them into a cul-de-sac, and ignorance, vanity, and selfishness on the part of their leaders prevented them admitting the truth, and retracing their steps.

O'Connell had one statesmanlike idea in his latter life. It flashed across his mind to summon the Irish Parliament to meet in Dublin, and, ignoring the illegal " Act " of Union, proceed to legislate for the country. There then existed a law known as the Convention Act, which forbade the assembly of delegates in Ireland, and the British Government attempted to counter O'Connell by its use. O'Connell sought to evade the provisions of the Act by calling his assembly the Council of Three Hundred, and the Young Irelanders, recognising the political wisdom of the move, enthusiastically supported O'Connell—they even for the moment thought they had misjudged the Tribune in holding him to be no statesman. " If the members be wise and brave," said John Mitchel, " Ireland will be saved." The British Government was alarmed as it had not been alarmed since 1798. " In six months," said Lord John Russell, " the power and functions of government will be wrested from our hands, and the Lord Lieutenant will sit powerless in Dublin Castle." The preparations for the meeting of the Council of Three Hundred proceeded apace. Thomas Davis was selected to sit for the County Down, John Mitchel for the town of Banbridge: then O'Connell discarded his own pro-

posal. The Council of Three Hundred never met—
the "Arbitration Courts," which had been formed
throughout the land to supersede the English Law
Courts, were abandoned, and the English Government breathed freely again. Had Ireland been led
by a statesman then, the end of the English government of Ireland was at hand. It is sixty years since,
and our population has decreased by one-half. Our
rights remain. The withdrawal of the Irish Parliamentary Party from the British Parliament and the
summoning of the Council of Three Hundred to meet
in Dublin are the initial steps for Ireland to take in
the application of a National Policy.

The Council of Three Hundred should meet in
Dublin during a period of the year, and initiate,
discuss, and pass measures calculated to benefit the
country. These measures once passed, the County
Councils, Urban Councils, Poor Law Boards, and
other representative bodies should, so far as they
have legal powers—and the powers of the Irish
County Councils and Poor Law Boards are more extensive than most Irishmen wot of—enforce them.
For instance, the County Councils have power to
make monetary grants and levy rates for desirable
purposes. If the Council of Three Hundred pass a
measure affecting the industries or agriculture of
Ireland, the County Councils can by united action
give the measure much of the legal force of an
Act passed by the British Parliament. Let it be
recollected that even under the Coercion Act, there
is no violation of the law committed by 300 gentlemen meeting in Dublin and recommending the adoption of measures to the Irish people calculated to
improve their condition, and that there is nothing
illegal in the Irish representative bodies using their
full powers to give force to these recommendations.
The County Councils of Hungary formed the strongest weapon of Kossuth in the Forties and Deak in
the Sixties against the Austrian Government. The
County Councils of Ireland possess in some respects

greater powers than the County Councils of Hungary; it needs but their united action, under the guidance of a directing mind, to render them as potent against English misgovernment as the Hungarian Councils were against Austrian oppression. A sum of £25,000 is raised annually for the upkeep of an impotent Irish Parliamentary Party in the British Parliament. This sum should continue to be raised, but be devoted to quite a different object, to the upkeep in all the great European capitals and important commercial centres of capable and patriotic Irish men of business, whose duties would be (1) to keep Europe acquainted with the truth about the struggle in Ireland, and (2) to secure a profitable market for Irish goods and produce abroad. The Hungarians adopted this plan with a success that would seem incredible to the average Irishman. From Paris to New York Hungary established its consuls during the years of its struggles against Austria, and the efforts of these consuls trebled the export trade of Hungary during the period of their work. What Hungary did Ireland can do, but at the present time Ireland has not a direct representative of her interests in any Continental capital, and she is the only country in Europe of which that fact is true. As a consequence our export trade to the Continent is insignificant and actually decreasing.

The institution of a system of Protection for Irish industries would be one of the principal duties of the Council of Three Hundred, and one that, by the co-operation of the Irish pubic bodies, could be made effective. The Hungarians inaugurated and carried out such a system by means of the "Vedegylet" association. The supersession of the English civil courts in this island, by the institution of "Arbitration Courts," such as the Young Irelanders projected and the Hungarians established, would be a matter of no difficulty and great profit to the nation. Voluntary Arbitration Courts are legal, and their decisions have all the binding force of law when the litigants sign an agreement to abide by them. The Irish abroad, especially in America, could form a valuable auxiliary, both by rendering aid to Irish industrial enterprises and obstructing and thwarting the designs of English foreign policy, as the Hungarian exiles did from 1849 to 1867 in the case of Austria—although far less in number than the Irish abroad. It would, of course, be a principal duty of the Council of Three Hundred to keep Irishmen out of the ranks of the English armed forces. In Hungary the County Councils saw so effectively to this that the Austrian army was rendered ineffective, and went to pieces in seven days before the Prussians.

We have but roughly indicated how the policy which made Hungary what it is to-day may be applied to Ireland; where the circumstances of the countries differ, it is a work of detail to adapt the policy. For its successful working clear-thinking, uncompromising men are required to lead. There is no doubt of the readiness of the people to follow. The people of Ireland are not less patriotic and not less intelligent than the people of Hungary—three-fourths of their misfortunes are traceable to their pusillanimous, incompetent, and sometimes corrupt leaders. An Irish Deak would have found in Ireland a support as loyal and as strong as Deak found in Hungary. But the Irish Deak never appeared, and shallow rhetoricians imposed themselves upon the people in his stead. Thus for a hundred years, with brief interruptions, Ireland has been consistently misled, and has paid for her weakness with the lives of half her people, and the loss of her fortune.

In the latter part of the eighteenth century, Ireland, by the determination and wisdom of her sons, was raised from the position of an insignificant and poverty-stricken province to the status of a nation and to a prosperity as great as that of any civilised country of her extent and population then existent. What Irishmen did in the eighteenth century, Irishmen are competent to do in the twentieth—what the Hungarians did for Hungary Irishmen can do for Ireland. None who reflect can doubt that, carried out with the same determination, the policy which resurrected Hungary from the tomb that Austria built for her in 1849 at Vilagos can end the usurped authority of England to rule our country.

APPENDICES.

I.

PITT'S POLICY.

IMPERIALISM AND IRELAND.

*The following articles with one exception appeared in
"Sinn Fein," in the year 1911, three years before the
outbreak of the war.*

I.

In 1783 England signed at Paris her renunciation of her
claim to govern the United States. In 1783 Mr. William
Pitt presented to the English Parliament a Bill renouncing
England's claim to govern Ireland. The Mr. William Pitt
who besought the King's Most Excellent Majesty, the Lords
Spiritual and Temporal, and the Faithful Commons of England to eat humble pie by declaring the right of Ireland
to be wholly free and independent of England for all time—
even as the United States—was the same Mr. William Pitt
who thereafter suppressed the Irish Constitution, strangled
the Irish Parliament, and to whom Ireland owes all her
miseries in the nineteenth century and all her woes to-day.

To Mr. William Pitt we owe the lost prestige of our nation,
our rags, our sores, our recriminations, our famines, our
abortive insurrections, our Orange Lodges and Boards of
Erin, our bigots and our Parliamentary squabbles, and our
nicknames. Because of Mr. Pitt we are calling each other
Factionists, Carrion Crows, Dollar Dictators, and other
fine things. Mr. Pitt being dead still pulls the strings to
which we puppets dance. England has had two policies in
three hundred years. Cromwell gave her one—which went
smash in 1775. Mr. William Pitt picked up some of the
pieces, welded them with pieces of his own, and gave England the other. Pitt's policy has been the policy of England
since 1785, and will continue to be the policy of England
until England produces another statesman or bursts. The
Russells, Palmerstons, Disraelis, Gladstones, Salisburys,
Balfours, and Asquiths, who have run the Empire since
William Pitt was gathered in, have not added one brick to
his edifice, and never were capable of adding half-a-brick.

Now, the evil consequences that have flowed to Ireland
from the fact that England in her direst need found in a
delicate young man who, drunk or sober, kept his head cool,
a statesman to patch her up on a new plan, may not
seem to all that large unthinking body of Irishmen who call
themselves Unionists, in obedience to Pitt's policy, very re-

grettable, for after all, some of these worthy people say, if Ireland has suffered, has not the Empire, our Empire, thriven apace? Look at its magnitude, its prosperity, its fine openings for our sons, who unfortunately can find nothing to do at home, its credit, its security. All these things we shall indeed look at with unsquinting eyes before we have done. Likewise we shall look at the present price of Consols, and his Imperial Majesty the German Kaiser, and before we are through we shall demonstrate that Pitt's policy, having been most undoubtedly successful in throttling Ireland, has as a consequence made Germany the nightmare which squats on every English Foreign Minister's chest at night. For Mr. Pitt, though a statesman, was not a first-rate prophet.

Can it be shown that Pitt's Imperialism, which demanded the destruction of Independent Ireland, has brought England to a pass in her history as grave as that from which Cromwell rescued her? So much we shall show.

Mr. William Pitt became the ruler of the English Nation at the age of 24, by the divine right of being the one man who could find a way out for her. In her dark day, England, with an instinct that saved her on many an occasion, turned away from amiable humbugs of the Fox type, and called to the helm a youth in years, cold-hearted and cool-headed—a man whose sole passion was ambition to rule—whose sole virtue was devotion to what he believed the interests of his country. His simple creed was England Over All—no law of God or man existed for him which conflicted with that creed. No sentiment of honour found room in his breast. Falsehood, fraud, corruption, bloodshed, were all justified to Pitt insofar as they served his England. Therefore when Mr. Pitt and his colleagues introduced the Renunciation Act into the English Parliament, Mr. Pitt and his colleagues did not dream of observing that international treaty, if haply thereafter they could evade it. England keeps no treaties she has power to break with advantage. Mr. Pitt acted as the creature of necessity. One hundred and twenty thousand drilled men, officered by the Irish aristocracy, sub-officered by veterans of the American War, were standing to arms in Ireland. The British fleet was out of action. The Lords Spiritual and Temporal and the Faithful Commons of England, therefore, without debate and without amendment, passed in record time the Act declaring:—

> "That the said right claimed by the people of Ireland to be bound only by laws enacted by His Majesty and the Parliament of that kingdom . . . . shall be and is hereby finally declared to be established and ascertained for ever, and shall at no time hereafter be questioned or questionable."

K

No talk of "subordinate legislatures," "Empire in danger," "loyalty," or humbug of any kind whatsoever. Whig and Tory swallowed the pill Ireland extended on the point of the national bayonet, and protested they relished the bitter taste. For the first time since Henry II. landed in Ireland, England admitted she had no right to rule in Ireland, and could never have any right to rule Ireland. When the news came to Ireland the national army fired off its cannon in salute and demobilised. Ireland felt she could trust the Englishman's written word. Ireland's capacity for trusting the Englishman's word survives all his perjuries. A very great, a very good, a very honest, and a very eloquent Irishman whom she deservedly loved, and whom she trusted, told her that the man who would doubt England now was an unnatural sceptic. There was one Irishman who continued to beg the people to doubt England. He was the statesman of the period, the man who knew his Englishman, but Henry Flood lacked the warm soul and burning eloquence of Henry Grattan, and the Orator won the generous nation against the man of state, who, as cold as Pitt, had eyes to pierce the mask all English politicians wear. Mr. Pitt had calculated that Ireland would listen to Grattan rather than to Flood. Mr. Pitt was right. Mr. Pitt was a man who knew how to wait. He waited until the trusting Irish ceased rifle practice and the Volunteers hung their uniforms up in the lumber-room. Then Mr. Pitt played his hand. It was not the hand he was destined to play later with success. The hand he played was "subordinate legislature." The independent Parliament of Ireland was to be reduced to a Home Rule Assembly. Mr. Pitt was in fact the first Home Ruler. Ireland was to have a subordinate Parliament. England was to rule the Empire. But Mr. Pitt miscalculated. Ireland was not asleep—she was only dozing. She wakened up with a cry, and Mr. Pitt was hard put to it to hold on to the English helm of State. Then Mr. Pitt made up his mind that as Ireland could not be tricked, she must be smashed. It took fifteen years to do the smashing, but he got there. The strength of Mr. Pitt lay in the fact that until he lay on his death-bed he never owned defeat. Beaten back down one line, he crawled up another. When the Irish Parliament spat on his proposal to Home-Rule-it Mr. Pitt made up his mind to garotte the Irish Nation.

II.—WHY MR. PITT MADE UP HIS MIND.

On the 20th January, 1785, the Parliament of Ireland met, and the Duke of Rutland, Lord Lieutenant, commended to its attention the regulation of trade and commerce with Great Britain. Five days later the Parliament of England

met, and George III. commended to its earnest attention
"the adjustment of such points in the commercial inter-
course between Great Britain and Ireland as are not yet
finally arranged." On the 2nd of February the Secretary
for Ireland—Orde—laid eleven resolutions to form the basis
of a treaty between two independent States before the Irish
House of Commons. As such the proposals were received
and discussed by the Parliament of Ireland. The nation was
in good humour—it was increasing each day in prestige and
prosperity. Three hundred commoners and two hundred
peers were resident in Dublin, which had become a centre of
culture and art as well as of commerce. The national vanity
was flattered by Mr. Pitt's proposal of an International
Treaty, and ten of the eleven resolutions proposed by Orde
could excite no reasonable opposition. The eleventh and
final one covered Mr. Pitt's design:—

That for the better protection of trade, whatever sum
the gross hereditary revenues of this Kingdom (after de-
ducting all drawbacks, repayments, or bounties granted
in the nature of drawbacks) shall produce over and above
the sum of £656,000 in each year of peace, wherein the
annual revenues shall be equal to the annual expenses,
and in each year of war, without regard to such equality,
should be appropriated towards the support of the naval
force of the Empire, in such manner as the Parliament of
this Kingdom shall direct.

This plausible resolution covered Mr. Pitt's design for undermining the Settlement of 1782. Beneath its apparent
ingenuousness lurked the reassertion of the principle that
Ireland was a subordinate Kingdom. Yet in February, 1785,
there was but one man in that trustful and good-humoured
Irish Parliament, which Pitt pleased by the subtle flattery
of approaching as he would have approached the Government of France or Spain, who saw into the English Minister's
design. Brownlow, of Armagh, a country gentleman, saw
what skilled lawyers failed to see—the design of reducing
Ireland to the status of a tributary nation lurking behind
the Eleventh Proposition. He protested with vehemence
against what he rightly declared was an attempt to en-
croach on the independence of Ireland. Mr. Grattan pooh-
poohed Mr. Brownlow. Englishmen had foresworn their
evil ways in statecraft. Whatever the past might have
been, English statesmen were now honourable men. The
heart of England and the heart of Ireland beat in unison—
in fact Mr. Grattan said and implied about English statesmen what other credulous orators say and imply about
English statesmen to-day. The Parliament of Ireland agreed
to the resolutions and transmitted them to the Parliament
of England.

Mr. Pitt had won his point. His point was not the destruction of the Irish Legislature—it was subordination of the Irish Legislature. Having won his point, his policy was not to alarm Ireland by any direct attack, but slowly and gradually work his commercial treaty to the end of returning the Parliament of Ireland to the subject position it formerly occupied. Mr. Pitt was not out after a Union of Legislatures. He was out to reassert the supremacy of the English Legislature over the Irish one. He saw clearly enough that if the Parliament of Ireland retained the independence it won in 1782, the government of the Empire must within 30 years be equally shared by the two countries. Mr. Pitt was determined that the Empire should remain England's private property. His Imperialism spelled England Absolute. Irish Independence was incompatible with English Absolutism—therefore Ireland must be again made dependent. But to unite the Parliaments of Ireland and Great Britain was in 1785 no part of Mr. Pitt's scheme. It was unnecessary and it was impossible in the spirit of the time. Mr. Pitt's policy in February, 1785, was aimed at—to use the words of a modern Irishman defining what he states Ireland wants and will be for ever happy and grateful to receive as a final settlement of her claims—" giving Ireland a Parliament to deal with purely Irish affairs and reserving all questions of Imperial concern for the British Parliament."

For it is to be recollected that the Parliament of Ireland at this period was no shadow of a Legislature. It was a sovereign assembly, with the power of establishing and maintaining its own army and fleet—with the power of making war and concluding peace—with absolute fiscal powers and right of concluding commercial treaties with any nation. It was as independent of the British Parliament as the Congress of the United States is to-day. It was the Parliament of an independent nation, and Mr. Pitt's design was to reduce it to be the legislature of a dependent state of Britain.

Mr. Pitt, however, made one muddle. He miscalculated the amount of brains which his Maker had bestowed on the English manufacturer, of whom all British Ministers are the most obedient servants. The honest manufacturers of England, whose jealousy and fear of Ireland grew with reason from day to day—since, as they bitterly complained, the Irish had beaten them not only out of Ireland, but were beating them out of many of the Continental markets—these honest fellows could not see that Mr. Pitt's design was a delicate and artistic way of ending the power of Ireland to compete against them. All they saw was the face-value of the Commercial Resolutions which placed Ireland permanently in a position to compete on fair terms for the

world's trade. When the Resolutions were transmitted from
the Irish Parliament Mr. Pitt made one of his best speeches
in favour of their adoption as a definitive treaty with Ireland. A murmur rose from manufacturing England and
grew and swelled. Lancashire roared that the measure
would be ruinous to England. The other manufacturing
centres roared that the statesman who would permit the
detested Irish to stand on an equal footing with the English
was a traitor to England. It was awkward for so thoroughly
English a statesman to be so amazingly misunderstood by
the very interests he was serving. It was quite impossible
for Mr. Pitt to explain, with Ireland looking on and listening, that his commercial propositions would induce the fall
of Irish commerce. Mr. Pitt spoke softly to his alarmed
countrymen. He begged them to trust him—to let the
propositions go. The roar grew into a menace, and Mr. Pitt
found the ground slipping from under his feet. Cursing
their stupidity under his breath, Mr. Pitt surrendered to the
English manufacturers, and introduced a series of new pro-
posials, which he doubted yet hoped that the Parliament of
Ireland would accept. Mr. Pitt had learned his last lesson—
never again would he, even in appearance, run counter to
the English man of commerce.

On the 12th of May, 1785, Pitt's new proposals were introduced in the English Parliament. They provided amongst
other things that Ireland should not trade with any country
where its trading might clash with the interests of England's
mightiest corporation—the East India Company; provided
that merchandise of certain of the West Indies should not
be imported into Great Britain through Ireland, and provided that the navigation laws which the British Parliament
adopted should be accepted by Ireland. Mr. Pitt was too
clever a statesman not to feel disgust that such a crude
method of destroying Irish commerce should have to be
openly proposed. It was left for an Irishman—that sublime
simpleton of British and Irish politics, Edmund Burke—to
grow enthusiastic over it, and describe England as "Ireland's Guardian Angel." The British Commons, always
subservient to the English manufacturers, passed at once
the propositions. The British Lords, over whom the manufacturers' power is feebler, passed them, after some strong
opposition. The opposition in the British Lords was based
on the belief that the propositions, being unjust to Ireland,
would be rejected by the Irish Parliament, and a hostile
feeling excited in Ireland. The Irish people, said Lord
Lansdowne, will certainly not give up their Parliament and
their share of the Empire, which these propositions aimed at
leading them to. It is interesting to remember that the
Lord Lansdowne of 1785 very clearly saw that if Ireland
gave up her Parliament she lost her rule of Empire. His

descendant protests in the name of Empire against Ireland
having a Parliament of any kind. Thus are the cats roused
to laughter.

On the 12th of August, Secretary Orde attempted to
bring into the Parliament of Ireland a Bill founded on the
new propositions. But Ireland was now awake. For
eighteen hours the Parliament House in College Green was
the theatre of vehement denunciations of Pitt's proposals.
Leave to bring in the Bill was only granted by a small majority, and the defeat of the Bill on its first reading was
assured. On the 15th of August Orde moved the first
reading of the Bill. Henry Flood moved a direct challenge
to England—" Resolved: That we hold ourselves bound not
to enter into engagement to give up **the sole and Excluusive
Right** of the Parliament of Ireland, in all cases whatsoever,
as well externally as commercially and internally." The
Bill was withdrawn, and Flood withdrew his motion. Thus
without deigning even to read it a first time the Parliament
of Ireland threw back in the face of Mr. Pitt his measure
for the subjugation of Irish trade.

Mr. Pitt would have been less than an Englishman if
he did not feel galled at the insult. He had attempted to
humble the Irish nation. It kicked him contemptuously out
of its house. The fault indeed was mainly due to the blundering dishonesty of the English manufacturer. But Mr.
Pitt would never again risk his political career by appearing
to play against the English manufacturers' interests. On
the 20th of August, 1785, Mr. Pitt learned the bad news
from Secretary Orde. On the 20th of August, 1785, Mr.
Pitt made up his mind and became a Unionist. As he could
not rule the Irish Parliament, he would smash it—as he
could not trick the Irish nation out of being co-ruler of
an Empire, he would trample it into an Imperial province.

III.—HOW PITT RESOLVED TO MAKE AN IRISH INSURRECTION.

When Mr. Pitt grasped the wheel of State, France and
Spain had crippled England's fleet and driven her out of
the fairest part of North America. Ireland had, after 600
years, asserted successfully its political independence. " The
sun of England's glory has set," quoth Pitt. But he was
solving the problem of how to make a sun rise again.

There were two courses open to Pitt. He could accept
as facts the loss of North America and the independence of
Ireland. He could substitute for the broken policy of
England's Absolutism a policy of Common Empire with
England and Ireland as joint rulers. A parallel situation
faced Count Beust in Austria 84 years later. Austria had

gone down before Prussia, and despoiled Hungary remained
to be reckoned with. Beust resolved to save the Empire by
sharing it. So he scrapped Austrian Absolutism and substituted it by the Dual Alliance ruling a Common Empire.
Pitt took the opposite course. He would preserve the
Empire—to England alone.

To do so it was necessary to reconquer Ireland and rebuild
English sea-power to overwhelm France. Ireland again
subjugated and France dethroned, England would be mistress
of the seas and arbiter of Europe. In the darkest hour of
England's fortunes it needed a strong man, a cool man,
an able man, an unscrupulous man to plan such a scheme
and devote his life to carrying it out. This Pitt did. He
was no Imperialist, although all that is called British
Imperialism comes from him to-day. He was an English
Absolutist. He succeeded. Ireland fell before him while
he lived. France fell before his policy when he had passed
to his grave. Less than forty years after he spoke and said
"The sun of England's glory has set," the sun of England
was blazing again. England, mistress of the seas and
arbiter of Europe, worshipped his memory. Minister after
Minister rose in England and guided its people by the light
of Pitt. Pitt's policy seemed to have made England omni-
potent—to-day the policy has failed. Ireland is down and
France is humbled, but England's voice no longer is the law
of Europe. Germany dominates the European Continent,
and England has exchanged omnipotence for the position of
a first-class Power. Pitt's policy sent her up and Pitt's
policy drags her down. Mr. Pitt was a more daring man
than Count Beust, but not so farseeing. Had he been so
an Anglo-Hibernian Dual Monarchy would be master of
the world to-day. To strike down Ireland—foolishly trusting
—was not too great a task. To hold her down implied a
permanent distraction of English politics and an imprisonment of English strength. This Pitt did not foresee. This
is the explanation of modern Germany.

Now we propose to show in these articles to all those
enamoured of Pitt's Imperialism that Pitt's policy has
brought England back after 120 years to the position in
which Pitt found her.

But first we shall finish with Pitt's dealings with this
country—with the successful issue of his conspiracy to overthrow the Constitution of Ireland.

Beaten by Ireland in his attempt to regain control of
her for England on the Commercial Propositions, Pitt laid
low awaiting another opportunity. It came in the madness
of King George III. When the King was mad it was necessary a Regent should rule. The natural Regent, the Prince
of Wales, was unfriendly to Pitt, and Pitt therefore proposed that the Prince should be invested with strictly limited

powers—powers that left the Government wholly in the hands of Mr. Pitt himself. Mr. Pitt knew how to carry his point, and he carried it in England. Then he despatched a message to his Viceroy in Ireland to use "unlimited discretion" to secure from the Parliament of Ireland a formal acknowledgment that whosoever the Parliament of England —being Mr. Pitt—should appoint as Regent, the Parliament of Ireland should also appoint with whatever limitations the Parliament of England imposed. Mr. Pitt calculated that the Parliament of Ireland would, the question being a delicate one, swallow the demand and thus admit implicitly the sole right and authority of the Parliament of Great Britain as the Imperial Parliament. Once again Mr. Pitt was out in his calculation. The corruption and threats of Buckingham failed to seduce or coerce. The Lords of Ireland by 45 to 26, the Commons of Ireland by 150 to 71 repudiated the right of the British Parliament alone to choose the Regent or to define his powers. Then by similar majorities our Lords and Commons adopted an address inviting the Prince of Wales to "assume the title of Prince Regent of Ireland . . . and to exercise unlimited regal powers." This declaration of the absolute independence of Ireland and its equal right and power to choose the Chief Governor of the Empire paralysed Pitt. Acting on his instruction, Buckingham, the Viceroy, refused to transmit the address of the Irish Parliament to the Prince. Ignoring the Lord Lieutenant, the Parliament of Ireland boldly appointed the Duke of Leinster and the Earl of Charlemont, on behalf of the House of Lords, and three Privy Councillors and a Member of Parliament on behalf of the House of Commons to proceed to the Prince of Wales with the address of the Parliament of Ireland. The Commissioners departed for London. The Prince of Wales received them effusively, but almost simultaneously with their arrival the mad King recovered his senses, and resumed governing. Thus ended an incident which must otherwise have led to the fall for ever from power of Mr. Pitt. For had George III. not unluckily recovered, England would have had no choice save to accept the Regency of the Prince of Wales under the conditions imposed by Ireland. She could not then have fought and conquered Ireland—she must have submitted to Ireland.

The second defeat of Pitt—the successful assertion of Ireland's equal right with England to choose the head of the Empire—flushed Ireland again with enthusiasm. The Irish ambassadors returned to Ireland in a blaze of glory. Pitt's Viceroy, Buckingham, skulked out of Dublin to Cork and took ship for England. But while Ireland was celebrating its victory Mr. Pitt was drafting a detailed scheme to end Ireland. He had found the man he wanted for the work in John Fitzgibbon—the ablest, strongest, and—with one dark exception—basest man in Ireland. Corruption alone Mr. Pitt had discovered would never enable him to overcome the Irish Parliament. However venal many of its members were, when the basic question of Irish independence was touched, the Parliament was incorruptible. Terror must be added to corruption, and Mr. Pitt made up his mind to induce a terrorism in Ireland that would draw the men of property into favouring a union with England. From the date of the Regency dispute, Mr. Pitt leaned on Black John Fitzgibbon, who faithfully set himself to rekindle the fires of sectarian bigotry and to open the way to scenes of blood and rapine calculated to make the timid and unthinking come to the conclusion that armed forces directed from Dublin Castle were a necessity. When Mr. Pitt got armed forces, independent of the authority of the Parliament of Ireland, on foot in Ireland, Mr. Pitt knew he could manage an insurrection by goading the peasantry. And after an insurrection Mr. Pitt felt assured he could bribe and terrify the Irish Parliament into voting its own extinction.

IV.—HOW JOHN FITZGIBBON CARRIED OUT PITT'S POLICY.

William Pitt was England's strong man—John Fitzgibbon the strong man in Ireland. England's strong man was England's champion, Ireland's strong man was Ireland's foe. Pitt rose with his country, Fitzgibbon rose on his country. False patriotism inspired Pitt's policy. He blackened his soul with a thousand crimes, but he sinned for his country. Fitzgibbon lived and sinned for himself. Patriotism, as he understood it, was Pitt's inspiring motive. Patriotism to John Fitzgibbon was a toy for grown-up children. Pitt found England down and raised it up. Fitzgibbon found Ireland up and pushed it down. No two men's outlook on country could more diverge, and each used the other to further his own ends.

The end Pitt sought was the necessary end of his false conception of Patriotism. He was an Englishman—Ireland and Scotland were foreign countries to him. The Empire was England's sole and exclusive property. Ireland had successfully challenged England's idea of Empire, and the rightful property of England must become a joint property if the Dual Monarchy continued to subsist. In England's interest the Dual Monarchy must cease. Therefore, the Constitution of 1782 must be overturned and London become the sole seat of Empire. An Empire equally governed from Dublin and London was possible of expansion beyond all

that the Empire had been.   But it would cease to be
England's Empire. It would be the Anglo-Hibernian Empire.
In the rule of Empire, England must bear no brother near
her throne.   Irishmen might be servants of Empire, but
they must not be co-rulers.   The Dual Monarchy must, therefore, be substituted by a single Monarchy and the legislative
power centred in the capital of England and in the hands
of Englishmen.   Granted Pitt's point of view, Pitt's policy
was the logical policy.   But what Irish Unionism—what that
strangely-named thing Irish Imperialism—has never realised
is that Pitt's point of view was not Imperial, but English.
It was not because danger threatened the Empire Pitt
planned the Union.   No danger threatened the Empire so
great as that which Pitt risked in carrying through his
anti-Irish policy.   Pitt planned the Union because without
the Union the relations that exist to-day between Hungary
and Austria must have supervened between Ireland and
England.   The Act of Union was passed to prevent Ireland
becoming an Imperial nation.   But the news has not yet
reached the Irishmen who cheer themselves hoarse over
that Empire out of which they have been cheated.

Pitt, despising Fitzgibbon's character, bought his strength.
The corrupting Viceroys and scheming Secretaries whom
Pitt   sent   over   to   Ireland   as   his   tools   were   placed
under the control of the Strong Irishman, who, had he had
even Pitt's perverted patriotism, would live to-day in Ireland's heart and shine with the great statesmen in the
history of modern Europe. There is in our modern history no
instance of a man with gifts so great as John Fitzgibbon's
who used them with such deadly effect against the country
that suckled him.

Pitt, baffled by Ireland on the Regency question, and
faced with the assertion of Ireland's equal right with England to control the Crown and Empire, made John Fitzgibbon Chancellor of Ireland and bade him compass the
Union.

Fitzgibbon struck with an iron fist.   Lords and Commoners who had opposed Pitt found themselves deprived of
office and of honours.   The fearful were intimidated, the
venal purchased in the open market.   The Lords and Commoners who had faced and beaten Pitt were paralysed by
the audacity of Fitgibbon.   Pitt had fenced with them in
the twilight gloom.   Fitzgibbon charged in among them
in the light of day with a club.   Before they had recovered
their wits, Fitzgibbon had won a battle.   Faced by a man
as strong as himself he would have been impeached and
overthrown or the country called to arms against the
onslaught on its Parliament.   But, as Fitzgibbon knew,
there was no man so strong as himself amongst his opponents.   Instead of stripping the Chancellor of his office, his

opponents protested and founded a Whig Club in sympathy with the English Whiggery that stood opposed to Pitt. Fitzgibbon scored a double triumph. He secured a majority in the Irish Parliament. He forced his opponents, in their weakness, to identify themselves with an English Party. The Whig Club charged the English Government quite truly with design to subvert the liberties of Ireland. But then it was a wicked English Tory Government. The good British Whigs were just men. The liberties of Ireland were again in danger, and the men who had seen the arms of the Volunteers re-establish them preferred to rely on sympathetic British Liberalism for aid to checkmate William Pitt than to meet the assault on the Constitution with the bayonets that won it and were still potent to uphold it. In the history of Ireland from that day forward reliance on British Liberalism has spelled Irish disaster.

Henry Grattan rising in the House to demand Fitzgibbon's political head and Lord Charlemont sounding his trumpet-call to the Volunteers, and Ireland could have been saved. Ireland heard neither the voice nor the trumpet. Instead of the swords of '82, the nation's leaders invoked a Whig Opposition. No aspersion rests on the courage and patriotism of the leaders. They loved Ireland well and served her faithfully and bravely. But there was not a man among them who realised the fact that when the Armed Man exists the Statesman's answer to violent assault on the Constitution is, and always must be, the Armed Man.

Fitzgibbon had cleared his path for the insurrection that Pitt needed—an **insurrection,** not a National War—not an united Ireland in arms against England for its Constitution, but an Ireland split in twain—fighting sect against sect. Mr. Pitt's insurrection was intended to be a Catholic v. Protestant bloody broil, with Honest England coming in at the end amidst the cheers of the exhausted faction-fighters to restore peace and to deal out Justice and Protection. Fitzgibbon got Mr. Pitt his insurrection eventually, but it was not the kind of insurrection he had planned. With whatever other feelings Irish Catholic and Irish Protestant recall it to-day, neither can recall the insurrection in shame. For the men who fought and failed in 1798 shed no drop of their blood to erect a sectarian ascendancy on the ruins of a free nation.

V.—HOW AN INSURRECTION WAS WORKED UP.

A common brawl in Armagh County developed into a series of faction fights between Presbyterians and Catholics, both of the illiterate classes. Fitzgibbon saw in this an opportunity. He held back the interference of Authority to quell the disturbance and encouraged it to spread. The row extended, and crossed the borders of the neighbouring counties. The illiterates of the Protestant side dubbed themselves Peep-o'-Day Boys—of the other, Defenders. When a disturbance that an act of vigour at the beginning would have squelched had spread, Fitzgibbon ordered troops to the spot and made a sham attempt to put out the fire he was privately fanning. Some bloodshed followed, and the work of the Castle went gaily on. In due time the two factions fought a pitched battle at a place called The Diamond, where the Peep-o'-Day Boys triumphed over the Defenders. Then the Peep-o'-Day Boys re-christened themselves Orangemen. Their opponents, after many changes of name, finally dubbed themselves Hibernians. By these names the descendants of the faction-fighters whom Pitt used to make the Union possible exist even to this day, mutually playing the game of Pitt's successors against their native country and holding themselves to be fine, independent fellows and patriots in place of the evil puppets of English statecraft they are, and ever have been.

Fitzgibbon's intention had been to use the Orangemen and Hibernians—or as they then called themselves, the Peep-o'-Day Boys and Defenders—for the insurrection which Pitt had planned. Peep-o'-Day Boyism was to be spread over Munster and Connaught, and Defenderism worked up against it until the two factions, having fought over three provinces, the general body of Irish Catholics and Protestants turned to Sister England for protection, and Sister England, stepping in, disarmed the faction-fighters and rushed a Union. The French Revolution overthrew Fitzgibbon's scheme in part. It found its most enthusiastic admirers in the Ulster Presbyterian townsmen, whose ideas of liberty and equality were brought up to the point of advocating Catholic Emancipation by Theobald Wolfe Tone, who, inspired by the French Revolution, dreamed of an Irish Republic. Neither the United Irishmen nor the Catholic Committee, to both of which he attached himself, shared his Republican enthusiasm. The United Irishmen were an improved edition of the Whig Club. A Reformed Parliament and Catholic Emancipation were the principles for which they stood. The Catholic Committee stood for Catholic Emancipation—the episcopal and titled section of it for a subordinate emancipation—"leaving to Parliament," to paraphrase a modern, "the decision of what was emancipation and how much they ought to be emancipated." The manly section, led by the Catholic merchants, Keogh and Sweetman, defined Emancipation as Emancipation, and demanded it in full. Outside the area where Pitt's deluded Defenders and Orangemen broke each other's heads in the name of religion, Catholic Ulster and Protestant Ulster united. In Dublin Catholics and Protestants fraternised.

The Volunteers refused to parade around King William's statue, lest their Catholic fellow-citizens might feel hurt. A new body of armed men sprang into being under the title of the National Guard. Then the French Republicans, with whom Pitt had coquetted, and who were in the beginning determined admirers of England, unconsciously fell athwart Pitt's Continental policy by occupying the Low Countries. Reluctantly Pitt was forced to go to war with France, for the Low Countries, as we shall hereafter see, form the pivot on which England's European policy revolves, and must not fall under the dominion of any Continental Power. A sectarian insurrection could not be organised in Ireland now, and any other kind of insurrection was too dangerous at the moment. Pitt resolved to break the union of Catholic and Protestant by a Catholic Relief Bill, to be passed with Protestant opposition speaking through the mouth of Fitzgibbon. In 1793, therefore, Catholics were admitted to all the professions and to the franchise, but excluded from Parliament. This appeared as a generous act of the Government in the Castle. The generosity bubble was pricked by the action of George Knox, a member of the Irish Commons. He moved "That Roman Catholics be empowered to sit and vote in the House of Commons." Major Doyle seconded the motion, which found strong support. The alarmed Castle friends of the Catholics thereupon were forced to come out in the open and vote against Catholic Emancipation. But 69 members of that Protestant Irish Parliament, to their eternal honour, were found to support, in an age when Religious Toleration was equally foreign to the ideas of Protestant and Catholic Governments, the motion for complete Emancipation. Had it been carried, as Pitt well knew, there would never have been an insurrection followed by a Union.

Fitzgibbon continued to play the role of ultra-Protestant even after the Act of 1793. His object was to prevent a working union of Catholic and Protestant for Parliamentary Reform. Such a measure once passed, the Union was impossible of achievement. In permitting the Catholic Relief Act, he had hurried through some highly desirable measures—the Convention Act, the Gunpowder Act, and so forth. These entitled him to make associations such as the United Irishmen illegal, to prohibit the importation of arms, and to raise armed forces responsible to the Castle. By the end of 1794 he had 36,000 armed men under his control. He had likewise suppressed the United Irishmen and forced it to become a secret society. A little later Pitt, with the aid of a scoundrel yclept Cokayne, whom he sent to Dublin with a Protestant clergyman named Jackson—an English revolutionist, the dupe of Pitt's machinations—succeeded in catching several of the formidable leaders of the Reform movement tripping—among them Wolfe Tone, who was allowed by Fitzgibbon to leave the country, for Tone had powerful friends. Tone sailed for America. The United Irishmen from Reformers became secret conspirators, but did not succeed in gaining much of the Catholic population to their side. Outside Ulster and Dublin the French Revolutionists were not enthusiastically admired in Ireland. The French Revolution had ruined Irish trade with France, and closed careers that had been open for a hundred years to the Catholic Irish. The Irish Brigade in France had remained strongly Royalist, and the Republican idea found no flaming response in the heart of the Gael, essentially a believer in aristocracy. To get a Catholic insurrection had become impossible, owing to the United Irish movement. Pitt now planned to get a Republican insurrection—to alarm the Irish Parliament into a Union out of the United Irish movement itself. As it stood, such an insurrection could not be had. United Irishism was chiefly Presbyterian, and an Ulster Presbyterian Republican rising whilst Catholic Munster, Connacht and Leinster either were passively or actively hostile to that rising would have defeated his object. The Catholic must be driven into the United Irish ranks, and made rise for Republicanism, too. Then the Minister could, indeed, tell the property of Ireland that it was faced with a formidable Jacobin conspiracy and force it to seek refuge in his arms.

To first raise the Catholic hopes to the highest and then dash them to earth was Pitt's plan. The reaction from hope to despair would drive sufficient Catholics into the Republican camp to make an insurrection sufficiently alarming for his purpose. Lord Fitzwilliam, the one honest English politician whose name appears in these times, was sent over to Ireland to open a new era. He was to emancipate the Catholics—he was to reform abuses—he was to pacify all Ireland with the blessing of Mr. Pitt. The poor nobleman enthusiastically set about his work. Ireland cheered for joy. United Irish, Reformers, Whigs, all embraced. Here was the New Era. When expectation was at its highest Fitzwilliam, to his astonishment, was recalled. Ireland stood stupefied. Her stupefaction was turned to rage when Lord Camden was sent to replace him—a man whose evil character was notorious and who, in the perfection of his unscrupulousness, equalled Fitzgibbon and Pitt.

Camden came to this country with instructions from Pitt to promote anti-Catholic feeling whilst apparently favouring the Catholics—to let the United Irish movement grow awhile and then dragoon and goad its supporters into armed revolt. He carried out his instructions to the letter. In the first few months of his administration many Leinster and Ulster Catholics flocked into the ranks of the United

Irishmen. At the end of 1796 the Castle was ready for the insurrection, and its bashi-bazouks were loosed to force it on.

VI.—THE INSURRECTION.

Not until the United Irish Society had been suppressed and declared illegal did the bulk of its supporters begin to dream of armed revolt and the establishment of a Republic. Not until after Earl Fitzwilliam's recall and the loosing on the country of hordes of British regulars and militia to harry and goad the peasantry did its leaders apply to France for aid. Not until the summer of 1796 did the United Irish movement become definitely wedded to the idea of a Republic established by force of arms. France listened favourably to the proposal that she should invade Ireland. But when France realised that the United Irishmen did not mean to connect Ireland to France, French enthusiasm cooled. An independent Ireland and an Ireland connected to France were different propositions. Wolfe Tone, however, succeeded in securing a French expedition of aid to be sent to Ireland. Most marvellous were the mishaps that befel it. Scarce had it lost sight of the French shore, the waters placidly reflecting the beams of the unclouded moon, than the ship containing the naval and military commanders of the expedition lost its way and was not thereafter heard of while the expedition was an expedition. Across the seas supposed to be infested with British war vessels the expedition passed unnoticed, and at Christmastide arrived in Bantry Bay, and loitered there long enough to permit preparations to be made to resist its landing by the people and the authorities who were alike hostile. While the French were in the bay the French Commanders-in-Chief remained not on the flagship, but together on a frigate, rendering communication with their staff difficult always, and sometimes impossible. Day by day the opposition to the expedition grew on shore, and day by day the strength of the expedition diminished. Wolfe Tone, fuming, submitted plans of landing to Grouchy—the gentleman whose late arrival at Waterloo nineteen years later lost the French Empire—which Grouchy highly approved. Then one morning Wolfe Tone awoke to find that the last of the French admirals had disappeared in the night, and the remnant of the expedition turned its ships' heads towards France. The neglect of the French to take the commonest precautions for their defence if an English fleet approached amazed Wolfe Tone. "I confess it passes my comprehension," he wrote. The disappearance of the vessel containing the Commanders-in-Chief in fair weather on a moonlight night astonished him. The Commanders who supplied their places and shut themselves up together in a frigate, "I cannot conceive for what reason," disgusted him. The aimless loitering, the dilatory tactics of the Frenchmen in the Bay infuriated him. "We have lost two Commanders-in-Chief—of four Admirals not one remains," he writes bitterly. And all this loss without meeting a British ship. Yet Wolfe Tone imputed no dishonesty to the French Commanders. He attributed all these things to coincidence. He was the man on the spot, and however the student of the history of this remarkably unfortunate expedition may feel suspicion aroused, the fact remains that the man on the spot most interested in the success of the expedition and most crushed by its failure did not suspect treachery in its conduct. We must, therefore, assume that fate, not the efficient Secret Service of Mr. Pitt, brought the French Expedition of 1796 to naught.

By this strange fatality the policy of Pitt was served. Alarm was spread throughout an Ireland opposed to "French principles." Fitzgibbon was easily able to bend an alarmed Parliament to sanction measures that would at other times have been hotly resisted. Yeomanry Corps were embodied partly of men genuinely aroused at the prospect of invasion, partly of the rapscallions that exist in every country. These men, inflamed with stories that the French were to be brought to Ireland by the United Irishmen to annex the country to France, confiscate property, and glut the guillotine, were incited to acts of cruelty and oppression on all whom they chose to suspect. In case they suspected wrongly, an Act of Indemnity protected them from the consequences. British troops, regulars and fencibles, were poured into the country, and free-quartered through the counties. The cruelty of the Yeomanry was tame compared with the acts of these men. The result was naturally what Pitt planned. The United Irishmen, who, outside Antrim and Down in 1796, were small in numbers, spread rapidly through Leinster, on which rapine had been loosed. In England and Scotland Republican conspiracies existed. In those countries Mr. Pitt stepped in and crushed them. He needed no insurrection in Great Britain. In Ireland, with all the details of conspiracy in the Government's possession, it held its hand, because it had planned a civil war.

Yet very unexpectedly Pitt in the end found himself hampered by the instruments he designed to use. Lord Carhampton was appointed Commander-in-Chief in Ireland for the performance of the tragedy. He was to produce the outburst, and then crush it in rivers of blood. Carhampton was a brutal soldier, but still a soldier. He conceived it was the duty of a soldier appointed to deal with an insurrectionary spirit to crush the insurrectionary spirit before it gathered strength to appear in the open. This he proceeded to do. The Lord Lieutenant hinted to him that this was not what was required. Carhampton ignored the hint, and proceeded with his business as a soldier. Again the Lord Lieutenant intervened. A second time Carhampton ignored him. Here was a pretty state of affairs. If Carhampton were not held up there would be no open insurrection, and if there were no open insurrection Mr. Pitt's Irish policy would fall to the ground. Mr. Pitt hastened to get King George, under his royal sign-manual, to order Carhampton to do as he (Mr. Pitt) wished him. Carhampton thereupon resigned, and, having resigned, publicly and bluntly declared that what Mr. Pitt wanted to do was not to suppress an insurrection, but to excite one.

Mr. Pitt made a second bad choice. General Abercrombie, a gallant soldier, was appointed Commander-in-Chief. He proceeded to spoil Mr. Pitt's plans by stopping the free-quartering, torturing, and rapine. Very much to the honest gentleman's astonishment, he found that the Government highly disapproved of this. Like Carhampton, he had believed that what Pitt wanted was tranquility when what Pitt wanted was insurrection. Abercrombie threw up his commission, took a parting shot at Pitt by issuing a General Order stating that the British army in Ireland was in a state of licentiousness, and went off to die in Egypt, fighting like a brave man against trained soldiers instead of playing the butcher of untrained peasants.

He was succeeded by General Lake, a man fit for the work of Pitt. With Lake in command, all was ready, and on the 12th of March, 1798, the Castle seized most of the leaders of the United Irishmen, and followed up the coup with a proclamation of general martial law throughout the land. One hundred and thirty thousand English and Scotch troops and Irish auxiliaries were now at the command of the Castle. Two regiments of German mercenaries were brought in and let loose on the people. On the 23rd of May the United Irishmen of half the Leinster counties rose in revolt. Their chief arms were pikes and pitchforks, and their leaders mainly private gentlemen destitute of military training. In courage they everywhere surpassed their opponents, but courage without arms and discipline and leadership cannot win battles. In a week the revolting counties were broken. Ulster, which had been looked on as the prop of the movement, did not rise in May. A fortnight after the rising in Leinster the Antrim and Down men took the field, and after a gallant seven-day fight were crushed. All this was in Mr. Pitt's programme. He had reckoned on a brief fight and assured success in Leinster and Ulster—a ten-day campaign. One county—Wexford—almost converted an abortive insurrection into a revolution—almost overturned Mr. Pitt's policy not only in Ireland, but throughout Europe.

The people of Wexford, being esteemed the most patient people in Ireland, had been treated to an exaggeration of the outrages inflicted in the adjoining counties. They did not resort to arms until several days after the other Leinster counties. When they took up arms they drove home the truth that the quiet man driven to combat is the most dogged of fighters. For nearly a month they held Wexford against all the forces Mr. Pitt could muster against them. Had a French expedition then made Wexford it would have gone hard with Mr. Pitt. But no French expedition made Wexford. Seven weeks after Wexford had been subdued, much to the relief of the alarmed Minister, who for a fortnight trembled in the thought that his insurrection might prove a revolution, a thousand Frenchmen under General Humbert succeeded in effecting a landing in the West, where the United Irish movement had small support. Nevertheless the French were joined by a couple of thousand of the people, and their initial triumphs induced some of the militia to declare for them. In attempting to penetrate into Leinster the French and their Irish allies, less than 2,500 men in all, succumbed to a British army 30,000 strong at Ballinamuck. Mr. Pitt's agents turned the incident of this little raid to profit by exhorting the opponents of French principles to consider that they could not rely on the Irish militia to protect them—they must rely on Sister England.

The last Gallic chapter in the history of Mr. Pitt's preparations for the Red Wedding of Ireland to England was the despatch of another miserable expedition to Ireland—nine ships and three thousand men—of which before it sailed a Paris newspaper published a full and minute account, with the additional information that Wolfe Tone himself was on board the flagship. This, however, does not prove that the Directory of France was composed of traitors. Rather we are to regard its members as political imbeciles. With this public information of the expedition and its strength the British arranged a reception for the French, who, after a brave battle against heavy odds in Lough Swilly, were defeated. Amongst the officers captured was Wolfe Tone. A month later he was sentenced to death in Dublin, and on the 19th of November he was dead.

On the same 19th of November Castlereagh wrote from Dublin Castle to Wickham that they "would soon have something to do," and that it was "most fortunate Parliament was not sitting." On the morning Wolfe Tone died in Newgate and the last act of the bloody tragedy of 1798 was played, Lord Castlereagh received in Dublin Castle Pitt's instruction to go ahead with the Union.

VII.—THE " UNION."

Castlereagh went ahead with the Union. The Irish militia
was drafted away to England—the English militia was
drafted into Ireland. A British military post was established opposite the Parliament House. People who met to
protest against the Union were dispersed at the muzzle of
the gun. The Irish military officers who declared against the
Union were cashiered, and with one hundred and thirty-
seven thousand armed men at his command Mr. Pitt proceeded to argue the question.

The Catholic ecclesiastics were secured by promises of
" Emancipation," the Orangemen were offered a perpetual
ascendency over the Papists. Yet the bulk of the Catholics
and the bulk of the Orangemen refused to support the
Union. The criminal who desired a free pardon got it by
signing a petition for the Union. The citizens who signed
petitions against it were treated as disloyal persons. The
civil officers who supported the Anti-Unionist side were
dismissed from office. Any blackguard of influence or ability
who cared to support it was rewarded in cash or office.

A Castle assassination club was established to pick off
the prominent Anti-Unionists. Expert duellists were to
provoke the Anti-Union leaders to quarrel and then finish
them off. Henry Grattan, then in feeble health, was the
first man marked down. He was challenged by Isaac Corry,
the rascal whom Castlereagh had made Chancellor of the
Exchequer after Sir John Parnell, refusing to support the
Union, had been dismissed Grattan and Corry met, and
Corry got shot. This unexpected result damped the ardour
of the Castle duellists, and thereafter they trod the path
of peace.

The bankers and merchants of Dublin met and denounced
the Union. The Bar of Ireland met, and by 164 to 32—all
the 32 being bribed—declared " The Minister shall not plant
another Sicily in the bosom of the Atlantic. Our patent to
be a State, not a Shire, comes direct from Heaven. The
God of Nature never intended that Ireland should be a
province, and by that God she never shall!" The Orangemen of Dublin denounced the Union. The Catholics of
Dublin denounced the Union. " Can the potion be sweetened
for Dublin?" wrote Cooke to Castlereagh. On the 21st of
January the first allusion to the Union was made in the
Irish Parliament in the address from the Throne. Mr.
Ponsonby replied to the invitation to Union with the declaration that neither that Legislature nor any power on earth
had right or authority to annihilate the Parliament of
Ireland. Ponsonby carried 105 votes with him—the Castle
106—it was saved by one. Forty-eight hours later the

Union proposals were defeated by 111 votes to 106 after an all-night debate. The majority comprised a score of men who had been dismissed from their places of emolument by the Government for refusing to support the Union.

Dublin illuminated itself in honour of the event, and despondency reigned at the Castle, but Pitt was not shaken. He had not provoked an insurrection and flooded Ireland with armed men to accept defeat. The Union must be carried, and by fifty votes. For eighteen months a campaign of corruption and intimidation was waged which in the end resulted in the passage of the infamous Act. To the last 124 of the 300 members of the Irish Commons resisted all intimidation and scorned all bribery.

One day in July, 1800, the Peers of Ireland entered their Parliament House rulers of a nation—co-rulers of an Empire —and came out less than the equals of the most illiterate Hodge in an English constituency. Mr. Pitt had destroyed the partnership of Ireland in the rule of Empire—he had made England not the predominant partner, but the owner of the firm.

Irishmen in their slavery have echoed the English lie that the Parliament of Ireland was devoid of virtue. To force that Parliament to its knees Pitt plunged this country in civil war, and with 140,000 bayonets at its throat failed to conquer that Parliament's resistance for two years. With Ireland in the grip of an English army of invasion, smuggled in under pretext of crushing an insurrection, and with the whole resources of English terrorism and English corruption let loose on Ireland, the Parliament of Ireland faced Pitt, and to the last 124 of its 300 members remained proof alike against bribe and menace. The history of England can show no parallel in public virtue. If hereafter the Kaiser of Germany should succeed in invading England and planting his armies securely in possession of London, if he should with half-a-million German bayonets at their throats invite the members of the English Parliament to take into consideration the question of union with Germany, and if in such circumstances there be found even fifty Englishmen to resist that Union—as 124 Irishmen resisted Pitt's Union —then, if we be anywhere on this earth, we shall proclaim that the English nation can beget good men.

On the 1st of January, 1801, the Union Jack we know to-day was hoisted for the first time in Ireland—Pitt's badge of conquest. Pitt's policy had trimphed in its Irish section. He had secured that England alone should rule the Empire. There should be no Anglo-Hibernian Empire—there should be henceforward and for ever a **British** Empire. To prevent all possibility of Ireland ever being able to control, direct or influence Imperial policy, he fixed the proportion of Irish representation in the Imperial Parliament at one hundred. He secured that so long as Ireland was "represented" in the Imperial Parliament Ireland should be outvoted by six to one. All the Irishmen who have written on the Union—for and against—have unanimously succeeded in missing the point of Pitt's policy. Rather than that Ireland should have an **effective** representation in the "Imperial Parliament," rather than that she should ever assert by such representation control over the Empire or Imperial policy, Pitt would have foregone the Union. "The number of representatives to be chosen by the Commons of Ireland is **upon no account whatever** to exceed one hundred," wrote Pitt's agent to the English Lord Lieutenant in Ireland. In this condition no relaxation, it was declared, could be permitted. A hundred men in the British Parliament would be always powerless. Two hundred and twenty men, which at the time was Ireland's proportion, would have prevented England from keeping the Empire for herself. So the Irish representation was fixed at 100 against 558, and Pitt, having thus deprived Irish Imperialists of all power in the Empire, still induces them a century after his death to speak of "our Empire," and to seriously believe that they exert influence on Imperial policy.

Pitt's policy was possible in Ireland because Grattan consented to the disbanding of the Volunteers—because he was content with leaving the Executive resident in the Castle when he had the power to make the Executive depend upon the Parliament. Grattan's mistake was the mistake of Irish leaders before and since him—reliance on the honour of England. Not until all Ireland realises that England has never kept a treaty with this or any other nation which it was within her power and it was her interest to break, shall we have adult politics in Ireland.

VIII.—THE END OF A PREFACE.

Thus far is but a preface to the consideration of the policy which Pitt gave England. Pitt struck down Ireland because Ireland declined to accept the Empire as England's private property. He correctly judged that the power of England could keep Ireland down. What he incorrectly judged we shall see hereafter.

We shall hereafter show that the Irish policy of Pitt induced the twentieth-century Germany. That Tenterden Steeple is the cause of Goodwin Sands sounds not more strangely in the ear than that the "Act of Union" begot the German world-power of the twentieth century. Yet we shall make that manifest. Henceforward in these articles Ireland will appear negatively, for Irish influence on England's fortunes has since the Union been purely negative. From the day the Union passed English policy in Ireland was directed with success to degrade Ireland morally and physically, and weaken her materially. All that England saw in Ireland was a possible rival in the government of Empire, a possible rival in trade. The Union secured England against such rivalries. The danger of Irish combination against English policy was averted by the establishment within Ireland of a Party made to feel its political importance depended upon English support. "By this means," as a candid English politician wrote in 1829, "division has been maintained between interests which might have been formidable if they were induced to combine."

We may now close the preface to Pitt's policy. When the Union had been carried the Catholic prelates and the Catholic noblemen whom Pitt hoodwinked into supporting him against their country by the promise of "Emancipation" found themselves deceived. Mr. Pitt was very sorry, but alas! the King would not hear of Catholic Emancipation. Mr. Pitt was very indignant. He resigned office. What could be greater proof of Mr. Pitt's sincerity in the eyes of his dupes, whom he thus double-duped. For Mr. Pitt resigned office in order to permit the Treaty of Peace with France, which it was necessary to make, to be signed by another hand than his own. So that if, in a revulsion of popular feeling, the terms of that Treaty were denounced, Mr. Pitt could not be held responsible. Mr. Pitt resigned office since he could not emancipate the Catholics. Mr. Addington pledged, not to emancipate the Catholics, was put in power by Mr. Pitt. Mr. Addington concluded the Treaty of Amiens, and when that Treaty became unpopular, Mr. Pitt kicked out Addington, returned to power in a blaze of glory and announced amid the applause of England that he would never again ask to emancipate the Catholics.

The three men who doomed this country to a hundred years of hell, perished miserably. Fitzgibbon, become Lord Clare, flushed with triumph, journeyed to England, was publicly derided by the peers of that land, and learned at the tail of his life that to the Englishman the negro is always a nigger and the Irishman a white negro. The triumphant Clare of 1801 died a broken man in 1802, praying on his deathbed for the forgiveness of the country he had destroyed. Pitt followed him to the grave five years later, believing his policy overthrown by Napoleon and his England doomed. "Oh, my country, how I leave my country," was the cry of despair with which Pitt met death. A darker fate was reserved for the meanest of the three men—Castlereagh. Pitt was Ireland's enemy—a deadlier enemy than Cromwell—but Pitt was not an Irishman. Fitzgibbon was an Irishman in blood, in genius, in temperament. He is the darkest Irish figure in Irish affairs since Mac Murrogh. All the vices of the Irish character backed by a lightning intellect and a man's strength were in Fitzgibbon. He was a bad Irishman in whom Irishmen will recognise the dark side of the national character attaining mastery over the noble. Not so Castlereagh. In his base character no likeness to the Irish nature can be found. The King of England commended him because "there was no trace of the Irishman to be found in him." That his Majesty was correct Castlereagh testified, for he cut his throat twenty years after the Union to escape the penalty of un-Irish sin.

So passed the authors of the Union. Their crime remains. What its effect has been upon the fortunes of that country for which they committed it we shall trace from the day when the Union flag was first hoisted in Ireland until this day, wherein Englishwomen have come to frighten their children with the name of Germany as the Carthagenian matrons terrified their infants with the name of Rome.

IX.—THE FUNDAMENTALS OF ENGLISH STATECRAFT.

When the Norman conquerors of England were definitely defeated in their attempt to seize the crown of France they were compelled to build a strong navy to secure themselves independence in the island to which they were then restricted.

As the commercial era followed the military era and England aimed at becoming a great trading nation it became vital to her that the countries facing her on the south-east should not be occupied by a strong naval or military power. The wars of England with Spain and of England with France in centuries past were waged to prevent Holland and Belgium becoming appanages of Spain or France. By the end of the seventeenth century Spain's strength was broken. The eighteenth century witnessed England concentrating her power to break France. It was at the moment when this traditional policy of England seemed to be defeated that William Pitt became Minister. The revolt of the American colonies gave France and Spain the opportunity of humbling England for ever. The combined Spanish and French fleets exceeded the strength of the English fleet. The English fleet was defeated, but owing to the gross mismanagement of the war by the Allies it was not conquered. England escaped destruction as a great naval Power in 1778-82 by the blunders of her foemen. She had invited it by permitting her fleet, for motives of economy, to fall below the standard of her traditional policy, i.e., equality with that of the combined fleets of the Bourbon Powers—

then the only Powers in Europe strong enough to thwart her.

Pitt was called to the helm at the time when as the first men in England despairingly proclaimed "the sun of England's glory had set." He must either give England a new policy or show her how to reassert the old.

He resolved to reassert the old. Ireland was on his flank. Ireland had profited by the collapse of English sea-power to reassert its independence. It remained, however, voluntarily associated with the Crown of England. The new policy was obvious. England had shown herself unequal to defending her Empire. Ireland had shown itself equal to defending itself. Ireland was filled with vigour, hope and enthusiasm, and produced in abundance the raw material of conquest. The new policy was, therefore, to accept the end of the English Empire as a fact and to reconstruct on its ruins an invincible naval and military Anglo-Hibernian Empire. This policy, which in similar circumstances eighty years later Austria accepted, Pitt rejected. He stood for England Absolute as those in Austria who opposed Beust's solution of the Hungarian problem stood for Austria absolute. There was no Beust in the England of Pitt. Pitt's policy was the policy of a daring gambler. He set the fate of his country on the chance of destroying the power of victorious France. Twice under his guidance England trembled on the brink of annihilation. He even died believing he had ruined his country, and his death alone saved him from denunciation in the English Parliament as the destroyer of the Empire. Yet in the end his policy won in so far as it involved the pulling down of France, and the restoration of English control of the seas. And for eighty years no man has been honoured and worshipped by England as William Pitt has been. Every English politician realises that Pitt performed an almost impossible feat when he preserved the Empire without admitting Ireland to be a co-partner.

To understand the last hundred years of history it is necessary to realise that the English foreign policy which went down in 1782 and was successfully revived by Pitt postulates four things, which are these:—

(1) In the control and direction of Empire England must be absolute.

(2) The maintenance of Empire depends upon the maintenance of an English fleet more powerful than the combined fleets of rival Powers.

(3) The Low Countries—Belgium and Holland—must not be permitted to become in themselves great naval Powers or to fall under the control of a great naval or military Power.

(4) No one Continental Power must be permitted to dominate the Continent. Against any Power seeking the hege-

mony of the Continent combinations of other Continental Powers supported by the English fleet must be formed.

This was England's policy for two centuries before Pitt. It was the policy that had failed when Pitt was called to power. Pitt restored it, and made it run for a century. It necessitated the Union. It necessitated the English policy that prevailed in Ireland for the whole of the nineteenth century. What we shall consider later on is whether it has failed—and why.

Since the two steps necessary to Pitt in the policy was the overthrow of France and the subjection of Ireland, Pitt's action in Ireland is explicable. His support of the French Revolution for four years is also explicable. The French Monarchy was the ancient enemy of England. Pitt backed the Revolution in order to overthrow the Monarchy. He did not believe that under a Republic France could remain a formidable Power. The invasion of the Low Countries by the French in 1793 awakened him to the fact that French Republicanism was not less imperialistic than French Monarchism. He therefore declared war against his former friends. The rise of Napoleon deranged his calculations, and he was forced in 1802 to face the fact that France was now in possession of the strongholds of the Low Countries, and that England's power of opposition was exhausted. To avoid the necessity of concluding peace on terms which admitted the failure of his policy, he resigned office, alleging that he did so on the Catholic question—and Addington concluded the Treaty of Amiens. Since this Treaty kept the Low Countries as a pistol at England's head, it was clear that England must by war or diplomacy secure the evacuation of these countries by France or England must go under. Diplomacy failed, although it offered Malta to France in exchange for the neutralisation of Holland. England then had no choice left. The war which followed the Peace of Amiens was England's fight for life.

If the impartial reader will keep before his mind the four fundamentals of Pitt's policy we shall conduct him to the conviction hereafter that that policy, which necessitated the Act of Union, has to-day failed, because of that Act of Union.

X.—THE ORIGIN OF FREE TRADE.

The battle of Austerlitz killed Pitt, and Fox, the man who might have reversed his policy, joined him in his grave. The disciples of Pitt regained power, and among them there was none so strong as Lord Castlereagh. Since the choice of Ministers lay between working Pitt's ideas to the full or abandoning them in favour of an agreement with France, the Pittite Ministry fell under the sway of Castlereagh.

He guided its policy, although never nominally its head. The one man to challenge his authority was a brother Irishman—George Canning. A duel between Castlereagh and Canning settled the question. Canning lost power in his party, and did not recover it whilst Castlereagh lived.

The history of England, then, from the death of Pitt until 1823 is little more than the history of an apostate Irishman carrying out resolutely the policy he had been taught by Pitt.

When in 1815 France fell before an embattled Europe, the Kingdom of the Netherlands was established with the Prince of Orange as Monarch. The Kingdom was given sixty million francs to construct a line of fortresses to keep France in check. Thus Pitt's policy seemed to have absolutely triumphed. England was not merely the chief naval Power in the world, but the **only** naval Power. France, her one serious rival in a hundred years, was dethroned and the Low Countries converted into sentinels on French ambition. To overthrow France, resume the Empire of the sea, establish suzerainty over the Low Countries, and kick Ireland into a cellar was not the end of a policy, but means to an end. The end was the commercial conquest of the world. In the early eighteenth century this aim was freely avowed. The subsequent misfortunes of England compelled her to wear a mask. Adam Smith, Mr. Pitt's mentor, supplied the mask. His "Wealth of Nations" was, is, and will remain the best example of a subtle scheme for English world-conquest put forward under the guise of an essay on political economy flavoured with that love of man which hooks in the sentimentalists of all countries. The fall of Napoleon left the way clear for England to monopolise the manufacturing power of the world. If she had thrown her ports open in 1815 instead of thirty years later there is no doubt all Europe would have gone down before her—rushing to exchange its raw materials for English manufactured goods. But, as Frederick List afterwards said, Providence has taken care that trees shall not grow quite up to the sky. Castlereagh gave over the commercial policy of England into the hands of the landed aristocracy, and it killed the goose which had laid the golden eggs. The Pittites preached open markets to the world, but kept their own closed. France, observing this, shut her ports against England, and to all remonstrances from the Friends of Man and Pioneers of Progress pointed to the closed ports of England. The Secret Service of England was able to incline Germany, Russia, and North America to the policy of opening their markets free to English manufactured goods. But France's resolute refusal blocked the way to the conquest of the Continent. The landed magnates who had backed Pitt refused assent to a policy of Free Trade which promised to decrease their importance whilst it increased that of the mercantile element. After the suicide of Castlereagh the dispute came to a head. All England—Whig and Tory— agreed that the glory of God and the interests of civilisation required that the Continent should buy its manufactures from England, whilst England in return would take raw material from the Continent—"and agricultural produce," added others. "No, no," shouted the landowners. Canning tried to avert a conflict between the English commercial and the English landed interests. He went to France himself and tried his power of cajolery on the Ministers, pointing out to them how much they had to gain by opening their ports. They told him they had resolved not to worry on the right or wrong of Free Trade until England herself opened her ports. He returned to England in a fury and threatened he would hang a mill-stone around France's neck. But France, unmoved, kept her ports fast locked. Thus England was forced to go to war within herself as a preliminary to the commercial conquest of Europe: The merchants and capitalists who believed that by opening the English ports France would be forced to open her own versus the landholders who didn't believe anything of the kind.

What Pitt would have done had he been alive in 1815 is uncertain. It is clear that with England's supremacy in Europe re-established and the commercial conquest of the Continent as the objective that the ports of England ought to have been thrown open in 1815. But there were powerful interests in England opposed to such a course, interests powerful enough to drag Pitt down. Castlereagh must have seen clearly enough that Pitt's policy pointed to Free Trade, and that Free Trade was the natural and immediate sequel of the overthrow of Napoleon by England, but the disciple shrank from the fate that awaited him if he attempted to carry to the end his master's policy.

France was the key of the position. To force France to open her ports the Free Trade movement was begun by the British industrialists and opposed by the British landholders. The year 1824 marks the definitive quarrel of Pitt's disciples as to the means of carrying out his policy and the birth of the parties we know to-day as Liberals and Conservatives as distinguished from the old hereditary parties of Whig and Tory.

XI.—LIST AND CAREY.

Up to the year 1824, when the commercial and the landed classes of England divided into hostile camps, England's economic policy had been the most rigidly protective in the world. Prohibitive duties were levied on the importation of the manufactures of the Continent, and the foodstuffs of these countries were all but interdicted. The navigation laws of England until the end of the Napoleonic wars provided that foreign commodities could only be imported in British ships or in ships of the country from which the goods were exported or of which they were the produce, and the trade of the British Colonies was restricted to British vessels. Goods exported could only be exported in British ships. The latter law was modified after the fall of Napoleon, but otherwise the navigation laws were kept intact. In 1824, when modern English history starts, the policy of England was to ensure that the foreigner bought from England and to prevent England buying from the foreigner. The doctrines of Adam Smith were sedulously promoted on the Continent by England while she kept her own ports closed. The Secret Service money of England was lavished with no niggard hand on Continental journalists and Continental theorists to influence them to advocate opening the Continental ports to English produce. Whilst the French Government stood firm against such a policy the French public was profoundly agitated in its favour by professors and progressive writers. Germany, enamoured of the beautiful theories spun for it inclined its eager ear. It was at this time a man appeared in Germany whose keen mind, intense patriotism, and fearless character laid the foundation for the German power of to-day.

The man was Frederich List, the son of a Wurtemberg tanner. Beginning life as an enthusiastic Free Trader, he was led to investigate more deeply, and arrived at the conclusion that what Germany stood in need of was a rigid Protection. In 1822 he appeared as the head of a German Commercial Union whose doctrines were a direct challenge to England. Fearing his propaganda would displease England, he was expelled from his native Wurtemberg by its servile Government. Seeking refuge in other States of Germany, he was in turn by the same influence expelled from them. Fleeing to France, he was welcomed, but later returning to his own country he was cast into prison. On his release he retired to America. Here he fell under the influence of the two Irishmen, Carey, whose ideas, incorporating with his own, formed the foundation of his doctrine of National Economy, on which modern Germany is built.

Carey the elder was an Irishman forced to flee his country by Mr. Pitt. Settling in America, he married, and his famous son, Henry Carey, elaborated the doctrine of Protection which the United States adopted in opposition to the doctrine of Smith. Henry Carey is the author of the United States as England's commercial rival. List, his colleague, is the author of Germany as England's competitor in sea power.

If at the end of the Napoleonic wars England, then standing supreme in manufacturing power, had itself

adopted Free Trade, it is humanly probable that all
Europe would have succumbed. The Ministers of England,
however, considered they could force the opening of foreign
ports without opening their own. For ten years they strove
to attain this end, and failed. Instead opposition grew in
strength on the Continent, and in 1824 England was faced
with the certainty that she could not force the Continental
ports to open to her Sesame without first modifying her own
prohibitive policy. The landed interest, which regarded the
free import of produce as certain to reduce its strength
and importance, stood rigidly opposed to any relaxation in
the English system. The manufacturing interest saw in the
open ports of Europe the road to a wealth and importance
unequalled in the history of the world. It had nothing to
fear from opening the ports to manufactured goods—the
Continent, it knew, was not able to compete with the home
manufacturer in the English market. If the landed interest
suffered some loss, the loss would be as nothing in comparison
with the prosperity England could acquire by such a policy.
The landed interest could not see this. It opposed doggedly.
Under the influence of the commercial interest the British
Government in 1824 began cautiously to move towards the
abrogation of its prohibitive policy. The opposition of the
landed interest proving too strong, the commercial interest
threw in its power on the side of "Reform," and the Reform
Act of the Thirties, breaking down the strength of the terri-
torialists, opened the way for the reversal of England's
ancient trade policy.

The history of British Parliamentary politics from 1824
to 1846 is the history of a struggle between the British
shipowners and manufacturers, in which they used the mul-
titude as their tool, and the British landed proprietors.
The "Reform and Anti-Corn Law" agitations were different phases of the fight between the two monied classes.
The commercials won in 1845, and Free Trade became the
declared policy of England. The English ports were thrown
open, and the English manufacturer, cheered on by Cobden,
who assured him that soon all the countries of Europe must
open their ports, went forth to the conquest of the world.
Incidentally some millions of Irish were famished or expa-
triated, and the price of food increased to their posterity.
The delusion that Free Trade has cheapened food in Ireland
is sedulously inculcated on a people ignorant of their history.
The following prices of food in Ireland outside Dublin in
the decade 1830-40, when Protection was in force, will dispel
the delusion:—Beef, 4d. per lb.; mutton, 5d. to 6d.; bacon,
2d. to 4d.; pork, 2d. to 5d.; butter, 9d. per lb.; fowls,
1s. the couple. In Dublin 10 to 20 per cent. might be added
to these prices. But this is of interest to none save the
Irish themselves.

France, refusing to fall in wit' Cobden's idea, was discovered to be living in an intolerable state of tyranny, and
the supersession of Louis Philippe by a Government of
Liberal ideas became an object of English policy. Of that
hereafter. The position of Germany requires a few words.
Frederich List, returning thither years after he had been
expelled, impressed its thoughtful people by his work on
"The National System of Political Economy." He promised his countrymen a glorious future if they would act
on his propositions, which were:—

"All nations have a common interest in protecting themselves against the destructive competition of England."

"All nations have a common interest in preventing England holding the absolute mastery of the seas."

"Germany's interest demanded that reciprocity treaties
should be entered into by her with the United States and
countries of the Continent, **but not with England.**

"An association of the States of Germany in a common
flag, a common fleet and a mercantile marine is politically
essential, and cannot be attained if the first three propositions are not accepted and acted on."

List was bitterly opposed in his own country, where Dr.
Bowring, paid by the British Government, lectured to dis-
credit him. In the reptile Press of List's native land he
was held up in turn as an ignoramus, an adventurer, as a
man who by bringing down England's displeasure on Germany endangered his country's safety, as at best a dreamer of
dreams. Uncowed by attack and unmoved by ingratitude,
List fought on against English policy, gaining recruits day
by day. But the opening of her own ports by England dealt
him a fatal blow. In holding the common mind of Germany
against open ports, he had always pointed to England's
keeping her own closed. When England flung them free,
boasting as she did so that within a few years all Europe
would be forced to follow her example, List, despairing of
his countrymen's virtue to resist, killed himself. Belittled
in his life, the dead man appeared to Germany in all his
greatness and patriotism. His tragic death achieved what
his continued life might have failed in. It impelled Germany to keep her sentinels on her ports and raise the call
for a German flag and a German fleet.

Modern Germany and modern America—England's political rivals and commercial competitors—are the creation of
List and Carey. We have turned somewhat aside to trace
the origin of Free Trade with which the children of Pitt
went forth to conquer the world. We shall now see how
Pitt's policy was faithfully carried on against France, while
despised Germany, silently working on the propositions of
List, gathered strength to set it at defiance.

XII.—PALMERSTON.

From the day of Canning's death until the end of his own days Palmerston dominated English foreign policy, and with small interruption it was confided to his direction. He slaughtered brown and yellow men for the benefit of British speculators and the opium trade, but these things were by the way, mere trade-wars. He bullied little Kingdoms such as Portugal and Greece and supplied munitions of war from his Government Ordnance factories to insurgents in countries whose rulers were too weak to make England respect international law. But such things the commonplace English Foreign Minister can always do. The enthusiasm that his name aroused in England—which sustained him for forty years against all combinations in that country—was due to his vigour in carrying out Pitt's propositions of English foreign policy, viz. :—

(1) In the control and direction of Empire England must be absolute.

(2) The maintenance of Empire depends upon the maintenance of an English fleet more powerful than the combined fleets of rival powers.

(3) The Low Countries—Belgium and Holland—must not be permitted to become in themselves great naval Powers or to fall under the control of a great naval or military Power.

(4) No one Continental Power must be permitted to dominate the Continent. Against any Power seeking the hegemony of the Continent combinations of other Continental Powers supported by the English fleet must be forced.

Palmerston added nothing to English foreign policy. But he enforced it as he had learned it from Pitt with the strength of Pitt.

When Belgium revolted against the role of Britain's policeman over French ambition, and France came to her aid, Palmerston effectively showed France that Pitt's policy had a strong man behind it. The French armies which marched to the assistance of Belgium marched out again when Palmerston pointed the guns of the British fleet towards the coast of France. The French dream of Belgium as a sword brandished against England vanished. "We have you down, gentlemen," said Palmerston to the French, "and down you stay."

France, baffled but unconquered. attempted to build up her power in the Mediterranean. She played for an independent Egypt, which as her ally would aid her to successfully dispute England's mastery of the centre sea. Palmerston let her play a while. Then he slipped in and knocked Egypt down with a club. "Gentlemen," said the English

Foreign Minister to the French, "the Mediterranean is an English lake, and an English lake it is going to remain."

France, held up in the Channel and held up in the Mediterranean, looked to alliance with Russia. Palmerston locked up Russia in the Black Sea, and retorted on France's attempt to find a Mediterranean ally by planning Italy a Mediterranean Netherlands. Liberty-loving England became aflame with enthusiasm for Italian freedom, and Austria, much annoyed, could only growl and swear.

The year 1848 brought matters in France to a head. The continued defeat of French foreign policy by Palmerston had aroused discontent against the Monarchy amongst Monarchists and Imperialists. who remembered in bitterness the days when France gave the law to Europe. The internal policy of the Government of Louis Philippe increased the discontent by striving to drive it beneath the surface. Republicans, Liberals and Bonapartists, mutually detesting each other, united in detesting Louis Philippe more. The unlucky Citizen-King resolved on a bold policy. France was to assert itself once again—by arms if necessary—against England. It asserted itself in connection with an affair of Spain, and Palmerston replied by a French Revolution. The British Embassy in Paris, with admirable skill, utilised French discontent to the end of firing Louis Philippe off the Throne. The French Republic of 1848 was inaugurated with great eclat and received with great enthusiasm. All that appeared to the public eye was that a somewhat mean and despotic monarch had been overthrown, and all that resounded in the public ear was "Tremble, Tyrants." Young Ireland, with a dream that this regenerate France would unsheathe its sword for Ireland, hastened to Paris to congratulate M. Lamartine, apostle of liberty and high priest of the Republic, and M. Lamartine bowed Young Ireland out, informing it, much to its astonishment, that the French Republic was on excellent terms with England, and could not dream of interfering with the right of that country to dispose as it pleased of its subjects—willing or unwilling. Thus did Lamartine pay some of the debt he owed England's Foreign Minister.

The French Revolution of 1848 saved England from the danger of a war with France at a time when England was not on good terms with Russia and Austria. Its echoes resounded through Europe, and inimical Austria found her hands so full with her own Republicans and with the insurgent Italians and Hungarians that her unfriendliness to England counted for nothing. Palmerston, having thus settled France and the Mediterranean, turned his attention to clipping the wings of Russia. Glancing at the States of Germany, in his wisdom he remarked that it would not be a bad thing if Prussia grew stronger and assumed their leadership—thus serving England as a guarantee against France and Austria—and then he passed on. Like his master Pitt, Lord Palmerston did not foresee the possibility of Germany playing a hand for itself, and discreet Prussia, silently plodding on its way as a humble second-rate Power void of ambition, gave him no hint that with France out of the way there could ever arise a Power in Europe to challenge British supremacy.

XIII.—THE CRIMEAN WAR.

The Crimean War was the work of Lord Palmerston. He believed some heavy blow should be struck at the naval and territorial power of Russia, and, in defiance of treaty and obligation, he made war on Russia ; for the war with Russia was a shameless violation of the secret arrangement of 1844 by which England had acknowledged the right of Russia on every point on which England afterwards declared war. Palmerston, who believed that with Louis Napoleon at the helm France was in his grasp—later on he revised his opinion of Louis Napoleon—induced France to make common cause with England. Napoleon was not loth to do so, for in the tangled state of affairs in France a foreign war was good policy. When England, France and Turkey went to war with Russia they were joined by Sardinia—a little Kingdon dominated by a great man. The adhesion of Sardinia was regarded by the combatants in the light of a joke. But Sardinia was the one country in the war which gained out of the war. The Crimean War ended in a nominal victory for England and France. In reality it left matters where they were. For Sardinia it ended most satisfactorily. As Cavour, who planned a Kingdom of Italy with Sardinia at the head, foresaw when he sent his little forces to the front, in the settlement of affairs after peace, Sardinia necessarily secured representation, and stood on an equal footing for the time with the Great Powers. Her representative was Cavour himself—the ablest man in the conference. He thus secured the foothold he wished in European affairs for his country and out of the blundering Crimean War built up the modern Kingdom of Italy.

The end of the Crimean War found Palmerston with his views of Louis Napoleon completely altered. He had regarded the Frenchman as his dupe—he found him cunning and dangerous. The Anglo-French Alliance went smash, and Palmerston roused England to the cry "Delenda est Carthagoi." This Heaven-sent Foreign Minister, as he was termed, carrying blindly on the anti-French policy of Pitt, openly advocated a "strong Germany with Prussia at the head." The strong Germany was to be England's catspaw in keeping France down. English policy set itself to back Prussia against Austria, which was precisely what Prussia wanted.

Palmerston in his day was acclaimed the greatest of European Ministers. Compared with Cavour and Bismarck he was a child. They used him to forward their own schemes—the one to make a united Italy, the other a German Empire. The united Italy did not matter to English policy, the German Empire mattered much.

Not until 1864 did any suspicion arise in England of Prussia—not for twenty years afterwards did she begin to take Prussia seriously. Her Heaven-sent statesman had learned from Pitt that France must be kept down. The possibility that another European Power could grow strong enough to challenge England as France had done never entered their minds. Palmerston for thirty years was the ruler of English foreign policy. He kept France in the place Pitt had designed for her and he let Germany get out of her bonds.

XIV.—THE DANISH WAR.

In 1850 Menzel wound up his history of Germany in a wail of despair. The idea of Germany one and strong was all but dead. Her nobles were indifferent, her people deserters. Emigrants. they sought abroad comfort for themselves and forgot their Fatherland. Germany was a dead lion.

How oddly this sounds sixty years later—yet there was much truth in it in the day of its writing. A few years before Mensel shed his tears List had died likewise despairing of the country in whose service he had spent his life and which repaid him with imprisonment, poverty and exile. Germany in 1850 counted for little or nothing. Twenty years later she was a Great Power. The man who worked the miracle was a private gentleman named Bismarck.

Bismarck had read his List and his Menzel. He went into politics to carry out their ideas—to re-make Germany a Great Power. In the making he became the best hated man in Germany and the best abused man in Europe. He fought his own King, his own Parliament, his own people, and the jealousy of Europe, and overcame all. German Nationalism had got itself mixed up with ideas of democracy and universal brotherhood. Bismarck candidly and brutally told Germany that democracy and universal brotherhood were not in his line. He had no use for them. All he cared about was making Germany Germany. He was a German, nothing more. He laughed at the doctrinaires and university professors who dominated German politics, and who sought to re-make Germany by drafting paper Constitutions. Germany, he told them, could be re-made only by blood and iron. When the German Parliament denounced him he crushed the German Parliament beneath his heel and went on to make Germany with his specific. He had no notion of letting the babblers drive him to death as they had driven List.

Bismarck did not come into leadership until the period of the Franco-Prussian War He was, as the head of Prussian politics before that time remarked. too much of an idealist for the positive art of politics. During the Franco-Austrian War the subordinate idealist influenced his leaders sufficiently to keep Prussia well out of the conflict. Later on his lot was cast in Paris and London, where the great politicians were highly amused at him "You are not a serious man," said Napoleon III. to Bismarck in Paris. Disraeli in London was highly diverted by the Prussian Baron who talked so frankly about a regenerated Germany. He caricatured him in the name of Count Ferroll, and gave him a place in one of his novels, where he made him say, "I will never have anything to do with new Constitutions. Instead of making a new Constitution I shall make a nation —by blood and iron." When Bismarck returned to Prussia the King made him his right-hand man. The Press of Europe was very much amused. The Press of Germany was savage. The Press of Europe spoke of Bismarck as a demented Minister. The Press of Germany represented him as a tyrant—which he was for Germany's sake. When the Parliament refused to vote him supplies to govern, he most unconstitutionally ignored the Parliament and took the supplies. When it frantically denounced him, he laughed in its face. He was there to make Germany, he told his enemies defiantly, and he would make it in spite of Parliaments and people who had no sense whatever. Probably no man ever exasperated his countrymen more than Bismarck did—they assailed his life, and he smiled back at them—loving them all the time. Nothing they could say, no blow they could strike him, made him swerve from his object. The Germans are children—they must be made into men—blood and iron is the medicine. That was Bismarck's creed.

In 1863 his first collision with England came. The Russian Poles had risen in revolt. Prussia had her own Poles to fear. England expressed great indignation at the action of Prussia. The Prussian Liberals and Democrats did the same. Bismarck remained unmoved. Napoleon III. suggested to England that France and England should jointly intervene. But this was not in the English programme. Her sympathy was not intended to be active. Instead she suggested to Russia that the Russians should permit the Poles to look after their own affairs. The Russian Press advised England to apply her own advice to Ireland first. England retired, and the Poles were speedily subdued. Bismarck became equally unpopular with the English and the majority of the Germans. To English criticism he made no reply—to his own countrymen he bluntly said his role was not the friend of man, but the friend of Germany.

The next year increased his unpopularity. The King of Denmark, who was also Duke of Schleswig-Holstein, as the Kings of England had at one time been also Kings of Hanover, died. Schleswig-Holstein was three-fourths German, and Denmark, holding that Schleswig-Holstein should be a part of Denmark, had been long engaged in its Danification. Bismarck desired the provinces principally because the possession of Kiel was essential to Germany becoming a naval Power. Denmark incorporated the provinces by Act of Parliament. Bismarck urged strong action. He found the King, the Parliament, and the people against him. and England threatening. "If," said Lord Palmerston in the English House of Commons, "any attempt be made to violate the rights of Denmark, those who make the attempt will find that it is not with Denmark only they have to count." The "Times" newspaper announced that if war were made on Denmark, Denmark could rely on England. War was made on Denmark. Denmark, relying on England, refused Bismarck's offer of compromise, and dared him to come on. Bismarck, by a dexterous move, induced Austria to join with him, and the two Powers fell upon the Danes, who fought bravely, waiting for England to come to their help. But England stayed at home and sent her sympathy instead. Lord Palmerston informed them that they had English public opinion with them, and "opinion was stronger than arms."

In the result Schleswig-Holstein was taken from Denmark and divided between Austria and Prussia. Bismarck had now the foundation on which to make Germany a sea Power. He applied to Parliament for money to start his navy with, and his Parliament, hating him, refused it—what did Germany want with warships? Bismarck then went ahead to make his navy without Parliament.

Why did England not go to the assistance of Denmark in 1864? Why did she permit Bismarck to get possession of Kiel? There were several reasons.

War with Prussia in 1864 meant war with Austria and all the States of Germany. This would have been a costly and expensive affair.

Bismarck's idea of a regenerated and powerful Germany was laughed at by all English statesmen, and formed food for jokes in "Punch" and satire in Disraeli's novels.

The possibility of a permanently united Germany with a powerful German fleet was never once contemplated.

France, in the tradition of Pitt, was regarded by all English statesmen as the enemy, and it was held that a weakened Germany would strengthen France.

The Fenian movement in Ireland was at its zenith, and a war between England and Prussia and Austria would have precipitated insurrection in Ireland, and necessitated a large part of the British army being kept in Ireland.

These were the considerations that induced England to break her pledges to the Danes in 1864. and let Prussia, by seizing Kiel, get her foot in the stirrup. Having got it there, Bismarck proceeded with the second part of his policy. His whole policy may be stated in four lines.

(1) To secure Kiel as a base for a German navy.

(2) To dethrone Austria from the hegemony of Germany and to weld the States of Germany together under the leadership of Prussia.

(3) Having thus secured German military unity, to attack and defeat France and make the German Empire the first land Power.

(4) Thereafter to build up German naval power to the end of challenging English dominance on the ocean.

Not a single statesman in Europe saw where Bismarck was going. Had they done so, Prussia would have been cut in pieces by England, France and Austria. The annexation of Kiel and the hegemony of Germany won at Sadowa meant little to English statesmanship. It was engaged in dragooning Ireland when Bismarck was engaged in clearing the way for Germany to seize England's place in the world. If there had been no Mr. Pitt to pass the Act of Union there would have been no Ireland whose necessary repression occupied English statesmen and blinded them to what the seizure of Kiel and the submission of the German States to the King of Prussia spelled.

XV.—THE FRANCO-PRUSSIAN WAR.

The Austro-Prussian war that followed on the defeat of Denmark was inevitable, yet Bismarck found difficulty in persuading Prussia to undertake it. Saxony, Bavaria, and some of the smaller States joined Austria against Prussia. Prussia secured Italy as an ally, and flung herself like a tornado on her foes. The Austrians went down before her like chaff before the wind. Austria had no friendly Hungary to help her this time. Six weeks after the declaration of war Prussia dictated the terms of peace in Prague. By the peace of Prague Austria lost her headship of the German Empire, Prussia became head of the North German States, but South Germany remained outside. Italy secured repossession of Venice. Hungary received back the Free Constitution which in 1848 Austria had suppressed.

Bismarck could not stop here. It was necessary to the unification of Germany that France should be met and beaten. So long as France remained the power she was, the South German States could not be combined in the grand Germany he had planned. The Franco-Prussian War was a sequel inevitable to the Austro-Prussian War. France recognised this, but despised her enemy. She counted on South Germany either actively supporting her or maintaining a benevolent neutrality. When war broke out, France found that the dislike of Prussia cherished by the South German States was not strong enough to make German war on German or even stand aside. The Southern States of Germany made common cause with Prussia, and France fell even more completely before the Prussian arms than Austria had done. On the 18th of January, 1871, the King of Prussia was crowned German Emperor in Versailles by the unanimous vote of all the German States.

The sympathy of England was with Germany in the Franco-Prussian War. Faithfully following out Pitt's idea that France was the one enemy to fear, England regarded France's annihilation as a gain to herself. She failed to realise at the time that the Germany which rose upon France's ruin would become a more serious menace than France had been since Napoleon's day. It was good policy from the English standpoint to let France be defeated. It was the worst of policy to let her be annihilated. A bold English statesman, not obsessed by the Pitt policy, would have followed one of two courses. He would either have joined the strength of England with that of Germany in attacking France and taken the lion's share of the fruits of victory, or he would have intervened on the French side when it was evident that France was bound to fail, and dictated the terms of peace. To let France be so utterly crushed that she no longer formed even a menace to Germany was the acme of stupidity when England gained nothing by the crushing. The intervention of England in the war in its middle stage would have forced Prussia to be content with much less than she obtained and secured that neither France nor Germany could hope for generations to effectively challenge English supremacy. France would have been stronger to-day than she is—Germany weaker, and the two Powers would have fairly balanced power on the Continent, leaving England to play the part Lord Palmerston described as the " Judicious Bottle-holder." The Franco-Prussian War made Germany a unit, as the Danish War made her a sea-power, and there was no statesman in England to understand the meaning in 1865 of the seizure of Kiel, or in 1871 of the Coronation of a German Emperor in

Versailles. All that England saw, in the light of the policy Pitt left her, was the annihilation of her old enemy, France. That Germany could ever menace her as France had done was unthinkable.

Bismarck, who understood the English politicians better than any man in Europe, foresaw this. He knew England would not intervene, for, as he implies in his memoirs, he knew England had no statesmen. He realised that if England joined with Germany in attacking France, Germany would not reap the reward he wished. He therefore refrained from anything that might induce her to do so, and he felt that English policy, obsessed by the vision of France as the enemy to fear, would keep England from coming to France's aid. His conclusions were fully justified.

English mobs in English towns cheered the news of Prussia's victories in 1870. In 1911 England is forced to arrange an entente cordiale with France, a treaty with Japan, and make overtures to the United States, to ensure her against the ultimate results of the victories she hailed with enthusiasm, believing with the man who garotted the Irish Parliament and made the Empire wholly an English possession, that with France humbled England must rule the world.

XVI.—MR. GLADSTONE.

The Franco-German War relieved England from serious fear of France, but it did not warn her of the obvious—the emergence of Germany as a rival. From 1870 to 1890 England entertained nothing stronger than dislike of Germany. Her active hostility was transferred to Russia. Disraeli was chiefly responsible for this policy. A brilliant and audacious man without depth, he inaugurated that era of dramatic statesmanship in English politics which has produced Mr. Balfour, Mr. Lloyd George, Mr. Churchill and Mr. Austen Chamberlain. Gladstone, a profounder type, who saw clearly that an anti-Russian policy could not serve England, saved English interests for the time by adopting Disraelian tactics, and raising a melodramatic agitation over " Bulgarian atrocities " which were chiefly manufactured at the English Liberal headquarters. Gladstone thus averted war with Russia, which, although England might have been nominally victorious, would have permanently injured her. In two years he beat Disraeli and assumed office. The policy he inaugurated was extension of the Empire without conflict with European Powers. By improving his friendship with Russia he got guarantees for his Indian frontier which the Disraelian wars in Afghanistan had endangered, and by his seizure of Egypt in 1882 he secured the only other real road to India against all rivals.

In South Africa his policy was marked by the same caution. The revolt of the Transvaal Boers, to whom after he had returned to office he broke his word, threatened at one time to interfere with the plans he had made for the subjugation of Egypt. After Majuba, when the Orange Free State Boers notified him privately that if he persisted they would go to the help of their Transvaal brethren, Gladstone had the courage to haul down his flag in Africa—a courage none of the limelight statesmen who succeeded him in office could ever display. Gladstone had to choose between South Africa and Egypt, and he chose Egypt. South Africa it was possible to get back later on, but Egypt not seized on at once was lost for ever.

Yet Gladstone, although infinitely superior to his rivals, the Disraelis and the Salisburys, as a statesman, was equally blind as them to the menace of Germany. Day by day that nation grew in strength—slowly but certainly its toy navy grew into the fifth class, then the fourth, then the third, and England did not read the meaning. In Africa and in Asia England extended her Empire, and did not understand the significance of Bismarck's pronouncement that Europe had become an armed camp because England was eating up the earth and leaving no outlet for other nations to expand. England seemed to grow in wealth and power each day, until when the Triple Alliance and the Dual Alliance were formed, and both sought England's partnership, she replied that she stood alone, supreme, in "Splendid Isolation."

It is little more than twenty years since that boast was made by the British Government and echoed by the British Press—England's haughty defiance of the whole world in arms. It is within the memory of every man of forty years of age that England with contempt refused alliance with every other Power, and asserted in her Press that she was in herself more than a match for Germany, Austria and Italy combined on the one hand, or France and Russia combined on the other. And not only did she believe her own boast, but the other nations believed it also. From that time until 1899 England was mistress of the world. She slighted Austria, snubbed Italy, insulted France, and ignored Russia and Germany. But all the time Germany continued building up her fleet.

In 1899, Gladstone being dead, she embarked on the South African War. While Gladstone lived it was impossible for any English Government to make such a war, for he had threatened to return to public life and oppose the Government that did so with the same methods, if necessary, with which he dished Disraeli. Gladstone's plan for the absorption of the Boer Republics did not include war. His plan was to hem the Boers in a ring-fence of British Colonies and permit them no outlet to the sea. In time he calculated

that as they could make no progress they would yield peace-
fully and take the status of British Colonies. This policy
had been tacitly agreed to by both Parties in England after
1881, but the discovery of gold in the Transvaal and the
impatience of Cecil Rhodes to become head of an United
States of South Africa, determined the South African War
once Gladstone was dead. So when Gladstone—her last semi-
statesman—had been a little over a year in his grave England embarked on the crowning blunder of her adherence to
the Pitt policy—the war against the Boer Republics.

XVII.—CONCLUSION.

England came back from the Boer War—which she entered
with the usual declaration from her Premier (Mr. Balfour)
that she was fighting for "Liberty and Righteousness"—
with her prestige lower than it had been for a hundred
years. "Splendid Isolation" was no longer possible, and
she was compelled to seek Alliances. She found Allies in her
old enemies France and Russia, and since she found them
her statesmen have been busy in encircling Germany in a
ring of steel.

This is Pitt—the A B C of Pitt's Continental policy—
" No one Continental Power must be permitted to dominate
the Continent. Against any Power seeking the hegemony
of the Continent combinations of other Continental Powers,
supported by the English fleet, must be formed." Germany
in the twentieth century is to England as France in the
eighteenth and nineteenth, and Spain in the sixteenth. It
is the fortune, or misfortune, of the German Kaiser to
stand in the same relation to English policy as did Philip
of Spain, Louis XIV., and Napoleon Bonaparte. One day
that ring of steel will be drawn tight, and then war will
happen. One day England will again stand at the head of
a strong European Coalition; and Germany, in its turn,
like France, must face a world in arms.

It needs no gift of prophecy to foresee so much. It is
plain to the student of English policy. It may be in a few
years, or it may not be for twenty, but the world will
assuredly rock with a war waged to secure the hegemony
of Europe—a war that Pitt's policy has made inevitable.
If England win that war, then for another century Pitt's
name will be glorified and Pitt's policy will continue to
rule and ruin our country. If England lose that war, then
the doctrine of England Over-All, which Pitt labelled
" Imperialism," will go out of fashion. England will realise
that the man who substituted Patriotism by Imperialism
was not a real statesman, but a very daring gambler.

In the day when England is again fighting for her absolutism her leaders will look for Ireland's aid, and they will

shriek " Loyalty to the Empire " in Ireland's ear. Thus Austria shrieked in Hungary's ear when Austria was grappling with Prussia. But Ireland, if she be in sanity, will not be deluded. The fruits of Pitt's policy to her have been the extermination of half her people, the paralysis of her commerce and industry, the devastation of her soil, and the loss of her place in Europe.

And now to the Irish Unionists—those so-called Imperialists—to whom I have really written these articles, I say: William Pitt, whose Act of Union you laud, was not only the destroyer of Ireland's organised nationhood. He will prove in time the destroyer of England's Empire. In his time there was an organised Irish nation co-equal with England. He struck it down. He served out to Ireland degradation and misery to the end that his England might be the more prosperous and exalted. He taught by example that the weakness of Ireland was the strength of England, and the statesmen of England have consistently followed his implicit teaching. A hundred years after his death they can look upon Ireland and say, " Behold. We graze the bullocks where the homesteads of four millions stood. We have made of Ireland the one country in Europe where the people yearly diminish. We have strengthened England. We have carried out Pitt's policy."

It is true. They have made England tenfold richer and Ireland tenfold poorer than when William Pitt walked the earth. But, while they were busy so doing, there grew up unnoticed in their pre-occupation a challenge to their life stronger than the challenge of Spain or France. The spectre of Germany to-day hagrides English statesmanship. When William Pitt struck down Ireland by the Act of Union he made modern Germany possible. When William Pitt made it certain that, instead of an independent and prosperous Ireland in the year A.D. 1911, with 20,000,000 of people in friendly relations with the neighbouring islanders, there should be an enslaved and impoverished Ireland with 4,000,000 of people hating most justifiably their neighbouring oppressors, he made the European situation of 1911. English Imperialism decreed that Ireland must be struck down and kept down. English Imperialism succeeded so well that England's rival will have no Irish enemy to face. England produced a Pitt—Austria produced a Beust. When England fights for its life there will be no Ireland to support her—when Austria fights for its life Hungary will stand with Austria. England has taught Ireland to abandon hope of freedom except through England's destruction. This teaching she has styled Imperialism. In the day of her stress she will find that Irishmen have learned the true lesson of her Imperialism, and that they will hail her defeat as their salvation.

II.

THE SINN FEIN POLICY.

At the First Annual Convention of the National Council held in the Rotunda, on Tuesday, **November 28th, 1905,** under the presidency of Mr. Edward Martyn, Mr. Arthur Griffith outlined the Sinn Fein programme. He said the Irish people were a free people, and must continue to possess the rights of a free people until, of their own free will, they renounce them. Any external power that attempted to control, or did by force control their free action, was a tyranny, and it was the first duty of the citizen to oppose and seek to end that tyranny. In Ireland this tyranny styled itself "the Government," and to prevent its real character from being apprehended by the nation, it had caused an educational system to be modelled and forced upon the people designed to make them oblivious of their rights as men and their duties as citizens. All departments of education in Ireland—primary, secondary, and university —were directly controlled by the British Government. The language of Ireland, the history of Ireland, the economics of Ireland, the possibilities of Ireland, the rights of Ireland, therefore found no place in their curricula. . . . The primary school system controlled by a Government Board was a system intended to perpetuate that ignorance which the British Penal Laws once made legally compulsory. The pupil was not taught to look out upon the world from his own country. It taught him he had no country, and therefore no national standard of comparison and value. He was forced to accept instead the standard of England. The secondary system of education in Ireland, controlled by a Board of British nominees was designed to prevent the trained intelligence of the country performing its duty to the Irish State. In other countries secondary education gives to each its leaders in industry and commerce, its great middle class which as society is constituted forms the equalising and harmonising element in the population. In Ireland secondary education causes aversion and contempt for industry and "trade" in the heads of young Irishmen, and fixes their eyes like the fool's, on the ends of the earth. The secondary system in Ireland draws away from industrial pursuits those who are best fitted for them, and sends them to be civil servants in England, or to swell the ranks of struggling clerkdom in Ireland.

The Object of Secondary Education

is to fit persons of average ability for those pursuits for

which they have aptitude. That is its object elsewhere than
in Ireland, where one Blitish Government Department
excuses itself at the cost of another—where the Department
of Agriculture defends its importation of foreigners to discharge the work which in cther countries is discharged by
the products of secondary education, on the ground that
secondary education in Ireland produces no men or women
capable of doing what its importations are asked to do.

University Education in Ireland

is regarded by the classes in Ireland as a means of washing
away the original sin of Irish birth. It is founded on the
inversion of Aristotle, as indeed the three systems of education in Ireland are. The young men who go to Trinity
College are told by Aristotle that the end of education is
to make men patriots ; and by the professors of Trinity not
to take Aristotle literally. Education in Ireland encumbers
the intellect, chills the fancy, debases the soul, and enervates
the body. It cuts off the Irishman from his tradition, and
by denying him a country debases his soul, it stores his mind
with lumber and nonsense, it destroys his fancy by depriving
him of tradition, and enervates his body by denying him
physical culture. Sir, this is the education which, as Aristotle says, ruins the individual and eventually the nation.
For he lays it down that any system of education which does
those things—which tends to debase the soul, chill the
fancy, encumber the intellect, enervate the body—is inju-
rious to the individual and destructive to the nation. If
he lived in our times and our country, Aristotle would be a
seditious person in the eyes of the British Government in
Ireland, which makes him useful to it now by standing him
on his head. The funds provided out of the pockets of the
Irish people for education in Ireland are invested to the
children's moral and national destruction. Out of the
primary schools come the recruits for the British armed
forces. . . . As the outcome of our secondary system of
education, the men who should be captains of the nation's
battalions are rendered unfit for service. As the outcome
of our University system we have bigotry and distrust.

How are we to Remedy These Things?

As to primary education, a friend of mine in London has
made suggestions which I believe are practicable. If the
control of primary education is not voluntarily transferred
from the British Government in Ireland to the Irish people,
let the Irish people take over the primary education system
themselves. They can do this . . by founding voluntary
schools, sustained in part by the contributions of the parents
and in part by a National Education Fund subscribed to
annually by the Irish people throughout the world. Is this

considered impossible? Hungary did it forty years ago—
Poland did it but yesterday, and the one overthrew Austria,
as the other is overthrowing Russian autocracy. But our
motto in this is festina lente. We cannot afford to withdraw
in a mass the school-going children of Ireland from the
National Schools. If we did so at present, we have no
sufficient resources at hand to cope with the educational
crisis that would be created. A period of educating public
opinion on the vital importance of the matter, and of pre-
paration for coping with the demand for a really national
system of education, will place us in the position we require;
and at the end of that period, if control of the primary
education system be withheld, then we may, as the Nationalists of Poland did within recent days, order a school strike,
and replace the present system by one which shall teach hte
Irish child to glory in his country and desire to serve her.
As to the Irishising of the secondary system, I look with
confidence for a beginning to the Irish Christian Brothers
to throw over the Intermediate Board and substitute it by
a system devised by themselves in conjunction with representatives of the Gaelic League and Irish educationists who
are also Irishmen. Pioneers in primary education the Irish
Christian Brothers were—let them gain again a noble dis-
tinction by pioneering a secondary system of education such
as Ireland needs. We can promise them that that Irish
nation which is coming into existence will see that they
do not suffer as a consequence of cutting themselves clear
from the Intermediate. . . . To substitute the de-nationalising
system of education in this country by a nationalising system
rests with ourselves, not with the British Legislature. If
it is worth having, it is worth making sacrifices to obtain,
and if the same spirit which prevail in Hungary, Finland,
and Poland—the spirit of self-reliance—be evoked in Ireland, it must be obtained. Next in importance to the education question in this country is

The Question of Our Industries,

and the greatest of these is agriculture; but agriculture in
Ireland is resolving itself into the cattle trade. The tilled
land of Ireland has decreased by one-fourth during the last
generation. Over a million acres which were crop-bearing
in 1871 are now grazing ground. . . If the soil of Ireland is
again to be brought into cultivation—and it is vital this
should be done—it is necessary that the County Councils,
which now by premiums encourage grazing, should withdraw
these premiums and allot them to tillage. A necessary orga-
nisation is an agricultural and manufacturing union—a
union of manufacturers and farmers—classes who at the
present time, through an extraordinary delusion, are
unfriendly to each other, and fail to realise their inter-

dependence. The farmer is indifferent about the industrial revival, failing to realise the increased market an Ireland with a manufacturing arm means to the agriculturist; the manufacturer is indifferent to the agricultural interest, failing to realise that the extension of agriculture—the extension of tillage—means the extension of the market for his products. It is one of the worst anomalies in this country that our manufacturing population should be largely subsisting on foreign food. There is no reason whatever for such a state of things. It is due to the ignorance of elementary economics. . . I am

In Economics

largely a follower of the man who thwarted England's dream of the commercial conquest of the world and who made the mighty confederaticn before which England has fallen commercially and is falling politically—Germany. His name is a famous one in the outside world, his works are the text-books of economic science in other countries—in Ireland his name is unheard and his works unknown—I refer to Frederich List, the real founder of the German Zollverein— the man whom England caused to be persecuted by the Government of his native country, and whom she hated and feared more than any man since Napoleon—the man who saved Germany from falling a prey to English economics, and whose brain conceived the great industrial and united Germany of to-day. Germany has hailed Frederich List by the title of Preserver of the Fatherland, Louis Kossuth hailed him as

The Economic Teacher of the Nations.

There is no room for him in the present educational system of Ireland. With List—whose work on the National System of Political Economy I would wish to see in the hands of every Irishman—I reject that so-called political economy which neither recognises the principle of nationality nor takes into consideration the satisfaction of its interests, which regards chiefly the mere exchangeable value of things without taking into consideration the mental and political, the present and the future interests and the productive powers of the nation, which ignores the nature and character of social labour and the operation of the union of powers in their higher consequences, considers private industry only as it would develop itself under a state of free interchange with the whole human race were it not divided into separate nations. Let me continue in the words of this great man to define the nation. Brushing aside the fallacies of Adam Smith and his tribe, List points out that

Between the Individual and Humanity stands, and must continue to stand, a great fact—the Nation.

The Nation, with its special language and literature, with

its peculiar origin and history, with its special manners and customs, laws and institutions, with the claims of all these for existence, independence, perfection, and continuance for the future, and with its separate territory, a society which, united by a thousand ties of minds and interests, combines itself into one independent whole, which recognises the law of right for and within itself, and in its united character is still opposed to other societies of a similar kind in their national liberty, and consequently can only, under the existing conditions of the world, maintain self-existence and independence by its own power and resources. As the individual chiefly obtains by means of the nation, and in the nation, mental culture, power of production, security and prosperity, so is the civilisation of the human race only conceivable and possible by means of the civilisation and development of individual nations. But as there are amongst men infinite differences in condition and circumstances, so are there in nations—some are strong, some are weak, some are highly civilised, some are half-civilised, but in all exists as in the unit the impulse of self-preservation and the desire for improvement

It is the task of National Politics to ensure existence and continuance to the Nation,

to make the weak strong, the half-civilised more civilised. It is the task of National Economics to accomplish the economic development of the nation and fit it for admission into the universal society of the future. I now take List's definition of a normal nation such as we desire to see Ireland. "It should," he says, "possess a common language and literature, a territory endowed with manifold natural resources, extensive and with convenient frontiers and a numerous population. Agriculture, manufactures, commerce and navigation must be all developed in it proportionately, arts and sciences, educational establishments, and universal cultivation must stand in it on equal footing with material production. Its constitution, laws and institutions must afford to those who belong to it a high degree of security and liberty, and must promote religion, morality, and prosperity. It must possess sufficient power to defend its independence and to protect its foreign commerce." Sir, in the economy of Adam Smith there is no place for the soul of a nation. To him the associations of its past possess no value; but in the economy of the man who made out of the petty and divided States of the Rhine the great Germany we see to-day there is a place, and it is the highest. True political economy recognises that prompt cash payment, to use Mitchel's phrase, is not the sole nexus between man and man—that there is a higher value than a cash value, and that higher value nationality possesses. When the German Commercial League sixty years ago exhorted all to stand together for a Germany such as we see to-day, it appealed to what its great economist had taught it was the highest value in economics—nationality. Can we imagine our manufacturers addressing our people as these German manufacturers did? Perhaps we can; but we can only imagine it occurring at some distant period when they have realised the value of a national spirit. Listen:—" Every misfortune that we have suffered for centuries past may be traced to one cause; and that is that we have ceased to consider ourselves a united nation of brothers, whose first duty is to exert our common efforts to oppose the common enemy. . . . More beautiful than the spring of nature—more beautiful than any picture created by poetical imagination—more beautiful than the death of the hero resigning his life for the benefit of his country, is the dawning of a new and glorious era for Germany. That which has been gradually vanishing from us since the days of the Hohenstauffen Emperors—that which is indespensable to enable us to fulfil the destiny marked out for us in the history of the world—that which alone is wanting to render us the mightiest of all the nations of the earth, viz., the feeling of national honour—we are now about to recover. For what object have our honoured patriots been striving? To imbue the people with the feeling of national honour." I shall detain you with Friedrich List, because he is unknown in the country which now needs his teaching most. We in Ireland have been taught by our English Lords Lieutenant our British Education Boards, and our Barrington Lecturers, that our destiny is to be the fruitful mother of flocks and herds—that it is not necessary for us to pay attention to our manufacturing arm, since our agricultural arm is all-sufficient. The fallacy dissolves before reflection—but it is a fallacy which has passed for truth in Ireland. With List I reply: A nation cannot promote and further its civilisation, its prosperity, and its social progress equally as well by exchanging agricultural products for manufactured goods as by establishing a manufacturing power of its own. A merely agricultural nation can never develop to any extent a home or a foreign commerce, with inland means of transport and foreign navigation, increase its population in due proportion to their well-being, or make notable progress in its moral, intellectual, social and political development: it will never acquire important political power or be placed in a position to influence the cultivation and progress of less advanced nations and to form colonies of its own. A mere agricultural state is infinitely less powerful than an agricultural-manufacturing state. The former is always economically and politically dependent on those foreign nations which take

from it agriculture in exchange for manufactured goods. It
cannot determine how much it will produce—it must wait
and see how much others will buy from it. The agricultural-
manufacturing states, on the contrary, produce for themselves large quantities of raw materials and provisions, and
supply merely the deficiency from importation. The purely
agricultural nations are thus dependent for the power of
effecting sales on the chances of a more or less bountiful
harvest in the agricultural-manufacturing nations. They
have, moreover, to compete in their sales with other purely
agricultural nations, whereby the power of sale in itself is
uncertain—they are exposed to the danger of ruin in their
trading with agricultural-manufacturing nations by war or
new tariffs, whereby they suffer the double disadvantage of
finding no buyers for their surplus agricultural products and
of failing to obtain supplies of the manufactured goods they
require. An agricultural nation is a man with one arm who
makes use of an arm belonging to another person, but cannot, of course, be sure of having it always available. An
agricultural-manufacturing nation is a man who has two
arms of his own at his own disposal. Again, List points out
that the relative cultivation of the agricultural and manufacturing arms of a country possessed of an ample and fertile
territory will give that country a population twice to three
times as large as it could secure by the development of the
agricultural arm alone, and maintain this vastly increased
population in a much higher degree of comfort. Surplus
agricultural produce, as he points out, is not necessarily
capital in an agricultural country. Countries which produce
such a surplus and remain dependent on manufacturing
countries are often obliged to purchase these manufactured
goods at an enhanced price. To warn his countrymen of the
effects of the as-good-and-as-cheap policy which England was
endeavouring to thrust on Europe, he pointed to the fate of
Poland, which, as Montesquieu has said, would have become
prosperous and stable if it had developed its manufacturing
arm—by, even if it could do so by no other means, introducing foreign manufacturers and foreign capital. Poland
did not do this; she lived idolently on her agriculture, and,
like Ireland, produced no middle class. She exported the
fruits of her soil to obtain the goods which she could have
manufactured on it. As a consequence she fell like a house
of cards when organised nations attacked her. List considers
that had she developed her manufacturing arm, besides retaining her national independence, she would have exceeded
any other European country in prosperity. To the advocates
of as-good-and-as-cheap economics he turns from the con-
templation of Poland, and says: "Go to fallen Poland, and
ask its hapless people now whether it is advisable for a
nation to buy the fabrics of a foreign country so long as its

N

native manufacturers are not sufficiently strengthened to be able to compete in price and quality with the foreigners."

Let the Irish people get out of their heads the insane idea that the agricultural and manufacturing industries are opposed. They are necessary to each other, and one cannot be injured without the other suffering hurt. We must further clear their minds of the pernicious idea that they are not entitled or called upon to give preferential aid to the manufacturing industries of their own country. Sir, if that idea were not met and combatted there would be an end to all hope of the development of an Irish manufacturing arm. "My object," said List, "is at all costs to save Germany from the destruction which the commercial policy of England designs for her." Our object is, at all costs, to save Ireland. "On the development of the German protective system," List wrote, "depends the existence, the independence, and the future of German nationality. Only in the soil of general prosperity does the national spirit strike its root, produce fine blossoms and rich fruits—only from the unity of material interests does mental power arise, and again, from both of them national power." The fruit of List's teaching is the Germany of to-day.

It is part of the Policy of the National Council to bring about that Unity of Material Interests which produces National Strength—

to convince the manufacturer that every improvement in agriculture will increase his home market, and the agriculturist that every extension of the manufacturing industry will promote his welfare—convince both that there can be no permanent prosperity for either unless the nation as a whole is prosperous. We must offer our producers protection where protection is necessary, and let it be clearly understood

What Protection is.

Protection does not mean the exclusion of foreign competition—it means rendering the native manufacturer equal to meeting foreign competition. It does not mean that we shall pay a higher profit to any Irish manufacturer, but that we must not stand by and see him crushed by mere weight of foreign capital. If an Irish manufacturer cannot produce an article as cheaply as an English or other foreigner, only because his foreign competitor has larger resources at his disposal, then it is the first duty of the Irish nation to accord protection to that Irish manufacturer. If, on the other hand, an Irish manufacturer can produce as cheaply, but charges an enhanced price, such a man deserves no support—he is, in plain words, a swindler. It is the duty of our public bodies, in whose hands the expenditure of

£4,000,000 annually is placed, to pay where necessary an enhanced price for Irish-manufactured articles, when the mnufacturers show that they cannot produce them at a lesser price—that is Protection. It is also the duty of the individual; but it is contrary to the principle of Protection and the interests of the country that a manufacturer in Ireland who can produce as cheaply as his foreign competitors should receive an enhanced price. The movement is one to give Ireland back her manufacturing arm, not to make fortunes for dishonest manufacturers. With the development of her manufacturing arm will proceed the rise of a national middle class in Ireland and a trained national democracy, and—I here again quote List against the charlatans who profess to see in a nation's language and traditions things of no economic value—" in every nation will the authority of national language and national literature, the civilising arts and the perfection of municipal institutions, keep pace with the development of the manufacturing arm."

How are we to accord Protection to and procure the Development of our Manufacturing Arm?

First, by ourselves individually; secondly, through our County, Urban, and District Councils and Poor Law Guardians; thirdly, by taking over the control of the inefficient bodies known as Harbour Commissioners; fourthly, by stimulating our manufacturers and our people to industrial enterprise; and fifthly, by inviting to aid in our development, on commercial lines, Irish capital. In the first case, every individual knows his duty, whether he practises it or not—it is, unless where fraud is attempted, to use where possible none but Irish goods. As to our public elective bodies, which annually control the expenditure of our local taxation, their duty is the same. The duty of our harbour bodies is to arrange the incidence of port dues so that they shall fall most heavily on manufactured goods coming into the country, and to keep and publish a table of all goods imported, and to whom consigned. In all these respects our Harbour Boards at present fail. They are in most cases composed of English shipping representatives and Irish traders in competing foreign goods, whose interests are diametrically opposed to the interests of the Irish nation. With some difficulty the Dublin Port and Docks Board has been forced to publish an annual return of the foreign goods imported into the capital of Ireland by sea, and the return has appalled all who read it; but the Cork Harbour Board has declined to do the same thing for Cork, and the other Harbour Boards around Ireland do as Cork does. Sir, is this to be tolerated? We want to know what the foreign goods are which come into every port in Ireland, we want to know whence they come, and we want to know who receives them—we want to

know what it is open to every citizen of a free country to
know, but which we are insolently denied. We want the
port taxation removed from raw materials and placed on
manufactured goods. We are told that this taxation is so
small that it would be inappreciable. Small it is, I know,
but not inappreciable. A few years ago some of us sought
to have the incidence of port taxation altered in Dublin; and
the Port and Docks Board, so far from considering the
matter insignificant, fought as fiercely as ever it fought to
prevent increased dues being placed upon manufactured
goods brought into the port of Dublin—very small, indeed,
the increase in taxation would have been, but

It would have given Ireland the Principle of Protection.

Our Harbour Boards must be manned for Ireland by men who
desire to benefit Ireland, not by the shipping agents of
English firms and importers of ready-made doors; a general
scheme of port taxation must be adopted throwing the bulk
of our port dues on manufactured goods, and a perfect tally
must be kept at our ports of such goods, whence they come,
to whom they are consigned and the tally must be published
once a month. Let this be done and the dullest of our
people will be forced to realise what is taking place in the
country industrially, and, perhaps, the spirit of nationality
will stir them to draw forth some of that £50,000,000 lodged
in the so-called Irish banks—which in turn lodge it in the
British and Colonial funds—and invest it in the industrial
enterprises of their own country. . . . We can offer the
investors of capital 400,000,000 tons of coal, the finest stone
in Europe, and an inexhaustible supply of peat to operate
on, and we can offer them all the facilities possessed by the
County Councils and Rural Councils of Ireland, and the
assistance and goodwill of the Irish people in turning our
coal, our stone, and our turf into gold. They can offer us
in return profitable employment for our people, and an enormous increase of strength socially, politically, and commercially. . . . . . I shall pass from this phase of our
situation by quoting the words List addressed to Germany
in its making:—"Let us only have courage to believe in a
great national future, and in the belief, march onward.
Above all, let us have national spirit enough to at once plant
and protect that tree which will yield its richest fruits to
the future generation. First, let us gain possession of the
home market, so far at least as respects articles of general
necessity; and secondly, let us try to procure the goods of
other countries direct from those countries and to pay for
them with our own manufactured goods" Naturally,

The Question of a Mercantile Marine

arises in this connection. Ireland has, practically speaking

no mercantile marine. A few coasting and cross-channel
vessels, and three small lines of steamers running to Continental ports, is all that is left of the once great commercial
fleet of Ireland. The mercantile marine of Ireland at one
time was important in the world. Between the end of the
sixteenth century and 1777 it dwindled as the consequences
of the laws directed against it by England—until at the latter date it was of no importance. The Volunteer movement,
by compelling England to cancel all her restrictive laws on
Irish commerce and shipping, brought again into existence a
powerful Irish mercantile marine, and its growth was so
rapid that within five years—in 1785—Tucker, the well-
known Dean of Gloucester, counselled English shipowners to
fit out vessels under the Irish national flag, since the
Irish marine was ousting the English out of several ports of
Europe. Sixty years ago Germany had little or no mercantile
marine, and shipped its goods in foreign bottoms. Friedrich
List urged upon his countrymen that it was vital they should
possess a marine of their own, and laid the foundation of the
magnificent marine Germany possesses to-day. The importance of a mercantile marine cannot be minimised—without the carrying trade England would be bankrupt and Norway non-existent. Norway with a population of less than
half our own, possesses a mercantile marine of 1,500,000
tons. Belgium, with a coast-line scarcely so long as that
of Dublin, is building up a good mercantile navy. The
American Government at the present time feels it so
essential to build up a great mercantile marine that it has
resolved to prohibit all commerce between the United States
and its foreign possessions except in American ships.
Through the lack of a mercantile marine we are debarred
from our best markets, deprived of our share in the world's
carrying trade, and are lost to Europe's interest. We lost
sixty years ago one of the greatest opportunities—a share in
the China trade—because we had no mercantile navy, and
as a consequence the China market knows nothing of our
linens, and we procure our tea through England. We lose for
the same reason to-day our share in the India trade, which
would be gladly given us if we had only a marine to work it,
and we are losing yearly our share in the European and
American trade for the same reason. What is our share?
Let us put it at the lowest, and say one per cent. The
countries from which we import outside England, comprise
the Republics of the Argentine, Chili, and the United States,
and the Dominion of Canada in America, eastward Australia
and Japan, and within Europe France, Germany, Belgium,
Holland, Spain, Portugal, Denmark, Italy, Austro-Hungary,
and Russia. The total annual imports of these countries
represents £2,000,000,000 sterling—one per cent. of that
trade would mean an increased revenue of £20,000,000 an-

nually to Ireland. Let us create an Irish marine and we shall obtain it. Why have we not this marine?

We have the Finest Naval Situation and the Best and Safest Harbours in Europe.

We have the material in abundance out of which sailors are made. We have £50,000,000 of money lying idle in our banks. It is because we have not the spirit of a free people —because we are taught to be dependent and look to and trust in a foreign Parliament when the people of other nations are taught to look to and trust in themselves. To establish such a marine, however, involves no extraordinary expense upon the nation. The great marine of Norway has been built up by its own people. There is scarcely a man in the towns and cities of Norway who is not part-owner of a ship. Instead of hoarding up their savings in banks, the workingmen of Norway and the shopkeepers of Norway invest it in ships. I have met many Norwegians—mostly workingmen—but I cannot remember that I ever met one who was not part-owner of a ship. Through the patriotism of her people, Norway has built up her great commercial navy, whose flag is familiar in every port in the world. A nearer country, Scotland, also possesses a very fine marine. Once in the Mediterranean I counted seventeen Scotch vessels of the "tramp" type. But I have seldom seen an Irish "tramp" steamer. A tramp line, for instance, between Ireland and South America, calling at French, Spanish. and other ports en route, could not fail to pay its owners, while it would open up for Ireland a lucrative trade and lower in Ireland itself the prices of those goods non-competing with our own which we now import via England. At the present time Ireland has little trade with any outside country, not because she does not produce many things which they require and which they buy, but because England blocks the way with her middleman's profit. So long as Ireland has no mercantile marine of her own and no

Consular Representation Abroad,

this must remain the case. The British Consular service is run solely in the interests of Britain, but Ireland is taxed to pay for its upkeep. The British Consul, of course, announces on his brass door-plate that he represents the United Kingdom of Great Britain and Ireland. The proportion he represents Great Britain and Ireland in the following figures show : Last year (1904) the "United Kingdom of Great Britain and Ireland " exported over three hundred and sixty million pounds' worth of goods ; of that total Great Britain exported three hundred and fifty-nine million pounds' worth, and Ireland one and a quarter million pounds' worth—that is, of the exports of "the United Kingdom of Great Britain and Ireland," Great Britain claims 99¾ per cent. and Ireland the remaining ¼. Of the total trade of the same "United Kingdom of Great Britain and Ireland" during the year, Great Britain's share was represented by 98.3 per cent. and Ireland's by 1.7—which means that out of every £100 worth of business done, as the result of the year's trading, Great Britain received £98 6s., and Ireland £1 14s., a result which equally exhibits the benefit Ireland derives from her connection with Great Britain and the efficiency of the Consular service—for Great Britain. The remedy for this state of affairs is for Ireland to appoint her own Consuls—to

Send Irishmen to act as Consuls in foreign countries, instead of sending them to orate in the British Parliament,

and to devote a portion of the £25,000 she at present expends in keeping eighty Irishmen in London to keeping about half that number of Irishmen stationed in the capitals and commercial centres of foreign countries, where a market may be found for Irish produce. At the present time Argentina procures one-third of her total imports from Great Britain, North America one-fifth, France one-seventh, Germany one-tenth, Spain, Russia, and Japan one-fifth each, Scandinavia one-fourth, Holland one-fourth, Hungary one-twelfth, Belgium one-twelfth, Australia one-third, and South Africa and India two-thirds. In return for giving Great Britain so much trade we in Ireland import from these countries, and consume, millions of pounds' worth of their products. We propose that in return for our consumption of the goods of the countries named, we should take our share in exporting goods to them. For this purpose, then, the National Assembly should choose and appoint from year to year competent men of business training, character, and linguistic knowledge to form

An Irish Consular Service,

and to act in all respects—save those which require the special exequatur granted to Consuls of independent nations —as the Consular servants of other countries do. The countries in which the appointment of Irish Consular representatives would, in all reasonable probability, lead to the opening up of profitable and extensive markets for the Irish producer are Argentina and Chili in South America, the United States, Canada, Australia, South Africa, France, Germany, Belgium, Holland, Spain, Russia, Japan, Denmark, Italy, and Austro-Hungary. There are possible fields for the Irish producer in every one of the countries named. One per cent. of the trade of these countries would, as I have said, mean an increased revenue of £20,000,000 annually for this country, and enable us to look forward to the near approach

of a time when the population of Ireland would again reach
the figure it stood at in 1845. The maintenance of a Consular
service of thirty or forty men would cost Ireland annually
about half the sum the maintenance of an Irish Parliamentary Party in London at present costs, and under no
circumstances could it fail to repay the outlay on it. So
much for oversea transit. Our internal system is as bad as
ignorance and selfishness can make it.

Owing to the attitude of our Railways the Development of the Country is materially hampered.

The Arigna coal mines, for instance, produce as good coal
as the best that Great Britain can produce, but owing to the
railway rates it is impossible to place it generally on the Irish
market. We cannot make up for the deficiency of the rail-
ways, but we can certainly do much to alleviate the present
situation by the popular utilisation of our semi-derelict canal
system. In this connection Ireland suffered a distinct loss
by the death of Mr. James M'Cann. A well-devised scheme
of canal and river service under the control of the County
Councils of Ireland will, however, go a considerable distance
in the direction of properly distributing the products of the
country. With

A Proper Transit System

in Ireland the interdependence of manufacturing and agricultural industry would become manifest, and a larger
market be created for both. By a proper transit system, as
the maker of industrial Germany pointed out, not merely
are the powers of labour of those who are employed in it
brought into activity, not only is the agricultural population
enabled to obtain from the natural resources which it possesses a greater return than before, but the wealth heretofore
lying idle in the earth becomes useful and profitable. Articles
such as coal, stone, salt, gypsum, marble, slate, timber,
which the freight of a few miles rendered before unprofitable
to work, become distributable over a whole country, and thus
the formerly valueless resources of a country become,
through good transit facilities, of a high importance in the
total of national production. This is what transit means to
our country. It is worth working hard to obtain. Now, let
us consider

The Poor Law System

of this country. Like the education system, it was forced
upon us by England, and with an equally sinister object. It
has been a potent instrument for pauperising and demoralising the people. From 1846 to 1849 it was used as a

machine for forcing the small farmers of Ireland into the workhouse or into the emigrant ship by the imposition of a crushing poor-rate. Since that period it has been used to impoverish the country by expending its money on foreign goods and by subsidising emigration, and to debase the spirit of the people by stamping pauper on the brow of every honest man and woman whom circumstances may for a period render dependent on the assistance of their fellow-citizens. In no other country in Europe—except in Great Britain itself—does such a degrading system exist. In France, in Italy, in Austro-Hungary, the State recognises the fact that periods may occur, and do occur, when industrious members of the community may, through circumstances for which they are not responsible, become impoverished, and it administers the necessary remedies without undermining the self-respect of the recipients. It does not strike them from the list of citizens or imprison them in a poorhouse. It fits them again to take a place in the industrial ranks. Neither do the Poor Law systems of the enlightened nations of Europe offer the poorhouse and a stigma to those who, after a life of honourable labour, are stricken by sickness or enfeebled by old age. They afford them, not as a charity but as a right, support in liberty. An ex-British Prime Minister last week (November, 1905) declared to his ignorant countrymen that in Germany the Government treated the poor as criminals. It is under the British flag that thing is done. The German system of Poor Law relief divides the poor into three classes —those who can and will work, those who are willing to work but are unable to do so, and those who can work and will not work. For the first class it finds work, for the second class it provides sustenance, not as charity, but as a right due to them; for the third class it provides the proper place, the prison. In Ireland for all classes the British Poor Law system provides the same remedy. Now, the position in Ireland is this: we have 159 Unions and 8,000 Guardians of the Poor elected by the people. It is not these Guardians' fault that the system is what I have described it, but it is their fault if they do not seek to neutralise its intention. When they vote the money of the Irish people to help on emigration and to purchase foreign goods they vote to further pauperise their country. Is there any land but this in which the Poor Law Guardians would dream of expending the poor-rate on purchasing foreign cloth to attire those who have been impoverished by lack of employment, and hire foreign tailors in foreign countries to make it up, or who would import from abroad the food to feed these people on, when their own country produced abundance of cloth and food? That which would be inconceivable in any other country, is the fact in Ireland. Above all taxes the poor-tax in other countries is directed to be expended within that country. In Ireland, the Guardians in the majority of instances expend it abroad, and thus keep continually adding to the total of pauperism with which they have to contend. As one of the means of extracting from the Poor Law system good for Ireland, we suggest that the 159 unions in Ireland, controlling the annual expenditure of a million and a-half of money, should in council draw up an official scale of union requirements, using uniform advertisements for goods of solely Irish material and manufacture, and print a scale of the various quantities necessary yearly for the collective unions. The action of the North Dublin Union in 1881 is an illustration of what could be done. In that year the Board decided to reverse the English as-good-and-as-cheap policy which it had heretofore pursued to the national injury, and to procure all its requisites, even though it had to pay an enhanced price, of Irish manufacture. When it could not procure what it exactly required of Irish manufacture, it procured something of Irish manufacture which served as a substitute. The result was, of course, that increased employment was provided in Dublin, and in the end the ratepayers gained to the extent of £800 a year. This year an attempt was made by the Local Government Board—one of whose primary duties is to push the interests of the British manufacturer in Ireland—to bluff the Irish Boards of Guardians into the acceptance of tenders for the supply of drugs sent by an English ring of manufacturers, whose object is to crush out the Irish druggists. In an excellent letter addressed to the Board of Guardians, the Cork Chemical and Drug Co., Ltd., put the issue clearly. It wrote:—" It is a comparatively simple matter for English capitalists to crush out their Irish competitors, and we know that this has been too often the fate of Irishmen striving to promote the manufactures of the country, but once the obstacles are removed it is easy enough for them to advance prices, and thus obtain compensation for preliminary losses. It is to this system we, as Irish manufacturers and large employers of labour, object ; but we are always ready to meet the ordinary competition of business, so long as this is conducted on fair lines." Many of the Irish Boards of Guardians have responded to this letter ; but, unfortunately, the bulk of the unions have fallen into the net spread by the English ring, and in consequence a very large sum of Irish money, not a penny of which need have passed out of the country, finds its way this year into England's pocket. Under the Sinn Fein policy such a deplorable error could not occur. The action of the Boards would, of course, be a united one, and no possibility would be left so far as they were concerned for a syndicate of unscrupulous English capitalists to crush out the home manufacturer and the home trader. Another example of what united action could achieve will suffice :

If the 159 unions of Ireland decided to-morrow to use no flour but Irish flour, twelve months hence many of the idle mills in Ireland would be again in full work, and hundreds of our people would be provided with employment. Under a National Government there would be no room for pauperism in Ireland, because under such a Government those unable, through no fault of their own, to work, would not be treated as paupers, and those able to work would be provided with it in plenty in reclaiming the four mil'ion acres of waste in this country. One half the victims of our present Poor Law system are able-bodied men and women. Did you ever hear of a free nation paying out its hundreds of thousands of pounds to keep in soul-destroying idleness tens of thousands of its able-bodied population while one-fourth of its soil remains awaiting reclamation? This is what occurs in Ireland—24 per cent. of the soil of this country awaits the plough or the tree, and meanwhile the people of the country are annually mulcted in millions to keep in soul-destroying prisons those who could carry out the work. The central plain of Ireland awaits only

Afforestation

to raise the mean temperature of Ireland four degrees, and thus render the soil of Ireland doubly fruitful; and our people are taxed not to carry on so noble a work, but to perpetuate pauperism. It lies, as I have shown elsewhere, within the powers of the County Councils to at least devote portion of the local taxation of this country to the purposes of such reclamation, and united action on the part of our County Councils and Poor Law Unions can serve to some extent to divert a portion of our iniquitous Poor Law taxation to reproductive labour.

The Poor Law Boards of Ireland employ about 4,000 officials, the Urban Councils and County Councils must employ at least 2,000 more. Here we have the materials for the formation of

A National Civil Service.

Of this great army of officials, paid by the ratepayers, the appointment of 75 per cent. is in the hands of men elected as Nationalists. At the present moment their appointment is determined, in the majority of cases, more by the amount of personal influence they can wield with the members of the Board under which they seek appointment than by any other consideration. The question of efficiency is often, though not always, a secondary consideration. It is evident such a state of affairs tends both to the impairing of efficient administration in our local government and to a lowering of the moral standard which should prevail in the conduct of our public bodies. These public bodies resent—and properly resent—any deprival of their right of "patronage." We do not propose they should be deprived of it. What we propose is that they should exercise it in the future, not in the interest of the individual, but in the interest of the nation. . . . . The cleverest and ablest men in the British Civil Service to-day are Irishmen. If we can deprive England of their services and secure them for Ireland, we shall be dealing a double blow against the foreign rule of this country. In the consular service I have suggested the abilities of many Irishmen who now fill positions in the higher grades of the British Civil Service would find adequate and congenial scope; for the hosts of young Irishmen who fill the secondary posts in the Civil Service, a National Civil Service under the local governing bodies of Ireland would provide scope. . . . . Institute a National Civil Service in Ireland, and the English education system of this country, designed to suppress in the breasts of its people the impulse of patriotism, is revolutionised. If no position in the public service of Ireland can after a period be obtained by those ignorant of Ireland, the schools must teach Ireland—and must teach their pupils Ireland's history, Ireland's language, and Ireland's possibilities. A National Civil Service in Ireland will prove a bulwark to the nation—it will revolutionise the so-called educational system—it will save for Ireland thousands of men who unwillingly leave it—it will necessarily cause the uprise of the most Irish-educated generation Ireland has known for centuries. It means an educated Ireland, and an educated Ireland is the harbinger of a free Ireland. And not less important to the nation than a National Civil Service are

National Courts of Law.

Hungary understood this and established Arbitration Courts, which superseded the courts which Austria sought to impose upon her. Ireland, before O'Connell retreated from the proposal of erecting a de facto Irish Parliament in Dublin, had established such courts. The prestige, the dignity, the strength such a national legal system would confer upon a movement for national independence is obvious; but in addition it would deprive the corrupt Bar of Ireland of much of its incentive to corruption, save the pockets of our people, and materially help in bringing about that spirit of brotherhood—of national one-ness in Ireland which all who love their country desire to see. The decision of an arbitration court is binding not only in morals, but in law, on those who appeal to it. I say to my countrymen, as the "Nation" said to them in 1843, "You have it in your power to resume popular courts and fix laws, and it is your duty to do so. It is the duty of every Irishman to himself, to his family, to his neighbour, his bounden duty to his country, to carry every legal dispute to the arbitrators, and to obey their decision. If you resort in any of your own disputes to any but your own judges, you injure yourselves and commit treason to your country." In one sentence the case may be put: Eighty per cent. of the cases which are now heard in the Civil Courts of Ireland, involving the expenditure by the people of an enormous sum of money which is utilised to keep up a corrupt judicial system, could be equally as **legally** decided in voluntary arbitration courts at practically no expense at all. . . . The course is legal and feasible—its advantages are great and obvious. Papineau took it in Canada, and Deak followed it in Hungary in the nineteenth century. Ireland can as easily follow it in the twentieth. . . . . The fiscal system of this country is the complement of the land system, and was designed and is conducted in the interests of England alone. In England the Stock Exchange, although the most powerful of its buttresses, is uncontrolled by the British Government. In Ireland it is different. English statesmen naturally understood that an independent and

National Stock Exchange

in Ireland would connote a degree of prosperity incompatible with English financial, if not with English political, interests. They, therefore, placed the Irish Stock Exchange directly under Government control. . . . . The Stock Exchange in Ireland has had no rival save the banks in ruining Irish industries in the interests of British ones, and in transferring to English pockets millions of Irish money. In every country except ours the primary function of the Stock Exchange is to create a market for local stocks, particularly the shares in manufacturing industries. In Ireland the primary function of the Stock Exchange is the reverse. Any limited liability company started in this country to create or develop industries or develop natural resources will not secure a quotation on the Stock Exchange, unless it be backed by unusual and powerful influences. The result of this is to render the small investor in eighty per cent. of cases unwilling to invest his money in Irish Industrial companies. To illustrate the reason, for those who may not be conversant with financial matters, let us assume that the townspeople of Trim, anxious to promote the prosperity of their town, anxious to benefit themselves, and anxious to advance the general prosperity of the country, decide to start a woollen factory in their midst. A company is formed with a capital of five or ten thousand pounds, the workingman subscribes for a pound share and the well-to-do shopkeeper for £100. The company may go on prosperously, but a few months later the workingman may be in need of money and be anxious to dispose of his share, or the shopkeeper

may find it imperative to turn his £100 stock into cash.
If the company possessed a Stock Exchange quotation, the
shopkeeper would have merely to telegraph to a stockbroker in Dublin to sell, and receive quickly the cash for
his shares at the prices current. But if the company be a
small Irish industrial company, there is no chance of the
Stock Exchange quotation, and the shopkeeper **cannot** turn
his stock into cash, unless by private treaty. His need for
the money may be urgent—his £100 stock may be worth
£150—but the market is closed against him by the **Government** stockbroker, and his only resource is to sell by private
negotiation, involving delay, and, invariably, loss. This is
the secret of why the small **Irish** capitalist will not invest in
companies for the initiation and development of Irish industries, and will invest in the shares of gold mines eight
thousand miles away, which he never saw, and never will
see.   The **Government** stockbrokers slam the gates of the
money market in his face if he invests in the one—they open
them wide if he speculates in the other. . . .   Shut out
from the natural investment of his money, the small capitalist has been transformed by the **Government** stockbrokers of
Ireland into a pure speculator—in other words, a gambler in
shares—and has been fleeced in turn by every species of
financial rascal England--fruitful mother—produces. "Fish
Oils" and their kindred have, within the past decade, transferred as many millions from the pockets of the small Irish
capitalist to the pockets of John Bull as would have
sufficed to set the idle mills of Ireland working, and have
provided a means of livelihood in their own country for the
scores of thousands who during that period steamed out of
the Cove of Cork. . .   If the Irish National Assembly,
representing the public bodies of Ireland, demands the
creation of a National Stock Exchange, that exchange must
come into existence. The Irish National Assembly has but
to order the public bodies it represents to transact all their
business in the buying and selling of stock through brokers
who are prepared to constitute themselves into a National
Exchange, and to insist on the banks with which it leaves
its custom supporting that National Exchange, to bring
about the desired result.   The Irish National Assembly
would control the banking of some millions per annum in
Ireland, and, consequently the banks dare not, if they
would, refuse to obey its mandates.   The existence of a
National Stock Exchange, providing a market and a security
for the investor in " Irish industrials," would entirely alter
the financial position of the country, and place the present
industrial revival on a basis too firm to be overturned.
Neither ninety nor nine hundred British Government stockbrokers could withstand for a year a National Exchange
backed by the public bodies of Ireland and performing the

primary function of a Stock Exchange—the commercial development of the country for the benefit of its inhabitants and their children.

The Banking System

in Ireland, combined with the Stock Exchange, prevents the development of Irish resources and hinders the Irish industrial revival. The Irish people deposited £50,000,000 into the Irish banks, the Irish banks put the bulk of that enormous sum into British stocks at 2½ per cent. or less. They have little money to put into Irish industrial enterprise, but they have millions to put into a war against the Boers. During the Boer War, the Bank of Ireland lent, free of interest, to the British Government the money of its Irish depositors to help in the extirpation of the Boer people. At the outbreak of the same war, the other banks in Ireland bought up British Consols at £115 per cent.—this stock is now worth less than £89 per cent.—and for every £100 stock so purchased, the shareholders in the Irish banks have lost £26.* We may take the instance of an Irish bank which bought half-a-million stock before the war. It paid for the half-million stock £575,000. The stock is now worth £445,000. Thus the bank has lost £130,000 on the transaction. It makes up its loss by squeezing its customers, and continues to lend to the British Government. The banks of Ireland, then, are willing to lend the money of the Irish people for British purposes, but not for Irish ones. Sixty-three years ago Louis Kossuth in Hungary, when he had successfully inaugurated the National industrial movement, found himself face to face with a similar state of affairs. The banks of Hungary were under the thumb of the Government in Vienna, and the gold of Hungary was drawn thither to fill the gold-reserve chests in the Austrian Treasury. The banks in Hungary acted then precisely as our own do. They lent the money of the Hungarian people to the Austrian Government—that is they sent the g**ld** coin of Hungary to Vienna, and took **paper** in exchange—at a low rate of interest, but they refused to lend money for the internal development of Hungary. Kossuth did not argue with the banks. He secured the support of the County Councils and the aid of those men of wealth who were true to the country, and founded a bank himself—

" The National Bank of Hungary."

This bank lent its funds, not to the Austrian Government, but to the Hungarian nation. What was possible to Kossuth in Hungary in 1842, is possible to us in Ireland sixty-four years later. If the public bodies in Ireland unitedly demand that the existing banks shall play

---

* British Government £100 stock has since fallen to 55.

the part of National banks—shall cease lending Irish money for the benefit of England, and shall begin to lend it for the benefit of Ireland, 1 doubt that they will refuse. If they do, our public bodies have simply to agree to withdraw their accounts and a national bank willl come into being. The bank in Ireland which has behind it the united support of the Irish public bodies, will be the premier bank in wealth and influence. With the establishment of a National Stock Exchange and a National Bank, the financial jugglery which withdraws from the service of the Irish nation the enormous sum of £50,000,000 and locks it up in the British Treasure-chest, will come to an end, and the shrivelled veins of Irish commerce be refilled with the blood of life. I have referred to the withdrawal of gold from Ireland. At the present time while there is nominally fifty million pounds in our banks there is not four million pounds in gold in the whole of Ireland. The Irish gold deposited in our banks is sent to London and there exchanged for paper. But when the Irishman presents an Irish bank note in a British Government office in London he is informed they cannot accept.

Paper Money.

The late Edmund Dwyer Gray very sensibly refused to accept payment in paper money from the banks in Ireland, and when the people individually and the public bodies in Ireland act with equal commonsense Ireland will retain her own gold within her own shores and permit England to sell paper for gold to some other country. . . . We propose the formation of

A Council of Three Hundred,

composed of the members of the General Council of County Councils and representatives of the Urban Councils, Rural Councils, Poor Law Boards, and Harbour Boards of the country to sit in Dublin and to form a de facto Irish Parliament. Associated and sitting and voting with this body, which might assemble in Dublin in the spring and in the autumn, could be the persons elected for Irish constituencies, who decline to confer on the affairs of Ireland with foreigners in a foreign city. On its gathering in Dublin this National Assembly should appoint committees to especially consider and report to the general body on all subjects appertaining to the country. On the reports of these committees the council should deliberate and formulate workable schemes, which, once formulated, it would be the duty of all County and Urban Councils, Rural Councils, Poor Law Boards, and other bodies to give legal effect to so far as their powers permit, and where these legal powers fell short, to give it the moral force of law by instructing and inducing those whom they represent to honour and obey the recommendations of the Council of Three Hundred individually and collectively. Over all the departments of our national life to which I have referred this Council of Three Hundred should be the directing authority. Our Councils can levy 1d. in the £ for Technical Instruction, and then demand and receive half as much again from the Board of Agriculture. The valuation of Ireland—the rateable valuation—is roughly £12,000,000, which would yield an annual grant for technical instruction of £50,000, plus £25,000 for the Department. The Councils have also the power, with the concurrence of the Rural Councils, to raise another 1d. in the £ for libraries, thus yielding another £50,000. Here, then, we have a total annual revenue of £125,000, which can be allocated, inside the limits prescribed in the Act, by direction of the Council of Three Hundred to objects intended to serve and strengthen the country, and aid in bringing about the triumph of the policy. Under the heading of Technical Instruction we can allocate money to train up the people in crafts useful to the country, and we can subsidise and offer

Bounties to New or Struggling Industries—

this is of the utmost importance. Under the heading Libraries, we can allocate money to the foundation of **National** Libraries throughout the country, the instruction of adults in **national** history and national subjects, the establishment of local **national** museums and of gymnasiums in which they may be physically trained and taught discipline. To illustrate: When the Council of Three Hundred meets in Dublin, it is proposed, let us say, that a certain fixed sum be devoted in that year in every part of Ireland to, we shall say, the physical training of the people and their instruction in Irish history; whereupon every County Council in Ireland levies the rate and allocates the portion as directed. Thus, uniformity of action and work is attained, and without in one iota infringing the British law, the **recommendation**—for these resolutions or **Acts** of the Council go forth as recommendations—is given the force and status of law. . . . We propose to extend the control of the Council of Three Hundred over the Department of Agriculture. We propose to make the six and a-half million pounds which is annually dealt with by our Irish elective bodies dealt with solely with a view to Ireland's interest and honour.

Our Policy, in a word, is to lead our People to Reliance in themselves, and to establish in Ireland's Capital a National Legislature endowed with the Moral Authority of the Irish Nation.

It is essential to the working of the Sinn Fein policy that its supporters in Ireland should secure their votes, and cast them for men who in Rural Council, Urban Council, and

District Council will carry out the Sinn Fein policy and
apply that policy in their local affairs as well as in the
national field. In Dublin and other cities, the British Local
Government Board, for instance, prevents our Corporation
from providing those facilities for education and recreation
which the municipalities in other countries are free to provide, by declining to sanction a rate struck for such purposes; but in many of our cities there is

A Borough Fund,

which, after a payment of certain fixed charges, is freely at
the disposal of the representatives of the people. But what
do we find the state of these funds to be? I take the
Dublin Borough Fund, which annually amounts to about
£30,000, and find it overdrawn, because while the people of
Dublin were keeping their eyes steadily fixed on London,
corrupt men were throwing burdens on the fund which
it should never have borne—and have thus rendered a fund
which properly directed would prevent the herding of the
poor of Dublin in fetid tenements and the consequent ab-
normal death-rate—would alleviate the distress which each
recurring winter brings in its train—and would provide for
the people means of rational enjoyment—have rendered that
fund unavailable. Let us try to make these municipal funds
again available for our people—and bring the policy of Sinn
Fein into every department of our social lives. I shall not
dwell on local policy—which must be largely determined by
local circumstance—further than to say, that I have seen
the war vessels of Ireland's enemy welcomed to Dublin and
entertained by the municipality, whilst I have seen the
war vessels of friendly nations—Argentina and Holland—
enter our harbours unwelcomed and unnoticed by the municipality of Dublin. I pass from the stain upon our soul and
the slur upon our character—and ask whether such a proceeding is calculated to advance the commercial interests of
Ireland in Argentina and Holland, and while I behold
British municipalities in order to further the commercial
interests of Great Britain inviting the German and French
municipal bodies to visit their cities, I can find no instance
of an Irish municipal body exhibiting similar commercial
instinct. The policy of Sinn Fein proposes to change all
this—to

To Bring Ireland out of the Corner.

and make her assert her existence in the world. I have
spoken of an essential; but the basis of the policy is national
self-reliance.

No Law and no series of Laws can make a Nation out of a People which distrusts itself.

If we believe in ourselves—if each individual in our ranks

believes in himself, we shall carry this policy to victory against all the forces that may be arrayed against it. If we realise the duties and responsibilities of the citizen and discharge them, we shall win. It is the duty of a free citizen to live so that his country may be the better of his existence. Let each Irishman do so much, and I have no fear for the ultimate triumph of our policy. I say ultimate, because no man can offer Ireland a speedy and comfortable road to freedom, and before the goal is attained many may have fallen and all will have suffered. Hungary, Finland, Poland, all have trodden or tread the road we seek to bring Ireland along, but none repine for the travail they have undergone. We go to build up the nation from within, and we deny the right of any but our own countrymen to shape its course. That course is not England's, and we shall not justify our course to England. The craven policy that has rotted our nation has been the policy of justifying our existence in our enemy's eyes. Our misfortunes are manifold, but we are still men and women of a common family, and we owe no nation an apology for living in accordance with the laws of our being. In the British Liberal as in the British Tory we see our enemy, and in those who talk of ending British misgovernment we see the helots. It is not British misgovernment, but British government in Ireland good or bad we stand opposed to, and in that holy opposition we seek to band all our fellow-countrymen. For the Orangeman of the North, ceasing to be the blind instrument of his own as well as his fellow-countrymen's destruction, we have the greeting of brotherhood as for the Nationalist of the South, long taught to measure himself by English standards and save the face of tyranny by sending Irishmen to sit impotently in a foreign legislature whilst it forges the instruments of his oppression Following the illustrious thinker of antiquity whom Trinity College inverts, I liken a nation to a ship's company, to whom different tasks are allotted, but all of whom are equally concerned in the safety of the vessel, and in a saying of his great predecessor I find summed up the spirit of Sinn Fein—"It is the part of the citizen not to be anxious about living, but about living well." If we realise this conception of citizenship in Ireland —if we place our duty to our country before our personal interests, and live not each for himself but each for all, the might of England cannot prevent our ultimate victory."

III.

THE ECONOMIC OPPRESSION OF IRELAND.

The history of Irish trade, commerce and industry has yet to be written. Ancient Ireland traded extensively with the Roman Empire, Gaul, Spain and Greece. In the Middle Ages Ireland carried on extensive commerce with France, Flanders, Italy, Spain, Portugal, Germany, and independent Scotland, Wales and England. The Guild merchants of the great Continental trade centres mostly included Irishmen—Bordeaux, Rouen, Bruges, and other cities contain memorials of the Irish merchants. A Flemish sixteenth-century writer records that in his time the Irish merchants held two fairs yearly in Bruges, where they sold friezes, serges, furs, skins, etc. An Italian poet of the Middle Ages sings the praise of Ireland for the " noble woollen stuffs " she sent to Italy, and Irish robes were used by the Queen of Hungary. The mercantile marine of Ireland was numerous and powerful. After the definitive establishment of English power in Ireland by Queen Elizabeth it was decreed treason to export Irish goods in Irish vessels; Irish shipping was destroyed or seized by England, and it was forbidden to an Irishman to own a ship. Subsequently Ireland was forbidden to export to America aught except victuals, horses, salt, and people. She was forbidden to export cattle, etc., to England. Ireland thereupon turned her attention to a Continental trade, and succeeded in wresting much of the market from England. Alarmed by this, England removed most of her embargoes; but after the Williamite Wars, Ireland being down, a Penal Code against Irish industry and commerce unparalleled in commercial history was enacted. Irish direct trade with the world was interdicted. The great Irish woollen trade was deliberately suppressed. The Irish cotton manufures were made subject to a duty of 25 per cent. in England, and it was decreed a punishable offence to wear Irish cotton in England or Scotland. The Irish linen manufacturer was practically excluded from England by an import duty of 30 per cent., and, while bounties were paid to English manufacturers for the export of linen, Ireland was forbidden to participate in such bounties. The Irish fisheries were deliberately impoverished, and a score of minor Irish industries, such as glassmaking, were legislated out of existence. In Ireland itself the farmers were forbidden to grow corn lest

164

they might undersell the English farmer.   In 1716 the unemancipated Irish Parliament sought to pass an Act entitling the farmer to cultivate five acres in every hundred, but the British Government vetoed the Act. Simultaneously civil rights, religious liberty, free tenures, and the right of education were interdicted to four-fifths of the Irish people.

The menace of the arms of the Irish Volunteers gained for Ireland restoration of the right to trade freely with the world, and power to protect and encourage Irish industry. In the twenty years 1780—1800 Ireland, on the admission of Lord Clare, Pitt's Chancellor, had advanced in cultivation, commerce and manufacture with more rapidity than any other European nation. The Irish woollen, cotton, linen and other trades had been restored or raised to a pitch of production and prosperity never equalled. Ireland had become a corn-exporting instead of a corn-importing country; the glass, metal and other manufactures were restored, and the Irish fisheries had become one of the first in Europe. In 1800 England forced the Union upon a flourishing Ireland through, as Lord Chief Justice Bushe said, a jealous intolerance of her prosperity.

Under the operation of that infamous Act, Ireland was once more turned back from tillage to grazing land, and one by one all her great industries, except linen, were again destroyed or reduced to skeletons of their former greatness. The Irish Exchequer and the Irish Custom House were suppressed by England. Some industries, such as the tobacco culture, were expressly forbidden by legislation.   Others were ruined by less open methods. Thus the Irish Government before the Union had paid bounties of a few hundred pounds yearly to encourage the exportation of Irish fish. England after the Union paid bounties of £2,000 a year for many years to encourage the importation of British fish into Ireland. In the fifteen years 1829—1844 grants of £200,000 were paid to Scotland for the development of her fisheries. In the same period the amount granted to Ireland was £13,000. The Scots fishermen were allowed a Government brand, but the English Parliament, by an overwhelming majority, refused the same right to the Irish fishermen.   A great Irish industry was ruined, and to-day the annual value of the Irish fisheries is but one-tenth the value of the Scots fisheries.

Thus were treated through the nineteenth century Irish industry and commerce until Ireland once more, as in the seventeenth, was confined to the English market and made subject to England's economic absolutism. Having thrice within three hundred years destroyed Irish commercial and industrial prosperity by force and fraud—having, in defiance of engagements, made Ireland jointly responsible for **England's** National Debt—having made, in the words of

Nassau Senior, Ireland the most heavily taxed and England the most lightly taxed country in Europe—England has represented Ireland to the world as a naturally poor and incapable country, kept from want by English benevolence. Ireland is not the only country whose commerce and industries were forcibly repressed by a jealous rival; nor is she the only country whose soil was confiscated to foreign adventurers; possibly she may not be the only country where a price was placed by its foreign rulers on the schoolmaster's head; but the Irish people are the one people on the earth to-day whose education, commerce and industry having been repressed, are held up by the repressors to the scorn of the world as a lazy, idle, poverty-stricken and illiterate people.

POPULATION.
Persons per Square Mile.

		1801.		1911.
Ireland	...	166	...	135
England	...	152	...	618

Prior to the "Union" Ireland was, it will be seen, more densely populated than England.   England is now over 4½ times more densely populated than Ireland.

Total Number of Persons.

			1801.		1911.
Ireland	...	...	5,395,456	...	4,390,219
England	...	...	8,892,536	...	36,070,492

The estimated population of Hungary was in 1801 7,750,000, as compared with Ireland's 5,400,000.   The present population of Hungary is 21,000,000.   Had Ireland progressed equally Ireland's present population would be 15,000,000.

NATIONAL DEBTS.
(From the British Parliamentary Paper 35 of 1819.)
1801.

		Debt.	Per Head of Population.
Ireland	...	£28,545,134	£5 6s. 0d.
Great Britain	...	£450,504,984	£42 18s. 0d.

On the basis of revenue, taxation per head in England in the financial year ending 31st March, 1917, was more than **four** times greater than the taxation per head in England in the year of the Union.   On the same basis the taxation per head in Ireland in the financial year ending

31st March, 1917, was almost **eleven** times greater than in the year of the Union. The placing of a three-fold burden on the Irishman had its origin in the suppression of the Irish Exchequer in 1816.

THE SMALL NATIONS.

		Area. (sq. miles.)	Population.	Revenue. £
Ireland	...	32,600	4,337,000	24,000,000
Holland	...	12,600	6,500,000	18,750,000
Belgium	...	11,600	7,500,000	32,000,000
Denmark	...	15,600	2,800,000	7,500,000
Switzerland	...	16,000	3,900,000	3,100,000
Norway	...	125,000	2,400,000	10,000,000
Greece	...	42,000	4,900,000	9,250,000
Bulgaria	...	43,500	4,750,000	10,300,000
Roumania	...	53,500	7,500,000	24,000,000
Sweden	...	173,000	5,700,000	22,000,000
Serbia	...	34,000	4,550,000	8,600,000
Montenegro	...	5,000	520,000	400,000

The figures are those for 1917 or the latest available.

IV.

ENGLAND'S SCRAP OF PAPER:
THE RENUNCIATION ACT, 1783.

GEORGII III. (ANNO VICESIMO TERTIO), CAP. XXVIII.

An act for removing and preventing all doubts which have arisen, or might arise, concerning the exclusive rights of the parliament and courts of IRELAND *in matters of legislation and judicature ; and for preventing any writ of error or appeal from any of his Majesty's courts in that kingdom from being received, heard, and adjudged, in any of his Majesty's courts in the kingdom of* GREAT BRITAIN.

Preamble 22 Geo. 3 c. 53 recited.

WHEREAS, *by an act of the last session of this present parliament (intituled* An act to repeal an act, made in the sixth year of the reign of his late majesty King *George* the *First,* intituled, *An act for the better securing the dependency of the kingdom of* IRELAND *upon the crown of* GREAT BRITAIN ;) *it was enacted, That the said last mentioned act, and all matters and things therein contained, should be repealed : and whereas doubts have arisen whether the provisions of the said act are sufficient to secure to the people of* IRELAND *the rights claimed by them to be bound only by laws enacted by his Majesty and the parliament of that kingdom, in all cases whatever, and to have all actions and suits at law or in equity, which may be instituted in that kingdom, decided in his Majesty's courts therein finally, and without appeal from thence :* therefore, for removing all doubts respecting the same, may it please your Majesty that it may be declared and enacted ; and be it declared and enacted by the King's most excellent majesty, by and with the advice and consent of the lords spiritual and temporal, and commons, in this present Parliament assembled, and by the au-

168

thority of the same, That the said right claimed by the people of *Ireland* to be bound only by laws enacted by his Majesty and the parliament of that kingdom, in all cases whatever, and to have all actions and suits at law or in equity, which may be instituted in that kingdom, decided in his Majesty's courts therein finally, and without appeal from thence, shall be, and *it is hereby declared* to be established, and ascertained *for ever, and shall, at no time hereafter, be questioned or questionable.*

The rights claimed by the people of Ireland firmly established.

II. And be it further enacted by the authority aforesaid, That no writ of error or appeal shall be received or adjudged, or any other proceeding be had by or in any of his Majesty's courts in this kingdom, in any action or suit at law or in equity, instituted in any of his Majesty's courts in the kingdom of *Ireland ;* and that all such writs, appeals or proceedings, shall be, and they are hereby declared null and void to all intents and purposes; and that all records, transcripts of records or proceedings, which have been transmitted from *Ireland to Great Britain,* by virtue of any writ of error or appeal, and upon which no judgment has been given or decree pronounced before the first day of *June,* one thousand seven hundred and eighty-two, shall, upon application made by or in behalf of the party in whose favour judgment was given, or decree pronounced, in *Ireland,* be delivered to such party, or any person by him authorised to apply for and receive the same.

No writ of error or appeal from the courts in Ireland, shall be received by any court in Great Britain.

HUNGARY'S SINN FEIN INSTITUTIONS

The institutions founded by Szechenyi, Deak, and Kossuth to combat the Austrocisation of Hungary included—(1) The National Academy of Sciences, which devoted itself mainly to the resuscitation of the Hungarian language as the language of literature, science, and industry in Hungary ; (2) The National Museum, designed to inspire reverence and pride in the past of Hungary, and to educate the people as to the possibilities of its future ; (3) The National Bank, intended to support Hungarian enterprise against Austrian financial opposition ; (4) The National Theatre, where all the plays were acted in the National language and dealt with Hungary, past, present, or future ; (5) The Company of Commerce, designed to promote Hungarian foreign trade, and free Hungary from economic dependence on Austria ; (6) The Agricultural Union (Kostelek), which devoted itself to the improvement of agriculture and to rendering Hungary entirely self-supporting ; (7) The Protective Union (Vedegylet), which accorded voluntary aid to Hungarian manufactures and vigorously discountenanced the use of the manufactures of Austria ; and (8) The National Casino (Club), which formed a common meeting ground for all working for Hungary's weal.